Lecture Notes in Economics and Mathematical Systems

Managing Editors: M. Beckmann and W. Krelle

350

Wei-Bin Zhang

⌊Economic Dynamics⌋

Growth and Development

Springer-Verlag

Berlin Heidelberg New York London
Paris Tokyo Hong Kong Barcelona

Managing Editors
Prof. Dr. M. Beckmann
Brown University
Providence, RI 02912, USA

Prof. Dr. W. Krelle
Institut für Gesellschafts- und Wirtschaftswissenschaften
der Universität Bonn
Adenauerallee 24−42, D-5300 Bonn, FRG

Author
Associate Prof., Ph. D. Wei-Bin Zhang
Institute for Futures Studies
Hagagatan 23 A, 3tr., S-113 47 Stockholm, Sweden

ISBN 3-540-53217-X Springer-Verlag Berlin Heidelberg New York
ISBN 0-387-53217-X Springer-Verlag New York Berlin Heidelberg

Printing and binding: Druckhaus Beltz, Hemsbach/Bergstr.
2142/3140-543210 – Printed on acid-free paper

To my teacher and friend:

Åke E Andersson

ACKNOWLEDGEMENT

First, I wish to thank Professor Åke E. Andersson for all of his help and inspiration. If I had not met with him at Kyoto University four years ago, economics would have remained a hobby for me. In fact, this book is a rewrite of my dissertation under his supervision.

I'm greatly grateful to Prof. Michio Morishima for his important comments.

I am greatly indebted to Professors David Batten, Börje Johansson, Kazuhiro Yoshikawa, Kiyoshi Kobayashi, Stig Andersson, for their comments. Without the kind help of Dr. Barbro, Eva, Gunilla, Ing-Marie, this study would have taken much longer to complete. In particular, I would like to thank Jennifer who checked my poor English. I am also very thankful for the friendship and hospitality extended to me by the staff of the Department of Economics at the University of Umeå and the staff of The Institute for Futures Studies at Stockholm.

I am very grateful to an anonymous referee for his many important comments, and to the economics editor of this series, Peter Schuster, for his effective cooperation.

Finally, I should like to take this opportunity to thank CERUM at the University of Umeå for the financial support.

CONTENTS

INTRODUCTION

The theory of economic development is a branch of economic dynamics. Any discussion of the theory must involve dynamics even though not all dynamic problems are necessarily related to economic development. The theory's primary locus is upon the nice paths of economic variables. Stationary states, which have been the main concern of modern economic development theory, are actually special cases of economic dynamics.

In this study, we propose an economic development theory within the framework of input-output systems and neoclassical economics. No political problems will be dealt with, although this does not mean that questions such as why Japan had a higher growth rate than China in the past are not important. Similarly, rather than dealing with the psychological and institutional aspects of in economic development processes we only suggest ways (or methods, as Hicks would call them) for analyzing what determines economic development from the point of view of "pure" economics.

Our main contribution to economic growth theory is that we investigate various nonlinear dynamic phenomena such as bifurcations and economic cycles. We emphasize that oscillations and structural changes are not rare but universal in a progressive economy. No economic system can be stabilized forever if change is permitted.

We make use of mathematics in order to explain and prove what we intuitively believe about economic development. Our proofs of periodic and bifurcating economic phenomena provide good illustrations of the usefulness of mathematics to economics. Mathematics is both a language and a tool - it is a means of communication and expression, and an implement for solving problems. Some problems cannot be solved without mathematics. In addition, mathematics can help us to organize our ideas about economic systems and to understand the interactions among economic variables. Even if one is poor at language and philosophy, one can still use mathematics. Kac (1969, p.699) once said that;

"Models are, for the most part, caricatures of reality, but if they are good, then, like good caricatures, they portray, though perhaps in distorted manner, some of the features of the real world. The main role of models is not so much to explain and to predict - though ultimately these are the main functions of science - as to popularize thinking and to pose sharp questions." This may help to explain the usefulness of mathematics in economic analysis.

In this study we make many simplifications. We omit factors such as international and regional interactions, public spending as well as fiscal and financial issues, even though all of these factors play a very important role in any practical economic development process. Furthermore, we discuss the whole economic system into weakly independent elements, despite our awareness of the dangers of this method. However if we try to take all of the conceivable interactions and dynamics into account, it is almost impossible to gain any deeper insight into the problems. In other words, our analytical capacity is rather limited. Even now that the human brain can be supported by the most powerful computers, we cannot understand all the possibilities of behavior described by a relatively simple three-dimensional nonlinear dynamic system such as, e.g., the relatively simple Lorenz equations. Appropriate simplification and isolation seems to be the most useful method in dynamic analysis. It is just because of this "unrealistic" method that we have come to understand something about the complexity of the structure of dynamic interactional systems. This method has been accepted in almost all of the important classical works in the sciences.

It should be noted that although some economists such as Schumpeter seem to consider the economic system as a whole interactive dynamic body, in a strict sense their main analytic methods are still to isolate each subsystem in a presumed static (or sometimes stationary) world. Before one can understand the whole body, one must master the subdivision of the system. There is, in other words, nothing wrong with simplification and isolation. However, it is important to accept the limitations of such methods. The main limitation is that any result from such theories can only be partially true in the real world. The attempt to discover "real truth" or "universal truth" can only result in either religion or skepticism - both are potentially very dangerous. It cannot be denied that the master of partial truth is in a superior position to the ignoramus and the skeptic.

We wish to emphasise that no theory can be so general as to explain all aspects of economic development. All scientific theories have some imperfections.

The economist must base any theory upon a series of assumptions which cannot hold indefinitely. Any social theory is only an approximation of the real world as it can only explain some of its aspects. Many economists (for example, Smith, 1776, Ricardo, 1817, Marx, 1867, and Schumpeter, 1934) have already developed their own theories of economic development. But it has become clear that each theory has only been partially succeeded in explaining this process.

The general linear theory of economic growth has been developed comprehensively in works of Walras (1874), Hicks (1965), Morishima ((1964, 1969), and others. There seems to be little need for further elaboration of this theory, although there is always the potential for improvements as analytic and computational capacity increases. It seems that any science usually experiences a phase of static/stationary growth between revolutionary periods during which new ideas are generated - although this phase appears to have become shorter in recent times. No one can claim that economics has a stable evolutionary path.

Rather than providing a unique approach to these problems, I will try to explain economic development from various points of view. This study consists of nine chapters which are arranged in the following manner:

In Chapter I, we discuss development problems, define some essential concepts, and provide a general historical sketch of economic growth theory. It is shown that choice of indicators depends upon the purpose of the study at hand. The length of the study period may also influence the development theory in different ways. For instance, different endogenous variables may need to be chosen for long-run and short-run studies; a variable in the long run may become a parameter in the short run. We also investigate how the adjustment speed of a variable determines its "role" in an economic dynamic system. Finally, we deal with equilibrium versus non-equilibrium, and stability versus instability within the framework of growth and development theory.

In Chapter II, we review some of the modern mathematical economic growth theories. This chapter is mainly concerned with quantitative approaches in which monetary terms are omitted. First, we confine ourselves to the simplest one sector growth model or "the standard neoclassical growth model", and its extensions. Then we demonstrate that technological change, endogenous population and natural resources have been introduced to the neoclassical growth model. We also examine the effects of income distributions on economic growth within this neoclassical approach. Then we review some of the multiple sector models. The

Uzawa two-sector model is used to show that the behavior of a "disaggregated" economic system may be different from that of an aggregated one. The behavior of the extended neoclassical model is also examined. Finally, the concept of production functions in dynamic analysis is discussed.

Chapter III reviews how monetary variables can be introduced into neoclassical growth theory. First, we simply explain some elementary issues about money in economic development. Fundamental ideas about classical monetary economics and (modern) monetarism are mentioned. Then, Tobin's analysis of money, which is one of the main approaches to money in neoclassical economics, is described. In particular, we prove the existence of endogenous oscillations in a generalized dynamic Tobin model.

Prices in the context of dynamic multiple sector models are dealt with in Chapter IV. First, we present some general illustrations of price problems in multiple sector models. We mainly confine ourselves to those interactions which occur amongst interest rate, growth rate and inflation rate - within the framework of multiple sector models. First, we are concerned with the determination of a short-run equilibrium of economic growth. The basic model accepted here is a dynamic Leontief system similar to the model presented in Morishima (1964), though we adhere to the original Leontief system in the sense that we do not differentiate between industries producing intermediary and capital goods.

Chapter V is concerned with a "mixed" economy with a combination of centralization and decentralization. The central government's behavior is assumed to maximize a social welfare function which depends on the economic growth rate. We readdress the problem of the existence, uniqueness and stability of dynamic models when they are subjected to different types of economic policy regimes. The discussion in this chapter is still limited to the framework of the dynamic input-output system. First, we analyze the problem of equilibrium and optimum properties of linear dynamic systems. Next, the problem of stability in situations of completely decentralized policy making according to the Marshallian and Walrasian adaption patterns is dealt with. Then we discuss what occurs when these basically decentralized reaction patterns are confronted with supplementary centralized policy making. We demonstrate that an economy which is unable to substitute between different inputs requires a combination of decentralized and centralized decision making if long term stable economic growth under conditions of equilibrium and optimality is to be achieved.

Chapter VI deals with the problem of the "choice of (exogenously given) alternatives or techniques". First, we explain how techniques can be chosen using a very simple equilibrium growth model. Then we analyze the problem within the framework of multiple sector models with Leontief technologies. The dynamic behavior of the primal and dual systems is examined. And finally, we show that the reswitching debate is not possible in the continuous substitution model.

Chapter VII examines the process endogenous technological changes. Dynamic interactions between human knowledge and economic variables are investigated. A growth model in this chapter is developed within the framework of neoclassical theory, and built upon a development problem in the economy of China. First, we explain the characteristics of the economic system and define the basic model. Next, we guarantee the existence of a unique equilibrium and state the stability conditions. Then the effects of some parameters are analyzed by traditional comparative static analysis. Finally, bifurcation analysis is applied with respect to population growth policy.

Chapter VIII explicitly introduces a new sector - called the knowledge or non-material sector - into the traditional input-output economic system. As in the preceding chapters, it is assumed that the growth of knowledge is the main source of technological change. Knowledge cannot be created as "manna from heaven"; in order to increase knowledge (or human capital) we need "inputs" and investments, just as we do to produce material capital. We attempt to develop models based upon the human capital theories of economics. This chapter proceeds as follows. First, we define the basic model, in which the K-set is explicitly introduced into the framework of input-output analysis. Then some properties of the model are investigated in relation to a fixed technology. We also show how the basic model is related to the traditional input-output model. Models of endogenous technical change are developed according to Arrow's "learning by doing" and "investment in training", respectively. We also develop a "hybrid" model of "learning by doing" and "investment in training". Finally, we suggest some directions for further studies.

Chapter IX summarizes the results of this study and suggests some mechanisms - the neoclassical, neo-Marxian and neo-Keynesian approaches - for "closing" an incomplete economic system which primarily consists of accounting equations.

I

THE ECONOMIC DEVELOPMENT PROBLEM

1. Economic Development

Since World War II, some countries have experienced rapid economic development, while others have suffered from slow economic growth. Why have there been uneven economic growth rates among different countries during the same period? What causes a country's growth rate to vary during different periods? Obviously, we cannot expect to get definitive answers to these questions since such problems can be analyzed from various points of view, using a number of disciplines such as history, sociology, psychology, and economics.

Development is a very complicated dynamic process which often contains elements of both success and failure. The complexity and subjectivity of the process leads to disagreements between "socialist" and "capitalist". Various countries emphasise different aspects of economic development. Some countries like to achieve high economic growth rates due to their strong work ethic, while countries in which leisure time is highly valued may experience more moderate economic growth. The emphasis depends upon material and cultural conditions. For instance, the Japanese ethos strongly influenced economic development of Japan (Morishima, 1982), while traditional Chinese culture appears to have exerted little influence upon the modern economic development of China (Russell, 1922).

Economists usually use the term development in its wider sense, which incorporates institutional and cultural change (Lewis, 1955). Classical economists, such as Smith, Malthus, Ricardo, Marx and Mill, are mainly concerned with how the whole social system can be developed. In this study, however, the concept of development is restricted to "pure" economic aspects. We are thus mainly concerned with dynamics of real variables such as capital and output, monetary variables such as prices and interest rates, and technological change.

The economic development theory suggested in this study is not limited to developed economies. We are looking for general principles in the development processes of any economy. From an economic point of view, it is difficult to classify an economy as developed or developing. One reason is that "development" is a comparative concept. Furthermore, it is argued that economic mechanisms in the developing countries do not work as "perfectly" as those in the developed countries. It may also be said that institutional changes in the developing countries are much slower than those in the developed countries. However, such institutional factors should not prevent us from proposing a general economic theory, since they only affect whether or not assumptions in a theory holds. Our theory can be applied to an economy in which institutional systems change very slowly or quickly in comparison to the economic variables under consideration.

It should be emphasized that the terms economic growth and development are not interchangeable. Both concepts are related to change and progress, but while growth is related to balanced change or expansion, development corresponds to evolution. The main difference of concern to this study is that development is associated with instabilities and stochastic behavior, while growth is related to stabilities and balanced expansion.

Another concept related to change is progress. Growth and development do not necessarily imply progress. Progress involves an improvement or an advance. Subjective evaluations are usually part of this process. The relationship between growth, development, and progress is subtle and complex. We, however, consider that growth and development generally constitute progress.

2. A General Historical Sketch of Growth Theory

Economic development is one of the classical fields of economics. Adam Smith, D. Ricardo, T. R. Malthus, Karl Marx, J. Mill, and various other classical economists have made significant contributions to the literature in this field.

In his the Wealth of Nations, Adam Smith argued that the division of labour can increase efficiency of the economic system. The division of labour between individuals, regions, and nations, was the most obvious aspect of the 19th century development among the North Atlantic economies. The economic potentials of linking resource-rich regions in North America with the labour-rich countries of Western Europe were significant enough to generate an enormous increase of trade, specialized production in new manufacturing cities, and massive increases in income per capita.

Adam Smith recognized the importance of exchange activities and the role of money. His emphasis on division of labour cannot result in improved efficient reallocation of resources unless exchange activities are efficient. He argued how money could facilitate exchange by allowing people to avoid the difficulties of attaining the double coincidence of wants. But Smith never explained how some one commodity or other had come to gain general acceptability in exchange.

The idea of specialization by division of labour, first formulated by Smith and Ricardo, became a macro and micro theory of economic organization. It provided guidelines for exploiting the comparative advantage principle from the individual factory floor to the industrial corporation as a home. The more limited the number of tasks performed by each worker the more comparative advantages would be used and the higher would be productivity and profitability of production. Marx had foreseen some of the political consequences of unrestricted division of labour. In the long run nobody would be able to set up competitive industries due to the complete fragmentation of the production process. Two classes would emerge - the fragmented and specialized labour class and the capitalist class with a complete overview of the whole production process. Limitless application of the principal of division of labour and the use of indivisible capital equipment would create a complete hierarchy of monopolistic production within each country. Only the size of the market would prevent such a system from becoming completely monopolistic. This amounts to the structuring of society by static principles alone.

Between 1870 and 1920 the partial equilibrium approach of Marshall and the general equilibrium approach of Walras dominated the literature. Great advances in the theories about capital and interest were also made by Böhm-Bawerk, Clark, Wicksell, and Fisher. However, their treatments are, at least in the light of present knowledge, frequently oversimplified in formulation and defective in reasoning.

It is well known that Walras provided the foundation of competitive equilibrium. However, his contribution to relations of monetary variables and economic growth is less known. Walras argued that the theory of money can be developed only after the real theory of growth. He believed that no money problem can be thoroughly discussed with a model where investment and saving are not made (see, Morishima, 1977). In Walras' model the demand for cash balances is a way of saving and is related to investment in commodity inventories. As there is no place for savings and investment in the system of pure exchange and that of simple reproduction, there is no need for money. There may be a numéraire in a static system of exchange and production, while "money" can appear only in dynamic systems in which individuals and firms are allowed to save and investment. Hence, Walras' money theory is related to the theory of saving, the theory of inventory investment, the theory of portfolio selection, and so on. However, as Morishima (1977) mentions, Walras' theory of money should be regarded as an unfinished work, "because it is incomplete and obscure in various points and even inconsistent, in that it contains a careless technical slip which has of course to be removed." Walras was concerned with an economy where capital goods and inventories directly owned by capitalists are rented to firms or entrepreneurs, and decisions concerning investment are made by capitalists (i.e., savers) themselves, so that there is no inconsistency between investment and saving such as Keynes emphasized. Moreover, Walras did not put explicit attention to the bond market: Keynes' system is also a model from which supply and demand for bonds have been eliminated. Hicks' model establishes equilibrium between supply and demand in the bond market and the money market, in addition to the ordinary commodity markets.

An important contribution in monetary economics is that of Wicksell. His celebrated "Interest and Prices" (1898) is concerned with restating and defending the quantity theory of money. One may divide neoclassical economics into two disciplines - the theory of value and the quantity theory of money. The first is concerned primarily with the determination of the system of relative or real prices that equate demand and supply for every commodity, guaranteeing the full employment of every scarce resource. The second is to fix the general level of nominal prices by an equilibrium relation between the demand and supply of money. Wicksell first challenged the real-monetary dichotomy of neoclassical economics and provided the key to the synthesis of these two theories. He attempted to explain the general movement of nominal prices from the perspective of the theory of the value.

In developing the quantity theory Wicksell was influenced by two things: (i) the capital theory of Jevons and Böhm-Bawerk, which had laid the foundations of a real theory of the rate of interest; and (ii) Tooke's objections to the quantity theory, which comprised both a number of puzzles and suggestions. We will explain Wicksell's work in detail later on.

The classical tradition is also expounded in J. A. Schumpeter's Capitalism, Socialism, and Democracy (1943), The Theory of Economic Development (1934). One of the most important contributions by Schumpeter is his emphasis on the role of technological change upon economic development. During the 19th and 20th centuries, two opposing assumptions have been accepted in the literature of economic growth. The first assumption is associated with Ricardo. In his world different regions were assumed to be endowed with differing sets of technological and commercial knowledge. Thus the availability of natural resources, agricultural traditions, and technological knowledge were assumed to have given Portugal an absolute advantage over England in the production of oats, wine and cloth. His riddle was then: would there be any mutual advantage in engaging in trade between these two potential trading partners, who were so unequal in productivity? Ricardo answered that the absolute productivity differential, however great, would never matter. As long as there were comparative productivity advantages in any field of production, there would be gains from trade for the sum of countries involved in international trade. Almost a century later, Eli Heckscher and Bertil Ohlin made the assumption of identical technological knowledge ruling everywhere. In such a world, it is possible to show that comparative advantages in terms of basic resource endowments were sufficient to generate comparative advantages from trade. Then it would even be possible to compensate for shortages in some immobile factors, such as sun or rain, by exchanging goods intensive in water and sundays in the process of cultivation and other production. Heckcher and Ohlin disregarded knowledge as an important factor determining trade and this productive specialization of different countries.

Schumpeter was the first economist to radically question this view of economic development. Although he admitted all of the principles of division of labour and the existence of a general equilibrium with a given structure, he considered all of these claims as a very limited case where all the natural dynamics of real economies are precluded. To him, knowledge was a dynamic factor of production potentially available in abundance. The synergetic combination of entrepreneurs and such potential technological knowledge was enough to make the general equilibrium unstable.

In Schumpeter's synthesis of economic growth and fluctuations, technological innovations are treated as the motor driving economic growth: without innovations an economy would reach a static equilibrium position of a circular flow. Schumpeter argues that technological change is not steady or even, but comes in waves. There is no single factor of causation, since a great diversity of events may affect the form and timing of the waves. Innovations are uneven at any time, exhibiting a tendency to concentrate in certain sectors.

Schumpeter provides a new view of competition based on innovation, which shows a departure from the neoclassical postulate that perfect competition is beneficial for the innovative climate and monopoly is detrimental. It emphasizes the creative role of the entrepreneur. Temporary monopolistic profit (real or expected) deriving from pioneering a new process/product is the major element pushing firms to innovate. Schumpeter emphasized dynamic interactions between the economic system and technical change, based on an evolutionary process in which technological change, firms' strategies and industrial structure mutually interact. The choice of a strategy is linked to the size of firm and its share of the market.

In The Theory of Economic Development , Schumpeter argues that development should be understood as only such changes in economic life as are not forced upon it from without but arise by its own initiative, from within. He identifies the key development process as the "carrying out of new combinations". In the competitive economy new combinations mean the competitive elimination of the old. It is the entrepreneur who carries out new combinations. The entrepreneur leans the means of production into new channels and may thereby reap an entrepreneurial profit. The entrepreneur "also leads in the sense that he draws other producers in his branch after him. But as they are his competitors, who first reduce and then annihilate his profit, this is, as it were, leadership against one's own will".

Schumpeter's theory of the entrepreneur is a part of a theory of the capitalist economic development. As mentioned above, according to Schumpeter, entrepreneurs are economic agents whose functions are the "carrying out of new combinations", the creative destruction of equilibria, thereby preparing the ground for a superior state of equilibrium.

An essential aspect of Schumpeter competition is that there are winners and losers and that the process is one of continuing disequilibrium. Firms facing the same market signals respond differently, and more so if the signals are relatively novel. In order to get entrepreneurial profits, firms have to solve many technical, economical and psychological problems. Firms participate innovative competition through product development, price or cost competition through process development, and marketing competition through sales or market promotion. Failures in any competitive field may affect incomes of the firms.

The General Theory of Keynes revived interest in macroeconomic growth theory, though the General Theory is characterized by statics rather than dynamics. It provides a picture of the interactions of aggregated macroeconomic variables. The works by Harrod (e.g., 1956, 1973) and Domar (e.g., 1946, 1951), who were much influenced by Keynes, made the long-run growth problems more rigorous and more statistically testable than the classical works. However, these models are crucially dependent upon the assumptions that the capital/output and capital/labour ratios are constant. This drawback was remedied by Solow (1956) and Swan (1956) who introduced production functions into growth theory, though this modification was seriously criticized by Robinson and Kaldor.

Keynes' The General Theory has provided the most influential work in modern monetary economics, irrespective of the fact that much of the General Theory's contents can be found in the writings of Pigou, Hawtrey and the Swedish school. The portfolio theory of demand for money which constitutes the kernel of Keynes' theory confines attention to the asset market and study the allocation of wealth among various types of assets, money being one of them. This is in contrast to the traditional quantity theory which focused attention to the relationship between the stock of money and the flow of magnitude - volume of transactions.

Since the publication of the General Theory, so-called monetarism has dominated modern static macroeconomics. Among others, Tobin (1955, 1965) and Friedman (1956) made important contributions to monetarism. We will study the models developed and extended within the framework of Tobin's analysis later on.

The works by Morishima (1964, 1969), Hicks (1965), Leontief (1949), Sraffa (1960), von Neumann (1937) and others have played a significant role in the development of modern economic growth theory. In fact, this work is a re-examination of these neo-classical approaches with the help of modern nonlinear dynamic theory.

It should be mentioned that the empirical facts which modern growth theory attempts to explain are quite different from those which the classical theory confronted. It appears that some of the most important empirical predications of, for example, the Malthus and Ricardo theories have not been realized. The share of land-owners did not seem to increase, and the population did not grow faster than output. The importance of agriculture relative to manufacturing declined markedly. On the other hand, the primary object of modern economic growth theory is to explain the movements in the output, employment, and capital stock of a growing economy and the interrelations among these variables. It also tries to explain the movements in the distribution of income among the factors of production. Modern growth theory aims to provide a conceptual framework within which much more meaningful empirical research can take place. The economies which it attempts to describe are essentially advanced and industrialized. In such economies, capital and labour are the two inputs upon which attention is focused. Land, which is an important input in classical growth theory, is usually ignored. In modern growth theory, it is the consumption-investment decision and not the allocation of resources among alternative investment or alternative consumption goods upon which the analysis has been primarily focused. In modern growth theory labor is usually assumed to grow exponentially, and technological progress is exogenous. Some efforts, however, have been made to relax these strict assumptions.

3. Development Indicators

In order to analyse economic development, we have to devise suitable measurements. Much work has been carried out to determine how to choose social indicators for measuring social change (e.g., Sheldon and Moore, 1968, Rossi and Gilmartin, 1980). It may be said that when we select a particular set of observations or measurements as indicators of some economic phenomena, we are introducing some selectivity into our perceptions of reality. Obviously, if an indicator that can represent a set of correlated changes can be found, and if intervention can be introduced, then the planner or analyst has access to a powerful analytical and policy tool.

Economic indicators provide an interpretation of the current state of some segment of the economic systems as well as past and future trends - whether progressive or regressive - according to some normative criteria. In this sense, an indicator should reflect time series that allows comparisons over an extended period. If an indicator can be indicated by a cardinal number, then the problem is easy. Difficulties arise if the indicator is not measurable. Furthermore, an indicator may be direct or indirect with respect to a particular variable of interest. A direct indicator is a measure of the variable itself. For example, if the variable of interest is physical economic growth, accumulation of capital could be the basis for a direct indicator. An indirect indicator is a measure of some other variable that is assumed to be closely related to the variable of interest. For instance, the number of years a student has spent in the education system would be an indirect indicator of the student's level of knowledge.

The choice of indicators is dependent upon the purpose of the study. An economic indicator can be used for: (1) describing the state of an economy; (2) analyzing; (3) forecasting; (4) evaluating; (5) setting social goals; and (6) managing and planning. Rossi and Gilmartin (1980) suggest the following four categories according to which the characteristics of indicators can be assessed and compared: (1) quality of data (validity, reliability, stability, responsiveness, availability, and scalability); (2) relation to other variables (disaggregatability, representativeness, and extent of overlap with other indicators; (3) breadth of comparability (intertemporal comparability, intergroup comparability, and breadth of application); and (4) usefulness (understandability, normative interest, timing).

In a theoretical work we can use economic indicators for which precise statistics are not currently available. It is, however, necessary to know that it would be possible to measure the indicators if we have a plenty of time and energy to collect the data.

In this study, we are interested in those indicators which can be used as interrelated components of mathematical models. Capital, prices, money, interest and inflation rates, population, human capital (knowledge) are the fundamental indicators in our study.

4. Short Term versus Long Term

In economic development theory, the time scale plays a central role in any discussion of economic growth and development. Approaches to long-run and short-run economic evolutionary processes may be completely different according to the time span under consideration. For a one year period, if the system is stable, it may be sufficient to look at the dynamics of prices, wages, consumption and so on. However, in a long term study technologies and institutional systems become endogenous variables. The duration of the study period influences the choice of exogenous parameters and endogenous variables in a dynamic system.

Although it is reasonable to treat technologies as parameters for the short-run, if we study the problems in the long term, there should exist interactions between technologies and economic variables. It may be said that in this case we are no longer faced with a problem of rationality, but with a process of learning.

In fact, if we want to understand real economic evolution in the long-run, economics seems to be narrow. Not only is technology changeable, but also institutions. For instance, the fiscal systems may change as the economy develops. This forms a kind of game between the government and economic development. In some countries where the institutional systems change very slowly are faced with slow economic growth, while in others the institutional systems change too rapidly to have any stable economic growth.

As an example of how the time scale may affect economic analysis, let us consider the interactions which occur between economic development and institutional systems. We should consider the case of economic development in China.

In China, one of the major current issues is the way in which the country will be opened to "Western" technologies and culture. We use "opening", denoted by y, to describe this policy. Although there are uncertainties in determining the speed of "opening", one cannot strictly assume the existence of interactions between economic development and the policy. To illustrate this, we suggest the following dynamics:

$$dx/dt = f(x,y),$$

$$dy/dt = s(x,y,t)[g(x,y,t) - y],$$

where x is a vector of the economic variables, and f and g are continuous with respect to the variables. The other countries are exogenous to our system. Of course, this assumption depends upon the strength of China's role in the world. The first equation means that the economic variables are dependent upon the opening of the country. The Chinese have benefited economically and technologically since the country was "partially" opened, though it is now experiencing new problems in its development. The second equation describes the behavior of the government. The function g is the "fittest opening level" of the country, which depends upon x, y and t. The functional form g cannot be determined uniquely from an economic point of view. Very complicated factors can influence its form. The variable s(x,y,t) is an adjustment speed. If s is zero, the opening policy will not be changed. This case can be observed during the period of "The Cultural Revolution". If s is very large, the government adjusts to the optimal situation very rapidly.

If the study period is very short and the system is stable, then it may be possible to disregard the opening policy in the economic analysis without affecting the qualitative results. However, if we want to analyse the evolutionary processes of economic development in the long term, we have to consider this factor.

The introduction of "opening" may change the characteristics of the pure economic system where y is fixed. For instance, the stability may be seriously affected. If we let s(x) change as fast as the economic variables, the country may become unstable though the growth rate may be very fast. On the other hand, if we close the country, it is possible to have a (local) stable society although the people suffer from poverty.

It is possible to specify the forms of f and g to a reasonable extent in order to obtain certain insights into the dynamic system. However, as we are not concerned with the institutional systems, further analysis is omitted.

We have made certain comments about institutional systems. Although we will not take these systems into account explicitly in this study, we must always remember their existence if we wish to understand actual economic evolutionary processes.

The time scale for economic modelling is a complex matter which requires exhaustive philosophical discussion in order to be understood. That which is wrong in the short term may be right in the long-run, and vice versa. The relations between the long-term and short-term horizons are as important as the relations between aggregated and disaggregated variables, and the relations of the whole and the parts.

5. Fast Variable versus Slow Variable

One of the serious debates in economic dynamics is related to the adjustment speeds of variables, which means the time it takes for the variables to adjust to an equilibrium. A variable is called fast if its adjustment speed is faster in comparison to these of other variables of the system. In a Keynesian economy wage rates are fixed, while in the classical model they become fast variables. In the Keynesian economy it is assumed that wages adjust to an equilibrium at a very slow speed.

The above example illustrates the importance of adjustment speeds in studies of economic development. The speed of a variable is dependent upon many factors including the institutional systems of a country. For instance, if we study the economic development which occurred during the period of "The Culture Revolution" in China, it is reasonable to assume that all prices and wages were fixed. However, if we study the current economic evolution in China, this assumption no longer holds because we are now faced with inflations due to various reforms, and wages are not fixed at all.

The adjustment speed of economic variables is closely related to the economic mechanisms which dominate a country. A structural change in an economy (e.g., from "capitalism to socialism", or from "socialism to capitalism") is always associated with changing adjustment speeds. From an economic point of view, all of the economic systems in the world are mixed in the sense that no country is purely planned or perfectly competitive, though the "degree of mix degrees" varies. It may be very important to study the correlations between the "degree of mix" and economic development. This makes the economic analysis more complicated. For instance, in a mixed economy like that in Japan, the adjustment speeds of wages may be very different among various industries or between large and small firms. In any economic analysis, it is necessary to take such differences into account.

There is also a relationship between the time scale and the adjustment speed of variables. For example, it has been argued that if there is a short study period, it may be reasonable to assume fixed wages, while the neoclassical model may be more appropriate if the study period is long term. To describe these relations, let us discuss the following system:

$$dx/dt = f(x,y), \quad dy/dt = sg(x,y),$$

where x is a vector of fast variables, y is a vector of slow variables, f and g are appropriate continuous functions, and s an adjustment speed parameter. In this case, s is sufficiently small. It is well known that in the neoclassical growth model, capital is a slow variable, while output, consumption, prices and wages are fast variables.

Obviously, if the study is limited to the short-run, y may be treated as a constant. Here we are concerned with long term development. Let us make a transformation of time: $t^* = st$ which transforms the system to

$$sdx/dt = f(x,y), \quad dy/dt = g(x,y),$$

in which the dot is differentiation with respect t^*. Under certain assumptions about the functions f and g, then $f(x,y) = 0$ holds almost everywhere. If the implicit function theorem holds globally for the function $f = 0$, we obtain $x = f^*(y)$. Substituting x into the second equation, the dynamics may be reduced to:

$$dy/dt = g(f^*(y),y) = g(y).$$

Hence, the variables x do not appear in the dynamic system. As soon as y are determined, x are given by $f^*(y)$. For example, in the neoclassical growth model, as soon as capital is determined, we have prices, wages, production and consumption.

It should be noted that this situation only holds when the system is stable. If the system is potentially unstable, the dynamic relationships may become very complicated since the behavior is very sensitive to small shifts of parameters.

6. Equilibrium versus Non-equilibrium

As we are generally concerned with dynamic systems, the concept of equilibrium will play a central role in understanding the properties of dynamic economic systems. It may be said that the modern growth theory literature has been characterized by the search for conditions which allow the existence of equilibrium and stability. The existence of a unique equilibrium seems to be a "necessary condition" for a model to be meaningful, though a few models which allow for instabilities do exist.

In this study we define equilibrium as the state of a dynamic system at which all the variables are invariant with respect to time. An equilibrium is often referred to as a steady state. It should be noted that in this study stationary states and balanced growth in which all the variables grow at a homogeneous rate are also included in equilibria.

A system is considered to be at nonequilibrium if the variables have different rates of change with respect to time. Limit cycles, aperiodic behavior and chaos belong to nonequilibria.

The concepts of equilibrium and nonequilibrium are not necessarily related to welfare economics. Nonequilibrium may be "bad" or "good". It is only a characteristic of an evolutionary economic system. Some people cannot accept the concept of equilibrium as they believe that it is impossible to observe such a state in an economic system. However, this concept can help us to gain insights into the properties of dynamic systems. In fact, although the concept of non-equilibrium is obviously more realistic than that of equilibrium, it is unlikely to be used as frequently because of our limited technical capacity. A concept's usefulness depends upon what can be gained from it.

The concept of disequilibrium is often used in the economic literature. Although we shall not employ this concept in our study, it is necessary to distinguish between equilibrium, non-equilibrium and disequilibrium. Disequilibrium is generally used to demonstrate that the "equilibrium" of a dynamic economic system can be different from Walrasian equilibrium. This concept is often used in disequilibrium macro-economics. In studies related to dynamics, disequilibrium is the steady state which is inconsistent with the Walrasian equilibrium of the system. Disequilibrium and non-equilibrium are even not the same in a dynamic system. For us, disequilibrium is a time-independent state, although there are also other definitions of disequilibria. For instance, in Stiglitz and Uzawa (1969) "a disequilibrium path is a path along which people behave according to certain expectations, but those expectations are not (in general) fulfilled." However, we do not think that these different definitions will cause any confusion when used in context.

7. Stability versus Instability

In the previous section, we defined the concepts of equilibrium and non-equilibrium. In studies of economic evolution, the concept of stability plays a very important role. In most traditional economic analyses, stability is considered to be a precondition, while instability is generally viewed as a nuisance or disturbance. However, we maintain that instability and nonlinearity may become sources of order and well-organized complicated phenomena such as limit cycles and chaos (Zhang, 1990, see also the Appendix to this book).

Economists have different points of view about how time dimension should be introduced into economic analysis. Some economists argue that static approach may be a good approximation of actual economic systems; while others think that it is necessary to explicitly introduce time dimension into economic analysis.

Those who believe in efficiency of static models usually hold that static analysis is a sufficient approximation of actual dynamic world in the sense that actual dynamic processes are not far from equilibrium states. Even if the actual system is temporally away from equilibrium states, the system will finally come back to the equilibrium if system is allowed to function for time long enough. From nonlinear dynamic theory, we know that this point of view may not be valid even if the actual system functions long enough without any exogenous shocks. It is possible for the system to run far enough from a static state even in the long run.

Even if economists agree upon the necessity of explicitly taking time dimension into account, their points of view about how dynamics can be effectively treated may be different. Although it is generally accepted that actual economic variables may have non-linear time-dependent interactions, linearization is often considered as a sufficient approximation of nonlinear systems. This belief in the efficiency of linearization is associated with stabilized belief in stable economies.

Although some economists have emphasized the significance of nonlinearity and instability in dynamic economic analysis, it can hardly be said that the ideas about economic evolution associated with instabilities have been transformed into education process. Students of economics are still educated with ideas of static equilibrium and linearization of dynamic systems. They are taught that regular and certain economic phenomena are universal; while irregularity and uncertainty are special cases. And irregular and uncertain phenomena will disappear if we allow systems to run in isolation for a long time. Whenever "irregular" economic phenomena are observed, they tend to be interpreted in terms of exogenous shocks. Decades of textbook use of stabilized world has convinced students, and even some teachers that our static model is an accurate description of the real economy.

There is a stabilized belief in stable economies. The acceptation of stability in economic analysis is strongly affected by development of natural sciences in which dynamic systems are required to be stable in order to make the analysis meaningful. For experimental sciences, this implies that a descriptive model must lead to the same qualitative result if the experiment is repeated in a minimally changed environment. The attitude toward reality from this requirement is that reality is indeed stable in such a structural sense. And the conviction that small variations in the environment of a real system do not lead to drastically and qualitatively different kinds of behavior is a heritage of the mechanically oriented 19th century. Guided by the idea of deterministic harmonics, complex phenomena which could not be explained by the usual models led either to the postulate that such phenomena should be analytically neglected, or that the system is superimposed by purely stochastic influences. Consequently, irregular phenomena in evolutionary systems are treated as temporal phenomena or mere disturbances to long-run equilibrium evolution. The attitude of most economists toward instabilities in economic analysis can be illustrated by Samuelson's recalls of his 1932-7 days as a classical theorist: "as an equilibrium theorist [I] naturally tended to think of models in which things settle down to a unique position independently of initial conditions ... technically speaking, we theorists hoped not to introduce hysteresis phenomena into our model, ... in our more realistic moods, we tacitly used models involving hysteresis: Spain would never be the same after Colombus ... obviously, in such models all real variables do not end up unchanged as a result of certain unbalanced introductions of new M into the system" (Samuelson, 1972, p. 540-1).

This point of view about stabilities has been changed. Stabilities are not presumed in sciences. It has been argued that small shifts in parameters may result in structural changes in dynamic systems. Such structural changes are not exceptional, but universal in evolutionary systems. Complex phenomena such as regular oscillations and chaos are characteristics of nonlinear unstable systems (see the Appendix to this book). The spontaneous formation of well organized structures out of chaos can be observed in a relatively simple nonlinear dynamic system. It has also been found that well organized spatial, temporal, or spatial-temporal structures arise out of chaotic states, and, in such self-organizing systems instead of finding stability and harmony, we discover evolutionary processes leading to diversification and complexity (Zhang, 1990).

The stabilized belief in stable economies may be partially due to the fact that it is only recently that we have become to understand some aspects of the complexity of behavior of nonlinear dynamic systems. Without the recent development of catastrophe theory, singularity theory, bifurcation theory, chaos theory and computer science, scientists could hardly satisfactorily explain complicated dynamic behavior such as regular and irregular oscillations. This book will apply nonlinear dynamic theory to explore nonlinear phenomena in economic evolution.

II

GROWTH THEORY REVISED
- FROM QUANTITATIVE ASPECT

There are two types of indicators of economic development. One is related to real variables such as goods, the population and the labour force. The other is related to monetary variables such as prices, money, wages, inflation and interest rates. When we analyse the economic development of any modern industrialized society, both quantitative and monetary variables have to be taken into account, since there are always interactions among these variables. Although we can find variables which are common to a number of different growth models, a particular variable may have to be treated very differently in each model. For instance, with the Keynesian approach the wage rate is fixed during the study period, while in the neoclassical growth approach it is determined endogenously as a function of inputs.

This chapter is only concerned with quantitative aspects of economic development. Monetary terms are explicitly omitted from the models. A growth model of real variables generally proceeds from the assumption that all of the essential phenomena in the economy can be described in terms of goods and services. Money only enters into the analysis in the modest role of a technical device to facilitate transactions. In quantitative approaches it is generally accepted that this device can become disordered. However, as long as it functions normally, it does not affect the economic process which behaves in the same way as it would in a "barter" economy. This is essentially what the concept of neutral money implies. Thus, money has been called a "veil" of the things that really matter to both households and firms in their everyday life. Accordingly, prices are nothing but symbols of the exchange ratios between the commodities under consideration. Similarly, income formation is analyzed in terms of an exchange of labour and the physical means of subsistence; savings and investments are interpreted to mean the saving of some real factors of production and their conversion into real capital goods.

This chapter revises some of the growth models which are related to quantitative aspects. The models which take monetary terms into account will be analyzed in the next chapter. In these chapters we do not analytically investigate the properties of these models as they are already well known in the literature. Rather, we focus upon the (mathematical) structures of these models. The structure of a model illustrates the way in which some economist sees the world in the abstract.

The models to be reviewed are not presented in their most "advanced" forms. Most of the models have been extended and generalized, but the main structure of the models has not changed by the generalizations; simple models are sufficient for our pedagogical purpose.

Our main focus is upon one-sector models. The Uzawa two sector model is presented to illustrate how the complexity of the economic system is increased by even the most modest "disaggregation". The multiple sector model of neoclassical production functions and the Solow-Samuelson model are also mentioned. However, multiple sector models of the von Neumann type and dynamic input-output systems are omitted as we deal with these models in a later chapter.

We omit some important approaches to economic growth problems in this study. For instance, the growth models by Harrod (1948, 1952) and Domar (1957), the life cycle model by Modigliani, the normative growth model, the disequilibrium model, are completely neglected except as ingredients or special versions of other models. The main reason is that this study has little relation to these approaches.

1. The Neoclassical Approach to Growth

It may be said that the neoclassical approach has played a central role in modern growth theory. Most neoclassical models are extensions and generalizations of the pioneering works of Solow (1956) and Swan (1956). For some unknown reason, Solow's work has received much more attention than Swan's. This section will focus on the Solow model and its extensions and generalizations, although we exclude any issues related to technological change, monetary mechanisms and unemployment. It should be noted that the following review of the model is fundamentally referred to Burmeister and Dobb (1970)

The model is fundamentally concerned with long-run economic growth. It is assumed that production conditions will appear to dominate the entire economic evolution in the sense that supply considerations, rather than demand conditions, dominates the evolution of the system. In the long run, the economy tends to operate close to potential output. In order to examine the longer run process of growth, the Solow model neglects shorter run processes of price adjustment or alternations in the rate of capacity utilization such as the unemployment rate.

The basic assumptions in the Solow model include perfect foresight among all individuals, and smooth adjustments in goods as well as labour and capital markets. These assumptions imply that both savings and investment plans are simultaneously fulfilled, and that neither miscalculated output nor misdirected investment can ever arise. Market clearance is usually achieved, while Keynesian unemployment is hardly possible. Solow believed that as Keynesian theory only applies in the short run, whereas the neoclassical theory is suitable for the long run, the neoclassical theory is at least equally relevant to the growth theory as Keynesian theory.

It is assumed that there is only one (durable) good. Factor markets work well; factors are inelastically supplied and the available factors are fully utilized at every moment. All savings volunteered by households are absorbed by firms for the accumulation of capital. There are two productive factors: capital, K, and labour, L. There is no technical change. The production process is described by some sufficiently smooth function

$$Y = F(K,L), \tag{2.1.1}$$

where Y is the output flow attainable with given amounts of K and L. In the Solow growth model, K and L refer to stocks of assets - stocks of physical and human capital, respectively - whereas the arguments of the production function are the flow rates of asset services. K is measured in units of the output good itself. Here, we assume that capital is malleable in the sense that one need distinguish neither its previous use nor the factor productions of its previous use. Malleable capital can be transferred quickly from a production process appropriate at one level of factor intensity to a different process appropriate to a different capital intensity. In this model labor is present and employed as a factor of production, but laborers are neither produced nor sold and need never be valued explicitly.

We assume that the production function F is neoclassical. A production function F is called a neoclassical production function if it satisfies the following conditions: (1) $F(K,L)$ is non-negative if K and L are non-negative; (2) $F(0,0) = 0$; (3) marginal products, $F_K =$ and F_L are non-negative; (4) There exist second partial derivatives of F with respect to K and L; (5) The function is homogeneous of degree one: $F(rK,rL) = rF(K,L)$, for all non-negative r; (6) The function is strictly quasi-concave. In what follows, we assume F to be neoclassical.

Before introducing dynamics of the variables, we consider the general equilibrium structure of the system. We assume that available supplies of factors are at very moment inelastically supplied and fully utilized. This means that the quantities of factor service do not vary with changes in factor prices or other shorter run economic considerations; at any moment, all existing labor and capital offers itself for use regardless of what wage or rental rates prevail. With this assumption, we may determine factor rewards from demand or productivity considerations. To derive relations between real and monetary variables, we imagine a competitive producer facing competitive markets for labor and capital services where, a price for his product, wage rate W for labor service and rental rate R for capital service prevail. The producer is to maximize the profit $\pi = PF - WL - RK$. Thus, the producer will select inputs K and L satisfying $R/P = F_K$ and $W/P = F_L$, which describe the producer's response to given factor and product prices. It should be noted that from the two relations just obtained, we could answer the question about what prices could clear the markets for factor services if endowments K of capital and L of labor are prescribed and the services of these offered inelastically at the fixed utilization rate.

We assume that the output good serves as a medium of exchange and is taken as numeraire. We thus set $P = 1$ and measure both wages and rental flows in units of the output good. As we assume that factor markets work quickly enough so that our system always displays competitive equilibrium in factor markets, one always has: $W = F_K$ and $R = F_K$.

In order to obtain the complete growth model, we further make two assumptions. It is assumed that the labour force grows at a fixed relative rate n independent of any economic variables in the system. The population growth is given by

$$dL/dt = nL, \quad L(0) > 0. \tag{2.1.2}$$

In order to have a growing economy, we assume that the agents regularly set aside some fairly predictable portion of its output for the purpose of capital accumulation. Since there is only one good, no question of changes in relative price can arise, nor can any questions of capital composition. We omit the possibility of hoarding of output in the form of non-productive inventories held by households. Thus, all savings volunteered by households is absorbed by firms for accumulation of capital. For simplicity, it is assumed that a constant fraction, s, of the total output flow is saved and set aside to be added to the capital stock. Neglecting depreciation of capital, we have

$$dK/dt = sY, \quad K(0) > 0. \tag{2.1.3}$$

The Solow (or standard neoclassical) growth model consists of (2.1.1)-(2.1.3). It should be noted that these equations take account of the real economic questions, such as markets for factor services, the reconciliation of independently determined saving and investment desires, production conditions, and determination of population growth and labor force participation rates into account.

Surely, we make many simplified assumptions about economic behavior of the agents. In the remainder of this book, we will gradually relax these assumptions.

As the production function is neoclassical, one can reduce the model into the following single differential equation

$$dk/dt = sf(k) - nk, \tag{2.1.4}$$

where $k = K/L$, $f(k) = F(K,L)/L = F(k,1)$. The function $f(k)$ has the properties: $f(0) = 0$, $f'(k) > 0$ if k is non-negative, $f''(k) < 0$ if k is non-negative.

The existence of solutions of the differential equation (2.1.4) can be guaranteed. In the Solow model, once the capital per capita is determined, all the variables in the system, such as K, Y, consumption, savings, wages and rentals, can be calculated accordingly. We will mention some properties of (2.1.4).

Theorem 2.1.1 (The Existence of a Unique Equilibrium)
If n and s satisfy

$$0 < n/s < f'(0), \tag{2.1.5}$$

then there exists a unique positive value k_0 such that $f(k_0)s/n = k_0$.

The proof of this theorem is referred to, for example, in Koopmans (1965).

The following theorem guarantees the stability of the equilibrium.

Theorem 2.1.2 (Stability of the Equilibrium)
The system is globally stable. Furthermore, the equilibrium is asymptotically stable in the region k > 0.

The asymptotical stability can be proved by defining the Lyapunov function: $V = U^2$, where $U = k - k^*$ where k^* is the equilibrium value of the capital intensity.

Economic development can be described as follows. In the long run the economy will always converge smoothly to the unique equilibrium capital/labour ratio from any positive starting point. Moreover, along the balanced growth path, capital expands at the same rate as the population grows. This is the simple and beautiful picture portrayed by the Solow growth model. The phase diagram of the Solow model is described in Fig. 2.1.1. The importance of this model lies in the fact that it supplies a very simple consistent system to simultaneously determine all significant variables - labour and capital inputs to production, outputs, savings, consumption, investment - in economic development. Irrespective of its oversimplified assumptions about production function, saving and investment behavior, the role of monetary variables and so on, it is a powerful tool since it gives us a logical framework to analyze some aspects of economic development.

There are many objections raised about the Solow model. Some of these objections about oversimplifications can be rejected by introducing technological change, monetary variables, endogenous population and natural resources, as shown below.

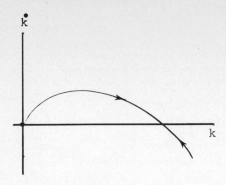

Fig. 2.1.1.
Dynamics of the Standard Neoclassical Model

One important objection is related to the so-called Keynesian difficulties, i.e., the liquidity trap, the downward inflexibility of wage rates, etc. Of course, these debates have to be considered from the point of view of more fundamental premises such as: whether or not the speed of monetary variables is fast in comparison to that of real variables. If the Solow model is not appropriate for analysis in the short run, there will be even more problems in the long run, provided that by the long run one does not simply mean that a perfect state is always the only concern of the study. As modern dynamic theory indicates, short-run perturbations might play a significant role in changing the long-run evolutionary paths of a dynamic system. As Solow believed that the economic system is stable, his model was acceptable if the assumption of stability were valid. It should be noted that in the neo-Marxian and neo-Keynesian theories there is no such faith in stability. However, the assumption of stability is not necessarily applicable in the neoclassical approach. As shown below, introducing any one of these factors - monetary variables, technological change, endogenous population growth or natural resources - to the standard neoclassical growth model may destroy the stability of the system.

In what follows, we review some of the extensions and generalizations of the standard neoclassical growth model. That is, we will relax some assumptions - such as fixed technologies, constant returns to scale, constant labour force growth, saving and investment behavior and so on - made in the standard model.

2. The One Sector Model of Technological Changes Within the Framework of the Neoclassical Approach

In the previous section, we reviewed the way in which neoclassical growth theory explains capital accumulation under the thrust of population growth. Technologies were fixed for the convenience of the analysis. However, as the standard neoclassical growth model seeks to explain long-term economic growth, it is obviously necessary to take account of the interactions between the economic variables and technological change. In neoclassical growth theory, technological change is usually reflected by shifts of the isoquant contours of the production function.

Technological change is usually characterized as either endogenous or exogenous, and embodied or disembodied. Endogenous changes which take place according to shifts in the input factors, while exogenous changes occur due to "manna from heaven".

First, we will discuss exogenous forms of technological change. In this case, the production function takes the form of

$$Y = F(K,L,t), \tag{2.2.1}$$

where F is continuous with respect to K, L and t. To classify disembodied and exogenous forms of technological change, let us define an index

$$I = (F_K K/F_L L)d(F_L L/F_K K)/dt.$$

Technological change is defined as: (1) neutral iff the relative shares remain constant and $I = 0$, (2) labour saving (labour using) iff the relative share of labour falls (rises) $I < 0$ ($I > 0$); and similarly (3) capital saving (capital using) iff $I > 0$ ($I < 0$). Here, the relative share of capital is defined as $F_K K/Y$, while the relative share of labour is defined as $F_L L/Y$. It should be noted that these definitions are crucially dependent upon the path which is designated. For instance, neutral forms of technological change can be further classified as: (1) Harrod neutral if the capital/output ratio is constant, (2) Hicks neutral if the capital/labour ratio is constant, and (3) Solow neutral if the labour/output ratio is constant. The effects of exogenous forms of technological change upon the neoclassical growth model are referred to in Burmeister and Dobell (1970).

Endogenous technological progress can be classified according to the way in which it originates: (1) through "inducement" by the factor prices; (2) through "experience" in production; (3) through education; and (4) through research activities. In what follows, we just mention a few of models with take account of some of these factors.

The comparison of English and American efficiency by Rothbarth (1946) led to the Habbakuk hypothesis which states that the higher level of capital intensity in America than England gave rise to America's faster rate of technological progress. Kennedy (1964), Weizsäcker (1966), Samuelson (1965), Drandakis and Phelps (1966) take account of the assumption of "inducement through the factor prices" in their studies. The second source is usually referred to as "learning by doing"; this was initially presented in a growth model by Arrow (1962), who had obtained his idea from the empirical works of Alchian (1963). Here, we will not discuss these approaches in detail since we will come back in our later discussions.

3. A Growth Model With Exhaustible Resources and Endogenous Population

This section deals with the way in which population and natural resources are related to economic development. Although this study is mainly concerned with the effects of monetary variables and technological change in economic development, it is also necessary to know how other aspects such as endogenous population growth, the distribution of income and wealth as well as natural resources can affect economic development. This section is based on work by Cigno (1981) and Cigno and Zhang (1988).

It was Stiglitz (1974) who first examined the implications of introducing exhaustible natural resources as an essential factor of production in the standard neoclassical growth model with a constant rate of population growth. He showed that if a steady-state solution exists, it is a saddle- point. That is, exhaustible natural resources have the effect of making a stable system highly unstable. However, Cigno (1981) argues that the assumption of a constant rate of population growth is implausible in an economy constrained by exhaustible resources. He also examines the implications of making the population growth rate a function of consumption and capital per capita and shows that the steady state is stable for a range of values of the savings/income ratio. Cigno and Zhang (1988) examine the behavior of the Cigno model when the system is unstable. They show that instability does not destroy the system, but it may mean that more complicated economic phenomena appear.

The production function takes on the form of

$$Y = K^{a_1} L^{a_2} R^{a_3} \exp(ht), \quad h > 0, \tag{2.3.1}$$

where

$$a_i > 0, \quad a_1 + a_2 + a_3 = 1, \tag{2.3.2}$$

and Y is output, K capital, L labour, R the rate of use of an exhaustible natural resource, and h the rate of disembodied technological progress. The factor prices are equal to marginal products

$$r = a_1 Y/K, \quad w = a_2 Y/L, \quad p = a_3 Y/R, \tag{2.3.3}$$

where r is the rental price of capital, w the wage rate, and p the price of the natural resource. The rates of change in the stocks of capital, labour and natural resources are given by

$$dK/dt = sY, \quad dL/dt = nL,$$

$$dS/dt = - uS = - R, \tag{2.3.4}$$

where s represents the propensity to save, n the rate of population growth, u the rate of resource extraction, and S the remaining stock of the natural resource. In general, we would expect n and s to be simultaneously determined by intertemporal utility maximization. In Cigno (1981) and Cigno and Zhang (1988), however, s is fixed and n is given by

$$n = [(1-s)Y/L]^{v_1} w^{-v_2}, \quad v_i > 0. \tag{2.3.5}$$

If we take one generation as the unit of time, (2.3.5) can be interpreted as the demand for children, increasing in current expenditure and decreasing in the wage rate. This is consistent with the microeconomic theory of fertility (Becker, 1981, Cigno, 1986), according to which wage rate changes have a negative substitution-effect and a positive income-effect on the demand for children, while changes in income from all other sources have only an income-effect.

The rate of the extraction of natural resources must be such as to make their owners indifferent as to whether they hold resources or capital. Thus, the price of the resource must remains equal to the rental price of capital. That is, the Hotelling law must hold

$$dp/dt/p = r. \qquad (2.3.6)$$

Letting $q = Y/K$, the model can be reduced to a system of three differential equations

$$dq/dt = Q(q,n) = - a(a_1a_3 + sa_2)q^2 + a(h + a_2n)q,$$

$$du/dt = U(q,u,n) = u^2 + a[h - a_1(1 - s)q + a_2n]q,$$

$$dn/dt = N(q,n) = a[v_2/a - a_1v_1]n^2 + a[hv_1 -$$

$$\{a_1(a_3 - s)v_1 + sv_2/a\}q]n, \qquad (2.3.7)$$

where $a = 1/(a_1 + a_2)$. For $0 < s < a_1$, the system has a steady state

$$q_0 = h/a_1a_3, \quad u_0 = (a_1 - s)q_0, \quad n_0 = sq_0. \qquad (2.3.8)$$

The eigenvalues of the Jacobian are determined by

$$z^3 + k_1z^2 + k_2z + k_3 = 0, \qquad (2.3.9)$$

where k_i are constants dependent on all the parameters of the model, including s (see Cigno and Zhang, 1988).

In order for the steady state to be locally stable the income elasticity of n must be smaller than the wage elasticity and the propensity to save must fall within a certain region determined by the other parameters, i.e.,

$$v_1 < v_2,$$

$$a_1a_3(v_2 - v_1)/[s(v_2 - a_2) + a_1(a_3 + sv_1)] < (a_1 - s)/s$$

$$< [1 - a_1(1+v_2 - v_1)a_2v_2]/(1 - 2a_3). \qquad (2.3.10)$$

Moreover, as Cigno and Zhang (1988) demonstrated, if (2.3.10) holds, then k_i (i = 1, 2, 3) are positive. Here, we are interested in the case in which the system becomes unstable as the parameter s is shifted.

Assumption 1.

For some value s_0 of s, one of the solutions of (2.3.9) is a negative real number, $z_1 < 0$, and the other two are purely imaginary numbers: $z_2 = iz_0$, $z_3 = -iz_0$, where z_0 is a real number explicitly given.

Theorem 2.3.1.

There exist limit cycles, bifurcating from the steady state, with the bifurcation parameter s of critical value s_0.

Let us then consider a perturbation

$$x = s - s_0 = -b^2 m_1/2m_0 + O(b^4), \qquad (2.3.11)$$

where h is an expansion amplitude parameter, m_0 and m_1 are constants dependent on the parameters of the model. The cycle of Theorem 2.3.1 has period $(2\pi/m)$, where

$$m = z_0 + b_1 m_2/2,$$

in which m_2 is a constant dependent on the parameters of the model.

Theorem 2.3.2.

If m_1 is negative, the bifurcating cycle is asymptotically stable, while if m_1 is positive, it is unstable.

Now, we will interpret these results. First, we note that the model contains a destabilizing feature: while equation $p = a_3 Y/R$ tells us that a constant level of p is required to persuade the producer of Y to use any particular amount of the natural resource R, $dS/dt = -R$ tells us that a constant growth rate of p is required to persuade resource owners to part with that R. If, at any instant of time, demand for the resource exceeds supply, the market could be cleared by raising the price p, but that would also increase the instantaneous growth rate of p, causing the natural resource deposits to become a more attractive asset than capital. Consequently, the supply (rate of extraction) of the resource would fall, necessitating a further rise in p, and so on. The opposite occurs if we start with an excess of supply. This phenomenon, first identified in Hahn (1966), is common to all economies with more than one asset, whether natural or man-made. In the absence of countervailing mechanisms, it can give rise to speculative price spirals in an upward or downward direction. In the present model, a speculative price boom would eventually bring resource extraction to a complete halt, as resource owners would hoard their possessions in anticipation of even higher resource prices; however, a price slump would lead to the complete exhaustion of resource deposits in finite time. Either way, the economy would vanish in finite time.

The model also contains a potentially stabilising mechanism. Suppose that we start from a situation of excess demand for the natural resource. As an alternative to a rise in p (which, as we have seen, could spark-off a speculative boom) the market could be cleared by a decline in w. This would induce producers to substitute R with L, thus reducing the demand for the natural resource. On the other hand, returning to the above-mentioned theory of fertility it would induce parents to have more children, thus increasing the supply of labour. However, the lower w is associated in equilibrium with a lower Y/L, which discourages reproduction (and may raise mortality). Another possible scenario suggests that the stock of capital is sufficient to meet demand at a particular instant at current prices. If r were to rise, the demand for K would be reduced. But, as capital would now be a less attractive asset to hold than natural resource deposits, resource owners would reduce the supply of R, throwing the resource market off balance and beginning the speculative spiral already discussed.

Simultaneous interactions between these mechanisms result in complicated cyclical behavior of the system.

In a "negative sense", these results confirm those obtained by simpler models: optimization and perfect foresight do not guarantee that the economy will follow a regular pattern, even in the long run. On the other hand, we can also draw a positive conclusion: if saving behavior can be manipulated by deliberate policy, the economy may be made to follow a regular pattern just by holding the fraction of income saved within a certain interval at a steady.

4. Distribution of Income and Wealth in the Neoclassical One Sector Growth Model

In the previous sections, different extended forms of the neoclassical one-sector growth model have been studied. Interactions which occur among various forms of technological change, population changes and economic development were investigated. This section will study another important aspect of economic development - the distribution of income and wealth. We are interested in the way in which long-term growth is affected by such factors. The discussion in this section is still limited to the framework of a one sector neoclassical model.

The neoclassical theorem, provided by Robinson and others, states that per capita consumption is maximized in the state of balanced growth or the Golden Age if the rate of profit is equal to the rate of growth. In such a state, the average saving ratio should be equal to the relative profit share. This theorem can be simply derived from the Solow model (see Section 2.1) as follows: in balanced growth, capital grows at the same rate as labour. Hence, along the balanced growth path net investment is given by nK and per capita consumption c is equal to:

$$c = f(k) - nk. \tag{2.4.1}$$

The function c is maximized at $k = k_0$, where $f'(k_0) = n$. Thus, when the neoclassical theorem holds, the equilibrium profit rate, i.e., the marginal product of capital, is equal to the growth rate. At the same time, net investment is equal to net profits.

In the preceding discussion, we did not take individual propensities to save or the distribution of income and wealth into account. However, in a "private-enterprise" economy, the savings of capitalists and workers lead to the accumulation of wealth and affect further distributions of income. In this sense, the neoclassical theorem may provide particular inferences about individual propensities to save and the distribution of income and wealth. Sato (1966) solved this problem by considering a case where capitalists remain capitalists and workers remain workers, no matter how much wealth they accumulate.

Sato shows that the situation envisaged by the neoclassical theorem requires that the capitalists' propensity to save should be unity, and that the workers' propensity to save should be equal to the relative profit share.

From the Solow model, we know that the wage rate w and the profit rate r are given, respectively, by

$$w = f(k) - kf'(k), \quad r = f'(k). \tag{2.4.2}$$

Output is distributed between wages and profits: $Y = wL + rK$. The relative share of capital is given by: $h = rK/Y$. Denote by K_c and K_w the equities held by capitalists and workers, respectively, i.e.,

$$K = K_c + K_w = zK + (1 - z)K, \tag{2.4.3}$$

where z is the capitalists' share of wealth, $z = K_c/K$. The workers' total income is given by $wL + rK_w$ and the capitalists' total income by rK_c. Assume that the capitalists' savings rate is s_c and the workers' savings rate is s_w and $1 \geq s_c > s_w \geq 0$. As

$$dK_c/dt = s_c rK_c, \quad dK_w/dt = s_w(wL + rK_w),$$ (2.4.4)

one has

$$dk/dt = k[(s_c - s_w)zf' + s_w f/k - n].$$ (2.4.5)

Differentiating $z = K_c/K$ yields

$$dz/dt = z[(s_c-s_w)(1-z)f' - s_w(f/k - f')],$$ (2.4.6)

The system consists of (2.4.5) and (2.4.6). In equilibrium the following equations hold:

$$f'(k_0) = n/s_c,$$ (2.4.7)

$$1 - z_0 = (1/h_0 - 1)s_w/(s_c-s_w),$$ (2.4.8)

which states that the equilibrium profit rate is equal to the ratio of the growth rate to the capitalists' propensity to save. Therefore, the profit rate is independent of the workers' propensity to save in an economy with balanced growth. From (2.4.7) one sees that per capita consumption is maximized when $s_c = 1$. We can thus conclude that for the neoclassical theorem to hold in this case, the capitalists' propensity to save must be unity, while the workers' propensity to save is not relevant. As the equilibrium solution is only economically meaningful if the relative share of wealth lies between zero and one, this condition is satisfied iff

$$s_w \leq s_c h_0.$$ (2.4.9)

It can also be shown that this is a sufficient condition for stability of the equilibrium. For $s_c = 1$ this condition implies that s_w does not exceed h_0. However, if the workers' propensity to save violates (2.4.9), the workers' equity holding increases faster than the capitalists' equity holding. The capitalists' share of wealth eventually converges to zero. This solution is obtained by putting $K_c = 0$ ($z = 0$). The equilibrium is determined by

$$f(k^*)/k^* = n/s_w. \tag{2.4.10}$$

The aggregate propensity to save is equal to s_w. Hence, we find that per capita consumption is maximized at $s_w = h_0$.

We have provided a simple example to show the effects of distribution on economic development. A comprehensive study of the relations between distribution and economic growth can be found in Marglin (1984).

5. The Two Sector Models

The one sector models in the preceding sections assume a homogeneous output. This implies that output can be transformed without cost into either consumption goods or capital goods. To overcome this unrealistic assumption, this section will consider a two sector growth model. The initial, most important contributions to the two sector economy were made by Uzawa (1961). This section is based upon his work.

In the two sector growth model, it is assumed that consumption and capital goods are different commodities which are produced in two distinct sectors. A two sector model may be equivalent to a one sector model if, for any given wage/rental ratio, the two sectors select the same capital/labour ratio.

As in the one sector models, it is assumed that labour is homogeneous, and grows at an exogenously given exponential rate, n. Unemployment is omitted. There is only one malleable capital good which can be used as an input in both sectors in the economy. Capital depreciates at a constant exponential rate, d, which is independent of the manner of use.

The economy consists of two production sectors: consumption and capital production. The technology of each sector is described by an production function. There are two kinds of production inputs: labour and capital. It is assumed that both capital and labour can be shifted instantaneously and without cost from either sector to the other. The production functions are obtained by aggregating the production functions of each sector's individual firms. The production functions are given by

$$Y_i = F_i(K_i, L_i), \quad i = 1, 2, \tag{2.5.1}$$

where Y_i are the output of the ith sector, K_i and L_i are the capital and labour used in the ith sector, respectively, F_i the production functions, the subscripts 1 and 2 denote the capital good sector and the consumption good sector, respectively. If we assume F_i to be neoclassical, then one has

$$y_i = f_i(k_i), \quad i = 1, 2, \tag{2.5.2}$$

where $y_i = Y_i/L_i$, $k_i = K_i/L_i$, $f_i' > 0$, $f_i'' < 0$.

It is assumed that the usual static efficiency conditions of pure competition, or Lerner-Lange socialism, hold at any time. This requirement means that the wages, w_i, and the wage/rental ratio, w_i^*, in the two sectors are equal, $w = w_1 = w_2$, $w^* = w_1^* = w_2^*$. As $w^* = F_L/F_K$, one has

$$w^* = f_i/f_i' - k_i, \quad i = 1, 2. \tag{2.5.3}$$

As full employment of labour and capital is assumed, one has: $K_1 + K_2 = K$, $L_1 + L_2 = L$, which can be re-written in the form of

$$n_1 k_1 + n_2 k_2 = k, \tag{2.5.4}$$

where $n_i = L_i/L$ $(i = 1, 2)$.

The savings behavior is described by the assumption that the gross savings propensities - both average and marginal - from wage incomes and profits are non-negative constants denoted by s_w and s_r, respectively. Thus, if the two propensities are equal (to s), then the consumption is equal to a constant fraction $(1 - s)$ of the gross national product. If we denote the rental rate of the two sectors by r, then the total gross savings in the economy is equal to $s_r rK + s_w wL$. As the investment in the economy comes from the production of new capital and savings is always equal to investment, we have

$$P_1 Y_1 = s_r rK + s_w wL, \tag{2.5.5}$$

where P_1 is the price of new capital. As $F_{1K} = r/P_1$, (2.5.5) can be rewritten in the form of

$$n_1 f_1(k_1) = f_1'(s_r k + s_w w^*). \tag{2.5.6}$$

As $dK/dt = Y_1 - dK$, one has

$$dk/dt = f_1'(s_r k + s_w w^*) - gk, \tag{2.5.7}$$

where $g = n + d$.

The dynamics of the economy is described by (2.5.7). Although it is similar to the Solow model, as shown below the functional form of the right-hand side is more complicated, which may result in some features that cannot be observed in the one sector models.

Under certain conditions, the dynamic system is "causal" (e.g., see Burmeister and Dobell, 1970). If we assume that the conditions are satisfied, then the right-hand side of (2.5.7) can be written as a function of k, i.e.,

$$dk/dt = H(k) = kh(k). \tag{2.5.8}$$

We will not give the functional form of h. Let us denote the "extended Jacobian" by J, and define two numbers a and b as

$$a = \max\{\lim[f_i/f_i' - k_i], i = 1, 2\},$$
$$k_i \to 0$$

$$b = \min\{\lim[f_i/f_i' - k_i], i = 1, 2\}.$$
$$k_i \to 0$$

Then the following theorems hold.

Theorem 2.5.1 (Local Stability)

Let k^* be any root of h = 0. If s_w/g is not larger than $k/f_1(k_1)$ or s_r/g is not less than $k/f_1(k_1)$, then the equilibrium is locally stable.

Theorem 2.5.2 (Uniqueness and Stability)

If any of the following conditions are satisfied for all $a < w^* < b$, then any equilibrium of the system is unique and stable:

(i) s_r is not less than s_w, while k_1 is not larger than k_2;

(ii) the wage elasticity of capital intensity $(w^*/k)(dk/dw^*)$ is not less than unity;

(iii) The substitution elasticity of the consumption sector is not less than unity;

(iv) $s_r = 1$ and $J > 0$;

(v) $s_w = 0$ and $J > 0$,

in which all functions and variables are evaluated at the equilibrium.

The economic interpretations of these results can be found in Uzawa (1961). It should be mentioned that even if all the conditions (i)-(v) are violated, it is still possible to find a unique and balanced growth path, and unstable balanced growth paths may exist.

Certain features of the two sector model can not be observed in the (standard Solow) one sector model. For instance, in the two sector model the existence of a positive unique equilibrium cannot always be asserted. The capital-/labour ratio may permanently oscillate around an unstable equilibrium (Inada, 1966).

Numerous extensions and generalizations of the Uzawa two sector model have been performed. Technological changes have been introduced into the system by, for example, Diamond (1965), Takayama (1965), Weizsäcker (1966). Drandakis (1963) demonstrated that the labour supply may be treated as a function of the real wage rate without significantly altering the structure of the two-sector model. Inada (1966) has examined a two-sector model in which it is assumed that capital cannot be shifted between sectors. This assumption means that once a machine is installed in a particular sector, it must remain in that sector for its lifetime. There are also some studies which replace the smooth neoclassical production functions by fixed coefficient production functions of the Leontief form (e.g., Shinkai, 1960, Corden, 1966). Stiglitz (1967) modified the two sector model so that labour is divided into two classes: capitalists who derive their income solely from the ownership of capital, and workers who receive both wage income and returns from capital ownership.

6. Multiple Sector Models
- The extended neoclassical model

This section presents some multiple sector models which involve the production of several types of durable goods. We will focus upon two models, which are characterized by nonlinear production technologies. For an introduction to multi-sector models see Morishima (1964, 1969) and Nikaido (1968).

First, we will illustrate the structure of the multisector neoclassical growth model. The model reviewed below is an extension of the Uzawa two sector model. Here we are only interested in certain aspects of the structure of the models, so we will not examine the model in detail.

The economy consists of n distinct capital goods and one consumption good. Joint production is excluded in this model. Hence, there are n + 1 production sectors and commodities. Let the subscripts 1, ... , n denote the sectors producing the capital goods, and the symbols K_i (i = 1, ... , n) denote the stocks of these capital goods. The sector producing the consumption good is expressed by the subscript 0. Each capital good and labour can be used in each of the n + 1 sectors. Labour is assumed to be homogeneous. Let K_{ij} denote the quantity of the ith capital good employed in the jth sector, and L_j the labour employed in the jth sector ($i = 0, 1, ... , n, j = 1, ... n$). The production of the jth sector is described by a neoclassical production function

$$Y_j = F^j(L_j, K_j), \quad j = 0, ... , n, \tag{2.6.1}$$

where Y_j ($j = 0, 1, ... , n$) are outputs of the jth sector, $K_j = (K_{1j}, ... , K_{nj})^T$. As the functions are homogeneous of degree one with respect to their arguments, one can rewrite (2.6.1) as

$$1 = F^j(a_{0j}, a_{1j}, ... , a_{nj}), \quad j = 0, 1, ... , n,$$

$$\tag{2.6.2}$$

where

$$a_{0j} = L_j/Y_j, \quad j = 0, 1, ..., n,$$

$$a_{ij} = K_{ij}/Y_j, \quad i = 1, ... , n, \quad j = 0, 1, ... , n.$$

The full employment conditions are given by

$$\sum_{j=0}^{n} a_{0j} Y_j = L,$$

$$\sum_{j=0}^{n} a_{ij} Y_j = K_i. \tag{2.6.3}$$

Capital accumulation is determined by

$$dK_i/dt = Y_i - d_i K_i, \quad i = 1, ... , n, \tag{2.6.4}$$

where d_i ($i = 1, ... , n$) are real depreciation rates of the ith capital.

We also wish to describe the following example of a non-linear multiple sector model.

This model assumes that all internal forms of allocation and optimization can be completely determined from knowledge of the stocks of factor endowments only. Hence, the results of these decisions may be described by functions in which only those total stocks appear as arguments. All outputs can be generally described by the equations

$$X_i(t+1) = H^i[X(t)] = H^i[X_1(t), \ldots , X_n(t)], \tag{2.6.5}$$

where $X_i(t)$ (i = 1, ... , n) denote output of the ith sector at time t. This model is completely self-contained and determined. The functions H^i are assumed to be continuous, homogeneous of degree one, and strictly increasing in each argument.

A sequence X(t) is said to be a balanced growth path or a steady growth path if for some g (> 0) we have

$$X(t+1) = gX(t), \text{ for any } t. \tag{2.6.6}$$

Because of the homogeneity of H, we are now reduced to finding a positive vector V such that

$$gV = H(V),$$

$$\sum_{j=1}^{n} V_i = 1. \tag{2.6.7}$$

The conditions for the existence and uniqueness of a balanced growth path are given in Nikaido (1968).

7. Production Functions in Growth Models

In all of the models mentioned above, we use the concept of 'production function'. Before studying how monetary variables are introduced into growth theory in the next chapter, we wish to discuss the production function controversy of the 1960. A discussion about whether or not individual production relations can legitimately be aggregated into a production function is referred to, for example, in Leontief (1947), Robinson (1953), Hicks (1965).

Hicks argued that this issue belongs to the field of the "static method in dynamic theory". In the economic literature, we can find many similar fundamental issues in this field. In addition to the production function, we have a demand function of money whose existence is the most basic assumption in "monetarism": a consumption function for goods, a savings function, a demand function for goods, and numerous other functions. All of these functions have been used in dynamic analysis. There should be some general reasons for using such static methods in a dynamic context.

If we accept the opinion that everything is changeable, we see that there are significant problems in assuming the existence of such functions, because each assumption is only valid if the relations these functions are assumed to describe are "structurally stable". For instance, the assumption of the existence of a production function F(K,L) means that during the study period the relations among the inputs and outputs are not subjected to great changes. Similarly, the existence of a money demand function means that the rules of the game between the government and individuals are invariant with respect to time. However, in the long term these assumptions cannot be sustained.

The problem is as follows. Suppose that we are concerned with a production unit such as an economy, an industry, or a firm. For simplicity, only the case of a single output is discussed. It is assumed that only labour, L, and capital, K, are used as "inputs" in producing "output", Y. We may pose the question: is there any relation $Y = F(L,K)$ which can be expected to hold, even very approximately, at any point of time during the study period. It should be noted that the form F may be determined in such a way that output Y is maximized from any given set of inputs L and K. Surely, if we wish to base the theory of production on the Jevons/Böhm-Bawerk theory of the "roundabout" process, we may introduce time explicitly into the production function: $Y = F(L,K,t)$. This form is also strongly suggested in Wicksell's treatment of capital problems.

In a static context, the assumption of the existence of a production function is quite acceptable, although there may be other questionable factors such as continuities (Hicks, 1965). However, there are problems if one assumes the existence of a production function in a dynamic analysis. Obviously, according to the definition the form of a production function is affected by various forms of technological change which is due to innovation (or imitation), management methods, institutional changes and other changeable factors. Now we will examine how such factors can be taken into account in a dynamic analysis.

The simplest method of introducing technological change in a production function is to assume that progress takes place according to some presumed order. As the change is exogenously determined, we can generally describe the changes by introducing a parameter (time) t as:

$$Y = F(K,L,t). \tag{2.7.1}$$

This form is mostly used in growth models such as those reviewed above. However, we are not so interested in these functions, as our main concern is with the endogenous factors which cause functional forms to change. Simple treatment of technological change as "manna from heaven" is nothing but a denial of our human efforts to change the world.

Production processes may improve as new theories are discovered. But it is to be expected that any immediate progress will be limited as it takes time for people to understand the new theories and to apply them in practice. Alternatively, productivity may be increased owing to innovations introduced by a firm. In order for production to increase to the full extent that the innovation makes possible, a process of adjustment will be needed - a process that will take time. The opportunities which new forms of technology produce take time to be fully realized as the ideas that are generated in this manner have to be transferred from firm to firm. Hicks called this the time needed for "informational diffusion". Similarly, it takes time for capital stock to be transmuted into a form which is appropriate to the new technology. This is termed "capital transmutation" (Hicks, 1965).

How can the processes of such adjustment be described in terms of a production function used in dynamic analysis? Hicks suggested that since there are stationary equilibria at dates both before and after the adjustment, it is possible to compare the new equilibrium with the old one. However, this method of comparison tells us little about the "dynamic process" of adjustment. Moreover, if a new stationary equilibrium does not exist, the method will fail completely. This could happen if chaotic behavior occurs after the adjustment.

If the innovation only occurs at the initial point of the study period and there is no other form of innovation to affect the production process during the whole period, we can take account of the effects of the adjustment process and imitation by assuming a functional form similar to (2.5.1), though some costs of learning must necessarily be considered. The problem is that we generally have no idea about when a new theory will be discovered or the time when an innovation may be introduced; they appear to be random to the analyst. In some cases, we may assume that the effects of innovation on production can be treated as small perturbations in a macro sense, and thus the effects can be neglected. We may also introduce a time distribution of innovation and thus the output determined from the production function becomes a random variable. In reality, innovation is more subtle and remains one of the main sources of mystery about technological progress.

Rather than dealing with "discrete" innovations, we can also assume that increases in productivity can be treated as continuous functions of "learning by doing" and education. Thus, in the long-run, the average effects of innovations are implicitly taken into account. We have already met with such approaches in previous sections. In fact, these approaches (implicitly) mean that there are certain deterministic laws which determine how knowledge can be converted into productivity. We can, at least empirically, know such laws.

Finally, we will consider the institutional factors which influence technological change in relation to recent reforms in socialist countries. The single common characteristic among the economic reforms in these countries is the introduction of competitive mechanisms into their economic systems. It is important to know whether it is reasonable to use a production function to describe an economy undergoing such a process. As the reform progresses, it may be difficult to guarantee the existence of a stable production function, because the production structure is changeable. Not only are new technologies introduced, the institutions are also being changed.

If, in some sense, productivity is only improved due to institutional changes we can overcome the difficulty in the following way. Let us assume the existence of a potential production function, $F(K,L)$, as described above. This function is determined by the condition that the whole social system functions "effectively" under existing levels of knowledge, the labor force and capital. Here, "effectively" means that the "potential" maximal output is obtained under the given social structure. In this case, we may assume that the production structure is always adjusted to the optimal structure (owing to the reform which has taken place). Hence, one has

$$dY/dt = s_1\{F(K,L) - Y\}, \tag{2.7.2}$$

where s_1 is an adjustment speed parameter. And it may be quite reasonable to assume that (2.7.2) is subjected to

$$F(K,L) \geq Y. \tag{2.7.3}$$

This implies that the actual output cannot be greater than the "designed capacity" $F(K,L)$. Owing to the reform, the actual output is always increased until it is equal to the designed capacity, even for fixed labour and capital inputs.

The parameter s_1 is affected by the efficiency of management and other "institutional" factors. It may also be a function of education (knowledge). The function F describes the technological potential of the production system. If the reform is effective, then the parameter s_1 may be very large, and vice versa.

Let us assume that the production system adjusts to the "optimal structure" very rapidly. That is, s_1 is very large. In this case, $Y = F$ may hold during the study period without affecting the qualitative properties of the dynamic system.

Consider the case in which the standard neoclassical growth model is extended to include (2.2.5). As is well known, the growth model is consistent in the sense that as soon as inputs are given, interest and wage rates are determined as:

$$w = F_L, \quad r = F_K, \tag{2.7.4}$$

where w and r are the wage rate and rate of interest, respectively. For simplicity, we assume that the price of goods is equal to unity during the study period. However, when (2.7.2) holds and s_1 is not very large, we have a new problem: how to determine the wage rate and rate of interest in the extended dynamics. Obviously, (2.7.4) does not hold generally. In this case, we may propose the following dynamics:

$$dw/dt = \alpha[F_L - w], \quad dr/dt = \beta[F_K - r]. \tag{2.7.5}$$

These equations imply that the actual wage rate and the rate of interest are adjusted to values which are determined by a perfectly competitive mechanism. Thus, the one-dimensional Solow model is extended to a four-dimensional dynamic system. From this example, we can see that the assumption of the existence of functional relations among variables may bring a great simplicity upon dynamic economic analysis. Such an assumption is often dependent upon whether we are interested in long run or short run dynamic behavior. However, it cannot be determined from the phenomenon under consideration itself. To some degree, the one-sector growth models are neither appropriate in the short run (as they neglect institutions) nor in the long run (due to the structural instabilities of the functional relations which have been discussed).

III

A REVISION OF REAL AND MONETARY DYNAMIC MODELS

In process of exchange and division of labour, money plays an essential role in any developed economy. Barter - the exchange of goods for goods, or of any nonmoney asset for any other - is important in primitive societies and is never wholly absent even in the most advanced economies. Pure barter has become less important in modern economic analysis. As there may be a considerable time interval between the receipt of money and its use in exchange, a complex society has need for a stable form of money that will provide a store of value. Although the store of value function may be shared with other liquid assets, there is no substitute for money as a medium of exchange. Things used as money reflect the simplicity or complexity of the economic life of the economic system under consideration. With the progressive increase in the volume and variety of goods and services in a community, the development of a convenient means of payment and the need for a standard to measure their values are very pressing. We will see that money and its role in society, like many other institutions, has become more and more complicated.

Money is a social tool. Its existence is due to the necessity of exchanges among different people. How it is used reflects the type of society in which one lives. The significance of money is reflected in its social functioning. In general, money has three functions, as a standard of value, as a generally accepted means of exchange, and as a store of value. These functions of money indicate that money must be generally acceptable in order to serve as a good medium of exchange and that it must be stable in value in order to serve satisfactorily as a standard of value and as a standard of deferred payments. Moreover, in analysis of a monetary system, desirable physical characteristics, such as convenience, durability, ease of recognition, uniformity in value, stability in value, are very important.

In order to study money, it is necessary to examine the social environment (or markets in a narrow sense) individuals live in. The utility of money to an individual depends essentially on the social environment as its value lies not in its value as a commodity but in its services in connection with his social act of exchange. For Robinson Crusoe, money is useless. It is also true that if the environment were such that the markets are complete and perfect in the sense of Arrow-Debreu, money will also be useless.

The role of money lies in its capacity to improve individuals: facilitate exchange and coordination among individual plans and generate a more efficient allocation of scare resources. The use of money permits the consumer to shift purchases from one commodity to a second, to buy certain goods today or to postpone purchases, to buy in one commodity or a second, or to buy from one merchant or another.

Because of so many functioning of monetary variables, it is not so easy to understand relations among these variables such as money, prices, interest rates, and not to say, relations among real variables and monetary variables. The amount of money and how it is used probably exerts a great influence on the general 'economic climate' in which businessmen and others live and work. Most economic decisions are related to monetary variables. Since money has a capacity to connect the present and the future, conflicts among long-run and short-run economic goals and uncertainties of the future make economic decisions very complicated.

The preceding chapter has investigated real aspects of economic development. Although the dynamic analysis of quantitative variables markets is important for understanding the complexity of economic development, one can hardly understanding the functioning of economic systems without examining the complexity of monetary systems. Effects of monetary variables such as quantity of money, interest rate, prices and rents upon economic development are very complicated. This chapter is to explore the complexity of monetary aspects of the economic systems.

1. Money in Economic Theory

In 1752, Hume made a pioneering contribution to monetary economics. There are two particularly important aspects of his study. First, he considered a trade imbalance which could cause specie (gold or silver) to flow either into or out of a country. This would then cause a change in price levels , which would alter the country's competitiveness in trade and in turn correct the initial imbalance. It follows that "mercantilism" policies designed to produce a trade surplus would be self-defeating; if a surplus were to be produced this would only be temporal since the resulting inflows would raise domestic price levels, reducing exports and increasing imports, thus eliminating the surplus. Second, he argued that monetary changes might have very different effects in the short run as opposed to the long run. In the short term an increase in the money supply might stimulate industry, for prices would rise faster than costs; but in the long run, when the relationship between prices and costs had returned to normal, the only effect of a monetary expansion would be to raise the price level. Although Smith was aware of Hume's monetary theory, he made little use of it in his Wealth of Nations.

Adam Smith recognized the importance of exchange activities and the role of money. His emphasis on division of labour cannot result in improved efficient reallocation of resources unless exchange activities are efficient. He argued how money could facilitate exchange by allowing people to avoid the difficulties of attaining the double coincidence of wants. But Smith never explained how some one commodity or other had come to gain general acceptability in exchange.

Henry Thornton also made a great contribution to the field of monetary economics. In his "Essay on the Nature of the Paper Credit of Great Britain" (1802), Thornton regarded paper credit (notes and bills of exchange) as one item in a balance sheet. Both notes and bills circulate - bills circulating more slowly because they bear interest, but the velocity of circulation of both bills and notes depends on confidence in a "season of distrust". Fluctuations in confidence might cause fluctuations in the demand for money, and hence in the price of bullion, irrespective of the Bank of England's actions. According to Thornton, the price of bullion might be independently affected by another factor - the balance of payments. Currency might flow abroad, depressing the exchanges (raising the price of bullion) as the result of exceptional remittances abroad. Thus, there was the possibility of an "external drain" of gold, due to an adverse balance of payments, together with the possibility of an "internal drain", caused by a loss of confidence in paper currency, either of which might alter the price of bullion.

Thornton also argued that monetary changes affected the economy and recognized that in the short run a monetary change might lead to changes in the level of activity. A monetary expansion might be caused by the banking system's reducing the cost of borrowing below the rate of profit that can be earned on capital. The increased availability of bank loans raises demand for goods and the price level rises. This process continues for as long as the rate of interest on loans remains below the rate of profit on capital. Such a process will stop as soon as the rate of interest returns to equality with the rate of profit. The economy will have a higher stock of money and a higher price level.

In "The High Price of Bullion" (1810), Ricardo argued that the sole cause of an unfavorable balance of trade, and of a high price of bullion, was the over-issue of currency. Although Ricardo made use of Thornton's indirect mechanism he focused on the long run where the rate of interest depends on the abundance or scarcity of that capital which does not consist of money. The rate of interest, according to Ricardo, could be kept low only by increasing the supply of capital, not by monetary expansion: Profits can only be lowered by a competition of capitals not consisting of circulating medium. Ricardo was assuming that Thornton's indirect mechanism worked itself out very quickly. The mainstreams of neoclassical theory accept this doctrine.

After Thornton, another major contribution in monetary economics is that of Wicksell. His celebrated "Interest and Prices" (1898) is concerned with restating and defending the quantity theory of money. In developing the quantity theory he was influenced by two things: (i) the capital theory of Jevons and Böhm-Bawerk, which had laid the foundations of a real theory of the rate of interest; and (ii) Tooke's objections to the quantity theory, which comprised both a number of puzzles and suggestions. We will explain Wicksell's work in detail later on.

Walras argued that the theory of money can be developed only after the real theory of growth. He believed that no money problem can be thoroughly discussed with a model where investment and saving are not made (see, Morishima, 1977). In Walras' model the demand for cash balances is a way of saving and is related to investment in commodity inventories. As there is no place for savings and investment in the system of pure exchange and that of simple reproduction, there is no need for money. There may be a numéraire in a static system of exchange and production, while "money" can appear only in dynamic systems in which individuals and firms are allowed to save and investment. Hence, Walras' money theory is related to the theory of saving, the theory of inventory investment, the theory of portfolio selection, and so on. However, as Morishima (1977) mentions, Walras' theory of money should be regarded as an unfinished work, "because it is incomplete and obscure in various points and even inconsistent, in that it contains a careless technical slip which has of course to be removed." Walras was concerned with an economy where capital goods and inventories directly owned by capitalists are rented to firms or entrepreneurs, and decisions concerning investment are made by capitalists (i.e., savers) themselves, so that there is no inconsistency between investment and saving such as Keynes emphasized. Moreover, Walras did not put explicit attention to the bond market: Keynes' system is also a model from which supply and demand for bonds have been eliminated. Hicks' model establishes equilibrium between supply and demand in the bond market and the money market, in addition to the ordinary commodity markets.

Menger (1892) argued that the fundamental problem of money is not why ceratin metals have become money, nor whether the society benefits from having a general medium of exchange, but how a general medium of exchange has evolved in a society through unconcerned actions of egoistic individuals. According to Menger, the central problem lies at the saleableness of goods. "These difficulties [of barter exchange] would have proved absolutely insurmountable obstacles to the progress of traffic, and at the same time to the production of goods not commanding a regular sale, had there not laid a remedy in the very nature of things, to wit, the different degrees of saleableness ... of commodities. The difference existing in this respect between articles of commerce is of the highest degree of the market in general. And the failure to turn it adequately to account in explaining the phenomenon of trade, constitutes not only as much a lamentable breach in our science, but also one of the essential causes of the backward state of monetary theory. The theory of money necessarily presupposes a theory of the saleableness of goods." According to Menger, evaluation of the saleableness appear to depend upon two measures. One is the difference between the purchase price of a good (the units of the most saleable good to be given up) and its selling price (the number of units of the most saleable good to be obtained on immediate resale). The other is the expected time cost involved in the sale of the good at an economic price. Basing upon the theory of the saleableness, Menger examines the genesis of media of exchange. His main points are as follows. First, there is the peculiar interdependence among individual tastes for a medium of exchange. One's willingness to accept it depends on his expectation about the same willingness on the part of his traders. Second, money is not a product of legal compulsion or of any social contrivance, but is a product of unconcerned efforts among individuals, each purchasing his own economic interests. Third, the evolution of money is a learning process on the part of generalizations of individuals. This dynamic theory in contrast with static discussions of barter and monetary exchange.

Irving Fisher (1911) attempted an explanation of money, using the most widely used version of the equation of exchange

$$MV = PT, \tag{3.1.1}$$

where M is the quantity of money, V its velocity of circulation, P the price level, and T the volume of transactions.

It should be noted that (3.1.1) is held at any point of time. Taking derivatives of both sides of (3.1.1) with respect to time, we obtain

$$dM/dt/M - dT/dt/T = dP/dt/P, \tag{3.1.2}$$

where the velocity is assumed to be fixed. This equation defines a dynamic relation among the rates of change in the money supply, transaction volumes and prices.

When bank deposits are brought in as well as currency, the equation (3.1.1) becomes

$$MV + M'V' = PT, \tag{3.1.3}$$

where M' and V' are the quantity and velocity of the circulation of bank deposits, respectively. Using the equation of exchange, Fisher analyzed the "permanent effect" of a change in the quantity of money, and "temporal effects during periods of transition". Permanent effects were obtained using a simple quantity theory: changes in the quantity of money would ultimately produce equiproportionate changes in the price level; the interest rate, velocity and the volume of transactions settling down to their normal values. During transition periods, however, monetary changes would produce changes in all the variables in the equation of exchange. The major reason for these temporary effects was, according to Fisher, the failure of the interest rate to respond sufficiently rapidly to price changes. For example, if M increased, this would increase the inflation rate, but if the money interest rate did not respond fully, the real interest rate would fall, and business would be stimulated. It should be noted that a similar way of analyzing money, using the equation of exchange, was accepted by the Cambridge school (e.g., Blackhouse, 1985), though a different formulation of the equation was defined. The Cambridge school puts greater stress on psychological factors and individual decisions.

The most influential work in modern monetary economics is Keynes' "The General Theory", irrespective of the fact that much of the General Theory's contents can be found in the writings of Pigou, Hawtrey and the Swedish school. The portfolio theory of demand for money which constitutes the kernel of Keynes' theory confines attention to the asset market and study the allocation of wealth among various types of assets, money being one of them. This is in contrast to the traditional quantity theory which focused attention to the relationship between the stock of money and the flow of magnitude - volume of transactions.

Since the publication of the General Theory, so-called monetarism has dominated modern static macroeconomics. Although it is difficult to exactly define the concept of modern monetarism, according to Laidler (1981) the key characteristics of monetarism are as follows: (I) A "quantity theory" approach to macroeconomic analysis in two distinct senses: to describe a theory of the demand for money by Milton Friedman (1956) and to consider fluctuations in the quantity of money as the dominant cause of fluctuations in money income; (II) The analysis of the division of money income fluctuations between price levels and real income in terms of an expectations augmented Philips curve; (III) A monetary approach to balance-of-payments and exchange-rate theory; (IV) (a) Antipathy to interventionist stabilization policy, either monetary or fiscal, and to wage and price controls, and (b) support for long-run monetary policy rules or at least prestated targets, cast in terms of the behavior of some monetary aggregate rather than of the level of interest rate.

Among others, Tobin (1955, 1965) and Friedman (1956) made important contributions to monetarism. Sections 3.2 and 3.3 will study the models developed and extended within the framework of Tobin's analysis.

Friedman's work on the demand for money should be viewed as a development of a fundamentally Keynesian capital theoretic approach to monetary theory (Johnson, 1962). Friedman assumed that money might have effects on economic growth because it is a financial asset. His approach is different from that of Tobin as it claims to be a theory of the total demand for money in the macro-economy rather than that of some component of that demand. Moreover, Friedman explicitly recognized the inflation rate as an own rate of return on money and postulated a well determined functional relationship between the expected inflation rate and the demand for money, a relationship whose existence Keynes explicitly denied (see, Laidler, 1981).

Friedman asserted that the demand for money was , as an empirical matter, a stable function of a few measurable arguments. It should be noted that Keynes did not believe this - his empirically stable relationship was the consumption function. It is with the publication of Friedman's essay that statements to the effect that the velocity of circulation is, as a practical matter, a stable function of a few arguments became central to debates about monetary economics. Its stress on this hypothesis makes monetarism a very different doctrine from classical and neoclassical economics, no matter what other similarities there may be.

This characteristic monetarist belief in a stable demand for money cannot be supported by empirical evidence. It has been suggested that the relationship has shifted in an unpredicted way in a number of countries. The instability in question is often present, particularly in the United States (Lainder, 1981). In fact, supplying money is nothing but a game between the government and individuals. If the rules of the game are changeable as they seem to be in the long-term, it is impossible to form a stable relationship. The discussion about production functions in dynamic analysis in Section 2.7 may shed some light on the implications and limitations of the assumption of a stable money supply function.

It should be mentioned that in neoclassical growth models monetary variables are (implicitly) assumed to be "fast", i.e., they are assumed to adjust rapidly to real terms. As soon as quantitative aspects are determined, monetary variables are given as the results of perfect competition. On the other hand, "monetarists" assume the speed of monetary variables to be in the same order as speed of certain real terms. This is one of the fundamental characteristics of monetary economics. By monetary theory, in this case we simply mean those doctrines which deny the "neutrality" of money in economic analysis. This implies that in monetary theory prices, incomes, and savings and investment decisions no longer only appear as expressions of quantities of commodities and of the exchange ratios between them. However, various monetary economists hold different points view about monetary variables. We will review some of these approaches.

Classical economists always assume that in the long run the economic system will function in such a way that it will remain structurally stable. In fact, for them a long-term analysis is the same as a static analysis because they assume that in the long-term everything works perfectly in a static world.

Real variables may be affected by monetary variables in the short run, although there is little (or at least a rather "weak") impact in the long run. In classical monetary economics it may be possible to observe that an economic system is out of "order" in the short run, but the historical path of economic development is not very seriously affected by such "fluctuations". Thus, all non-liner phenomena such a "disorders" or temporal phenomena are omitted in any long-term analysis.

The insights provided by modern (nonlinear) dynamic theory show that such an approach is invalid. Small fluctuations can drive essentially nonlinear systems well away from their original equilibrium development paths; i.e., they may cause large scale changes in the variables. This implies that if economic systems are potentially unstable and monetary variables can drive them out of order, then in the long term monetary variables should play an important role in changing the evolutionary paths of economic development.

In the recent literature monetarism appears to have become increasingly important, but many significant contributions to modern growth theory have been obtained from real analysis. It is doubtful whether the criticisms made by monetarists about real analysis focus upon the relevant aspects of quantitative growth analysis. As real analysis is always concerned with stabilized economies, its premises about the role of money might be reasonable as long as the assumption of stability is valid. The reason is that stable economic development is always associated with long-run equilibrium in which forecasting can be correctly made.

The monetarists do not base their attack on real analysis upon the relaxation of the assumption of stability. The (modern) monetary approach is fundamentally based on empirical studies in which the assumption of stability is still presumed, although the studies by Grandmont (1985) and those economists concerned with business cycles and economic chaos are exceptions. Significant progress in understanding the role of monetary variables in unstable economies - in both the theoretical and practical sense - may be made once we gain more knowledge about chaotic economies, although this will probably be a slow process.

In the remainder of this chapter, we will introduce some models to show how monetary variables can be introduced to growth theory. As in the preceding chapter, we do not deal with the problems of capacity utilization and unemployment, or disequilibrium phenomena.

2. The One Sector Model With Money Within the Framework of the Neoclassical Approach

This section introduces some of the features of a monetary economy.

We assume the presence of a paper currency in addition to a single capital good; wealth may be held in either of these two forms. The production side is identical to the neoclassical growth model just described. That is, the capital good and the labour force are combined to produce a homogeneous output which can be used either for consumption or for investment. It is assumed that the price level and capital stock are set by past conditions. However, at each moment the rates of change of price level and the capital stock are determined. The change rates are determined in such a way that a money market equilibrium condition and a saving hypothesis are satisfied. Thus, the price level and the capital stock for the "next instant" are given. This implies that rather than the price level, it is the "inflation rate" that is directly determined in the system. It is assumed that our study period is long enough for prices to adjust fully to a stationary equilibrium value.

Money, issued by the government without cost, is assumed to serve as numeraire. Money is desired for current investment and transaction purposes. The demand for money is affected by the distribution of income and wealth. However, for simplicity we assume that the per capita demand for money is a function of per capita money income, per capita money wealth, and the expected yield on capital. The money market is assumed to be always at an equilibrium, that is, money demand per capita m^d always equals the actual money supply per capita:

$$m^d = G(y,w,r) = m, \tag{3.2.1}$$

where m (= M/L where M is money stock, L labour force) is per capita money stock supply, G is a continuous function with regard to the arguments, y per capita value of output, w (= pk + m) per capita money wealth; r is the expected money yield on the capital good (r = f'(k) - d + E[dp/dt/p], where p is price of output in terms of money as numeraire, k is per capital stock, d is the depreciation rate, E[dp/dt/p] is the expected inflation rate). We assume the absence of "money illusion", which means that G(y,w,r) is homogeneous of degree one in its first two arguments.

Different authors assume various forms of the money demand-supply function. If G is taken on the form of G(pk,w,r) which is homogeneous in the first two arguments, then one obtains: m/pk = g(1,r) = q(r) (q' < 0). This is the liquidity preference model concerned with portfolio balance, first introduced by Tobin (1955, 1965). If (3.2.1) is altered to m = m(pf(k),r) where m is homogeneous of degree one, one has: Mv(r) = pF(K,L), where v(r) = m(1,r), v' > 0. This is a transaction demand model in which the velocity of circulation is an increasing function of r. In the classical Cambridge model the velocity is (an institutionally) determined constant. In the pure speculation model (e.g., Hahn, 1969), one has: r = u(k,m/p) = 0. Finally, it should be mentioned that in the Keynesian tradition, money is decided both for speculative and transaction purposes, but the function G/p = g(k,r) is not necessarily homogeneous in k.

These cases represent different assumptions about monetary economic behavior. In our model we will choose the final case, not only because it is in the Keynesian tradition but because it also provides the most general representation in the sense that it includes all the behavioral motivations that underlie the other cases.

As we have assumed the absence of "money illusion", from (3.2.1) one has m/p = G(y/p,w/p,r) or x = G[f(k),k+x,r], where x is real per capita money holdings defined as: x = m/p. Solving this equation yields

$$x = g(k,r), \qquad g_k > 0, \quad g_r < 0. \tag{3.2.2}$$

or

$$r = u(k,x), \quad u_k > 0, u_x < 0. \tag{3.2.3}$$

For any positive, finite value of the capital/labour ratio the (positive) expected yield on capital may be so low that no one would wish to hold their wealth in the form of capital. The equilibrium level of per capita real money balances thus may become indefinitely large. This situation is termed the traditional Keynesian liquidity trap.

As we assume that the money market is always in equilibrium with equality between the exogenously given m and the money demand m^d, whether the trap can be arrived at for different values of k is of no consequence in the model. In fact, as shown in Burmeister and Dobell (1970), the equality in equilibrium is achieved by instantaneous adjustments in the expected rate of inflation. As such perfectly flexible prices are (implicitly) assumed, a full-employment solution is ensured even if there are liquidity traps.

The real wealth, W, and real disposable income, Y_d, are defined as

$$W = K + M/p, \qquad\qquad (3.2.4)$$

$$Y_d = F(K,L) - dK + d(M/p)/dt, \qquad\qquad (3.2.5)$$

respectively. As $F(K,L) = C + dK + dK/dt$ where C is the consumption, one has

$$Y_d = dW/dt + C. \qquad\qquad (3.2.6)$$

That is, real net disposable income is equal to the change in real wealth plus real consumption. It is assumed that real consumption is always a constant fraction of real net disposable income

$$C = cY_d, \quad 0 < c < 1, \qquad\qquad (3.2.7)$$

where c is the propensity to consume. This is a flow equilibrium condition satisfied at all points of time. From (3.2.6) and (3.2.7), one obtains

$$dW/dt = sY_d, \qquad\qquad (3.2.8)$$

where $s = (1 - c)$. This implies that

$$dK/dt = s[Y + d(M/p)/dt - dK] - d(M/p)/dt$$

$$= s(y - dk) - (1 - s)d(M/p)/dt,$$

which is often referred to as Tobin's fundamental equation.

Taking the derivative of $x = M/pL$ yields

$$x = (z - n - dp/dt/p)x, \qquad (3.2.9)$$

or, $dp/dt/p = z - n - dx/dt/x$, where n is the fixed population growth rate and z is the constant proportional rate of increase in the nominal stock of money. The parameter z is fixed by the government. This, of course, may imply money illusion on the part of the government (monetary authority), because it is assumed to change the nominal quantity of money at a constant rate, irrespective of the rate of inflation. However, money illusion is not assumed for individuals.

To formulate the dynamics of price, let us assume the perfect myopic foresight which states that the expected inflation rate is equal to the actual rate, $E[dp/dt/p] = dp/dt/p$. People correctly expect the actually realized rate of inflation or deflation. Two interpretations can be given: first that people have perfect myopic foresight; second that people expect that tomorrow the rate of inflation will be what it is today. Under the assumption of "perfect foresight" one has

$$dp/dt = p[r - f'(k) + d]. \qquad (3.2.10)$$

As $r = u(k,x)$, the price dynamics is given by

$$dp/dt/p = u(k,x) - f'(k) + d. \qquad (3.2.11)$$

Thus (3.2.9) can be written as

$$dx/dt = [f'(k) + v - u(k,x)]x = H(k,x)x, \qquad (3.2.12)$$

where $v = z - d - n$.

It is not difficult to identify the following equation for capital

$$dk/dt = sf(k) - (n + sd)k - c[f'(k) - d + z -$$

$$u(k,x)]x. \qquad (3.2.13)$$

Our model consists of (3.2.12) and (3.2.13). This model is called the Tobin model because it was initially suggested by Tobin. The system is an equilibrium monetary growth model in the sense that at every moment of time all the markets are cleared and expectations are fulfilled. This is also a full employment model since the assumption is made that the labour market is instantaneously cleared through perfect flexibility of wages. Whether, however, the model is capable of arriving at equilibrium is another matter.

Our discussion is limited to the domain of values of the parameters such that the system is economically meaningful. Under appropriate conditions, the existence of a positive unique equilibrium can be guaranteed (Burmeister and Dobell, p. 175, 1970). In the equilibrium, the rate of price change may be either positive, negative, or zero, which depends upon the sign of $(z - n)$. It can be proved that the equilibrium value of k without money $(x = 0)$ is higher than the equilibrium capital/labour ratio with money. This result denies the neutrality of money, if "neutrality" means that the long-run capital density is the same for both the monetary and the "idealized" economy. Here, when we say that money is not neutral, we mean that the capital intensity of a monetary economy is different from that of the "idealized" - idealized in that it runs smoothly without money because there are no transaction costs and, therefore, no reasons to hold money.

The equilibrium is a saddle point. From the comparative static analysis with respect to z, one can obtain that as z is increased: (1) the equilibrium capital/labour ratio k becomes higher; (2) the equilibrium value of x is indeterminate; (3) the equilibrium rate of the inflation rate is always increased.

Finally, it should be noted that the model we have presented does not deal with some important issues. We have assumed that there are no aggregate demand deficiencies and that labour is fully employed. It would be desirable if the savings function and the demand function for postulated real cash balances could be derived by maximizing the behavior of the economic units.

3. On the Generalized Tobin Model

The model in the preceding section is carried out within the framework of Tobin's analysis. Before Tobin published his works on economic growth with monetary variables (1955, 1965), many notable achievements of economic growth theory had not been incorporated in monetary economics and neoclassical growth theory dominated the literature. Tobin revolutionized dynamic monetary theory. The main conclusions in Tobin's analysis , which have already been presented in the preceding model, are: (i) long run (steady-state) capital intensity is lower in a monetary economy than in a non-monetary economy; and (ii) by altering the rate of change of the nominal quantity of money the monetary authorities can vary the steady-state capital intensity of the economy. These results have been challenged by a number of authors. For instance, Stein (1969) challenged Tobin's conclusion that an increase in the rate of change of the nominal quantity of money will raise the capital intensity, by proving that the same policy may raise, lower, or leave it unchanged in the long-run. However, Stein's model is different from Tobin's model. Hahn (1969) challenged the non-neutrality issue by changing one assumption in Tobin's analysis. The short-run perfect foresight assumption in Tobin's analysis is relaxed and it is replaced by the adaptive expectations hypothesis. Levhari and Patinkin (1969) also challenged the two conclusions by means of a model that introduces money into either the utility or in the production function.

This section reexamines Tobin's analysis. The generalized model given in this section is defined in Hadjimichalakis (1971a, or 1971b). As many basic issues in monetary economics can be addressed within this model, we discuss it in some detail. In Tobin's original analysis, stability problems are not discussed. The main focus is upon the existence of a long-run equilibrium. Although the following model - called the generalized Tobin model - is similar to the original model in many aspects, it is different in some other aspects including price dynamics and stability properties.

3-1. The generalized Tobin model

In this section we extend the previous model in such a way that Tobin's models become special cases of the generalized model. Sections 3-1 to 3-3 are closely related to the work of Hadjimichalakis (1971a, 1971b). We provide some important propositions in Section 3-4.

The production side is identical to that in the Solow model. The output per capita is given by: $y = f(k)$. Using the same symbols as in the previous section and omitting depreciation factors (i.e., $d = 0$), we have eqs. (3.2.9) and (3.2.12)

$$dk/dt = sf(k) - c(z - q)x - nk,$$

$$dx/dt = (z - n - dp/dt/p)x. \qquad (3.3.1)$$

In the generalized Tobin model, the view that price changes reflect both excess demand (or excess supply) and adaptive expectations is accepted.

To complete the system, we have to specify dp/dt. We modify the assumption of equilibrium monetary growth to allow for disequilibrium. Ideally, we should permit all markets, as well as expectations, to be out of equilibrium.

However, as the problem will become mathematically intractable, at this stage we still assume that the labour market is instantaneously cleared. This assumption leaves us two markets - the market for goods and services and the money market.

We permit the market for goods and services and the money market to be out of equilibrium and the actual rate of inflation to be different from the expected one. We adopt the Walrasian view that when there is excess demand the price rises, and when there is excess supply the price falls. According to Walras's law, the excess demand for goods and services is equal to the (flow) excess supply of real balances. Without taking account of expected inflation, we can thus propose the following dynamics

$$dp/dt = \alpha p[x - g(.)], \tag{3.3.2}$$

where α is a positive constant parameter, and the function g is to be specified. This implies that (3.2.2) may be invalid at some point of time. The parameter $1/\alpha$ is the time needed for the discrepancy between the demand for and the supply of real balances to disappear. If this is done immediately, then $1/\alpha = 0$ and in this case we have $x = g(.)$; i.e., (3.2.2) holds.

For convenience, we denote the expected inflation rate $E[dp/dt/p]$ by q. Taking account of the effects of the expected rate of inflation upon actual price changes, we can generalize the dynamics of price as follows

$$dp/dt = \alpha p[x - g(.)] + q. \tag{3.3.2}'$$

For simplicity, our analysis is limited to the special case (3.3.2).

It is assumed that the expected inflation rate may be different from the actual inflation rate. The dynamics is specified as

$$dq/dt = \text{ß}[dp/dt/p - q], \tag{3.3.3}$$

where ß is the so-called "expectation coefficient". This is the "adaptive expectation" equation initially introduced by Cagan (1956). It states that expectations change a constant proportion of the "error" between the actual rate of inflation and the expected one. If $\text{ß} \to \infty$, we again have the perfect foresight equation.

We now come to the problem of specifying the demand function for money. In the case in which the demand for real balances is only for asset purposes, then it is a function of the opportunity cost of holding them, $f'(k) + q$. We now examine the cases in which the two assets of our model, capital and real cash balances are perfect and imperfect substitutes.

In the first case, the yields of both assets have to be the same. Otherwise, when $f'(k) + q > 0$ only capital is demanded, and when $f'(k) + q < 0$ only real cash balances are demanded. In this case we have $g'(.) \longrightarrow -\infty$, where the derivative is related to $f'(k) + q$. In the second case $f'(k) + q > 0$ because of the obvious superiority of real cash balances. The demand function is negatively related to $f'(k) + q$. Tobin attributed this difference to a risk element involved in asset capital as compared to the risklessness of real cash balances, while Friedman et al attributed this difference to what they call the utility yield of real cash balances.

We also have to take account of money which is demanded for transaction purposes. The proxy for per capita transaction demand usually found in the literature is the per capita output $f(k)$; the higher the per capita output, the higher the per capita transaction demand. We thus can generally write g as

$$g = G^*(f(k),f'(k)+q)),$$

or

$$g = g(k,q). \tag{3.3.4}$$

It can be shown that $g_k = +\infty$, and $g_q = -\infty$, in the case of perfect substitutability, while $g_k > 0$ and $g_q < 0$ in the case of imperfect substitutability. We thus complete the formulation of the model. The remainder of this section investigates the behavior of the system.

3-2. Short-run analysis

We will study the case in which the markets are cleared and expectations are fulfilled in every period of time. Whether, and under what conditions, equilibrium can be reached in every period will be examined. For this reason we will investigate the short-run model, following the Hicksian method of temporary equilibrium. Short-run is defined as a period during which the capital intensity is fixed at k^* and the labour force is given, i.e., $n = 0$. The short-run model is given by

$$dx/dt = x\{z - \alpha[x - g(q)]\}, \tag{3.3.5}$$

$$dq/dt = \beta\{\alpha[x - g(q)] - q\}. \tag{3.3.6}$$

To examine whether the short-run model is capable of equilibrium, set $dx/dt =$

dq/dt = 0, whose solution is denoted by (x_0, q_0). It can be easily shown that in equilibrium:

$$\det A = \alpha\beta x > 0,$$

$$\text{trace } A = -\alpha\beta(x/\beta + 1/\alpha + g'), \tag{3.3.7}$$

where A is the Jacobian, det A the determinant of A. A necessary and sufficient condition for stability of the equilibrium is that det A > 0 and trace A < 0. This short-run model excludes the possibility of saddle-points. A local analysis can easily show

Theorem 3.3.1.

(i) If both α and $\beta \rightarrow \infty$, then the short-run model is locally unstable,

(ii) Even if neither α nor $\beta \rightarrow \infty$, if money is a perfect substitute for capital, the short-run model is locally unstable.

Later we show that this theorem is also true for the long-run problem. The two models examined in Tobin (1965) made the assumption that α and $\beta \rightarrow \infty$. One model treats money as a perfect substitute for capital, and the other treats money as an imperfect substitute for capital.

Theorem 3.3.2.

(i) The short run model is locally stable if and only if: $g/\beta + 1/\alpha + g' > 0$;

(ii) If $\beta \rightarrow \infty$, $\alpha < \infty$, then the condition of stability is: $\alpha < -1/g'$;

(iii) If $\alpha \rightarrow \infty$, $\beta < \infty$, then the condition of stability is: $\beta < -g/g'$.

These two theorems give the necessary and sufficient condition for stability. Hadjimichalakis (1971b) applies this condition to the studies by Tobin (1965) and Shell-Sidrauski-Stiglitz (1969).

Consider the phase plane of this dynamics. First we can show that along dx/dt = 0 the following result holds

$$dx/dq = g' - 1/\alpha < 0,$$

i.e., dx/dt = 0 is a downward-sloping curve. Moreover, above the curve dx/dt = 0, dx/dt < 0 and below it dx/dt > 0. We can similarly examine the properties of dq/dt. The behavior is illustrated in Fig. 3.3.1 below.

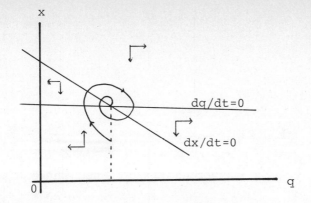

Fig. 3.3.1. The Case of a Stable Focus

So far we have worked in the x-q plane. The short-run model can also be defined on the p-q plane (see Hadjimichalakis, 1971b). Corresponding to Fig. 3.3.1, the dynamics in the p-q plane is illustrated in Fig. 3.3.2.

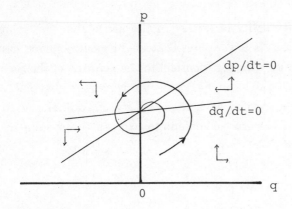

Fig. 3.3.2. The Stable Focus in the p-q Plane

3-3. Long-run analysis

In this section we carry out a long-run analysis. During the study period, capital accumulation and population growth take place. The rate of growth of the nominal quantity of money is assumed to be fixed at rate z. It is interesting to note that the introduction of capital accumulation will affect the stability of the system.

The generalized Tobin model can be rewritten in the form of

$$dk/dt = sf(k) - (1 - s)(z - q)x - nk,$$

$$dx/dt = x(z - \alpha[x - g(k,q)] - n),$$

$$dq/dt = \beta(\alpha[x - g(k,q)] - q). \tag{3.3.8}$$

A positive long-run equilibrium (k_0, x_0, q_0) is determined as a solution of

$$sf(k_0) - (1 - s)n(z - q)x_0 - nk_0 = 0,$$

$$\alpha[x_0 - g(k_0, q_0)] = z + n = q_0. \tag{3.3.9}$$

From (3.3.6) we have

$$x_0 = \{sf(k_0) - nk_0\}/(1 - s)n,$$

which exhibits the non-neutrality of money in the sense that the capital-labour ratio of the monetary model is lower than that of the non-monetary one. If $x_0 = 0$, then one has: $sf(k_0)/n = k_0$, which is identical to the solution of the Solow model. If x_0 is positive, then $sf(k_0)/n > k_0$, or $f(k_0)/k_0 > n/s$. Non-neutrality follows.

As we are only concerned with the stability of equilibria and the local behavior of the system, it is very convenient to express the system in the local form near the equilibrium. Introduce

$$U_1 = k - k_0, \quad U_2 = x - x_0, \quad U_3 = q - q_0, \tag{3.3.10}$$

where (k,x,q) satisfies (3.3.5), and U $(= (U_1, U_2, U_3)^T)$ are sufficiently small. Substituting (3.3.7) into (3.3.5) yields

$$dU/dt = AU + N(U,U) + O(|U|^3), \tag{3.3.11}$$

where A is the Jacobian evaluated at the equilibrium and $N(U,U)$ is the quadratic term. A is given by

$$A = \begin{bmatrix} sf'-n & -(1-s)n & cx_0 \\ \alpha x_0 g_k & -\alpha x_0 & \alpha x_0 g_q \\ -\alpha \beta g_k & \alpha \beta & -\beta(1+\alpha g_q) \end{bmatrix} .$$

$$(3.3.12)$$

$N(U,U)$ is not explicitly given since we rarely use them in the remainder of the study.

Introduce

$$a_1 = \text{trace } A = sf' - n - \alpha m - \beta(1 + \alpha g_q),$$

$$a_2 = \begin{bmatrix} sf'-n & -(1-s)n \\ \alpha x_0 g_k & -\alpha x_0 \end{bmatrix} +$$

$$\begin{bmatrix} -\alpha x_0 & \alpha x_0 g_q \\ \alpha \beta & -\beta(1+\alpha g_q) \end{bmatrix} + \begin{bmatrix} sf'-n & cx_0 \\ -\alpha \beta g_k & -\beta(1+\alpha g_q) \end{bmatrix} ,$$

$$a_3 = - |A| . \qquad (3.3.13)$$

The eigenvalues of the Jacobian are determined by

$$Z^3 + a_1 Z^2 + a_2 Z + a_3 = 0. \qquad (3.3.14)$$

The necessary and sufficient conditions for stability are known as the Routh-Hurwitz criterion: (i) $a_i > 0$; (ii) $a_1 a_2 - a_3 > 0$. We thus immediately have

Theorem 3.3.3.
(i) If both α and $\beta \to \infty$, then the long-run model is locally unstable,
(ii) Even if either α nor $\beta \to \infty$, if money is aperfect substitute for capital, the long-run model is locally unstable.

From Theorem 3.3.3, we see that if a model is unstable in the short-run, due to the conditions in Theorem 3.3.1, it cannot be stabilized by introducing capital accumulation into the long-run model. As shown from the comparative analysis by Hadjimichalakis (1971b), if the equilibrium is stable, an increase in the rate of change of the nominal quantity of money increases the long run capital intensity and the expected rate of inflation, and the sign of dx_0/dz is the same as that of $sf' - n$.

The following theorem is proved in Benhabib and Miyao (1981).

Theorem 3.3.4.

The equilibrium point is locally asymptotically stable if the following conditions are satisfied

$$ß[- q_0 g_q/g(z-n) + 1/\alpha x_0] + (1-s)n/\alpha k_0 \leq 1,$$

$$k_0 g_k/g \geq 1.$$

Since the equilibrium values k_0, x_0, and q_0 are not affected by changes in α and $ß$, we can state from Theorem 3.3.4 that the smaller the value of $ß$ or the greater the value of α, the more likely is stability. Also, the smaller the elasticity of the money demand function with respect to q, or the greater the elasticity with respect to k, the more likely is stability.

Theorems 3.3.3 and 3.3.4 imply that the equilibrium may be either stable or unstable; this is dependent on the parameter values. For instance, if we move from adaptive expectations towards perfect foresight, saddle-point instability may appear as it does in the Tobin model. For the sake of illustration, consider an increase in the stock of money at the equilibrium. The immediate impact of this is to increase the price level while the real money stock tends to fall back to its original level; but the initial increase in the stock of money also tends to increase price expectations and reduce the capital stock. The latter two effects reinforce the decrease in the money supply and may cause the money stock to overshoot its long-run equilibrium. As the money supply keeps falling beyond its equilibrium level, the effects on the two variables are reversed: the capital stock rises and expectations fall. Combined with the direct effect of the money stock on the accumulation of money, the fall of the money stock will now be reversed. This discussion hints at the possibility of oscillations in the long run. We now prove precisely the existence of business cycles in the generalized Tobin model.

3-4. Instability and the business cycle

Much of the literature concerning with money is mainly related to the existence of steady states and the effects of monetary policies. As traditional comparative statics only deal with the movement of time-independent equilibrium when parameters are changed, the effect of shifting a policy parameter upon a variable is not changeable with time. We now know that such conclusions are invalid if the system is located near a critical point (Zhang, 1990). For instance, if the Jacobian of the dynamic economic system evaluated in an equilibrium point has a pair of purely imaginary eigenvalues, then a small change in the parameter may result in time-dependent limit cycles (Hopf bifurcation). The values of the variables on the cycle may be either greater or smaller than the values of the variables in the equilibrium, which are dependent on the phase of motion of the dynamic system. In this, effects of the parameter change are uncertain, or more precisely time-dependent.

The existence of Hopf bifurcations in the generalized Tobin model has been identified by Benhibib and Miyao (1981). Their results can be summarized as follows.

Theorem 3.3.5

If there exist a set of parameter values which guarantee the stability of the equilibrium, we can find a value of ß, denoted by $ß_0$, such that the Jacobian of the system has a pair of purely imaginary eigenvalues. Moreover, there exists a continuous function $v(\varepsilon)$ ($v(0) = 0$) of a parameter ε such that when ε is sufficiently small, the generalized Tobin model has a continuous family of periodic solutions $(k(t,\varepsilon),x(t,\varepsilon),q(t,\varepsilon))^T$, which collapse to the equilibrium point $(k_0,x_0,q_0)^T$ as $\varepsilon --> 0$.

This theorem is very important since it proves the existence of regular oscillations in the system. Such oscillations will continue permanently if the stability of the cycles can be identified. Non-equilibrium economic development is no longer a short-run phenomenon. The generalized Tobin model can thus be applied to explain business cycles. We seek to improve the results obtained by Benhabib and Miyao in the following aspects: (i) to find stability conditions of the cycle; (ii) to explicitly interpret the parameter h; (iii) to find the explicit expression of the cycle; and (iv) to discuss whether the Hopf bifurcation is supercritical or subcritical.

Firstly, we show that if the Jacobian has a pair of purely imaginary eigenvalues, then the three eigenvalues are given by

$$Z_1 = -a_1, \quad Z_{2,3} = \pm ia_2^{1/2} = \pm iZ_0, \tag{3.3.15}$$

where a_i are defined in (3.3.13). As discussed in Benhabib and Miyao, we know that a_i (i = 1, 2, 3) are all positive.

The existence of purely imaginary eigenvalues means that (3.3.14) can be written in the following form:

$$Z^3 + a_1Z^2 + a_2Z + a_3 = (Z^2 + a^*)(Z + a')$$

$$= Z^3 + a'Z^2 + a^*Z + a'a^* = 0. \tag{3.3.16}$$

Thus (3.3.15) is true.

In the following bifurcation analysis we select $ß$ as a bifurcation parameter. The value of $ß$ in which (3.3.16) is held is denoted by $ß_0$. A small shift of $ß$ from $ß_0$ is expressed by v, i.e.,

$$v = ß - ß_0. \tag{3.3.17}$$

The eigenvalues are continuous functions of $ß$. We denote $Z(v)$ the eigenvalue which equals iZ_0 at v = 0 (i.e., $ß = ß_0$). In Zhang (1989), I explicitly calculate $Z_v(0)$. It is shown there that the assumption of $Z_v(0)$ being unequal to zero is quite acceptable.

Introduce the following real numbers

$$G_1 = \alpha^2 g^*[(1 - s)x_0g_k + (n - sf')g_q](x_0 - ng_q)$$

$$+ \alpha g^* g_q Z_0^2,$$

$$G_2 = \alpha g^* Z_0[g_q(\alpha x_0 - \alpha ng_q) - (1 - s)x_0g_k - (n - sf')g_q],$$

$$\tag{3.3.18}$$

where $g^* = 1/[(1 - s)\{Z_0^2 + (\alpha x_0 - \alpha ng_q)^2\}]$. Then we have our main results:

Theorem. 3.3.6.

The bifurcated cycle in the generalized Tobin model has period $2\pi/d(\varepsilon)$, and can be approximately expressed as

$$k(t,\varepsilon) = k_0 + 2\varepsilon\cos[d(\varepsilon)t] + O(\varepsilon^2),$$

$$x(t,\varepsilon) = x_0 + 2\varepsilon G_1\cos[d(\varepsilon)t] - 2\varepsilon G_2\sin[d(\varepsilon)t] + O(\varepsilon^2),$$

$$q(t,\varepsilon) = q_0 + \varepsilon\{(n-sf')/x_0(1-s) + nG_1/x_0\}\cos[d(\varepsilon)t] -$$

$$\varepsilon\{Z_0/x_0(1-s) + nG_2/x_0\}\sin[d(\varepsilon)t] + O(\varepsilon^2), \qquad (3.3.19)$$

in which ε is the expansion amplitude parameter and

$$v(\varepsilon) = \text{ß} - \text{ß}_0 = \varepsilon^2 v_2/2 + O(\varepsilon^4),$$

$$d(\varepsilon) = Z_0 + \varepsilon^2 d_2/2 + O(\varepsilon^4), \qquad (3.3.20)$$

where v_2 and d_2 are constants yet to be given. When $\text{Re}(Z_v) > 0$, if $v_2 > 0$ the cycle is supercritically stable, while if $v_2 < 0$, the cycle is unstable. When $\text{Re}(Z_v) < 0$, if v_2 is negative, the cycle is subcritically stable, while if v_2 is positive, the cycle is unstable.

The theorem is proved by Zhang (1989).

In Theorem 3.3.6 we omit the higher order approximations since the expressions are too complicated. Supercritical bifurcations mean that if the bifurcation parameter b is increased, the system is stabilized, while if it is decreased, the system becomes unstable and bifurcations may take place. Fig. 3.3.3 describes the behavior when the Hopf bifurcation is supercritical.

This theorem gives a complete description of the Hopf bifurcations near the equilibrium. At the equilibrium point, the system is very sensitive to changes of the parameter b. Even when perturbations in b are sufficiently small, structural changes take place, resulting in limit cycles. Moreover, it may be interesting to compare the above theorem with the early results on adaptive expectations by Cagan (1956) and their application to the generalized Tobin model by Hadjimichalakis (1971a, 1971b). This theorem shows that the loss of stability that occurs as expectations adjust is associated with the emergence of bounded, persistent oscillations in prices, output and expectations. This holds no matter how quickly prices adjust since there always exists a value of b at which the stability of the equilibrium is lost.

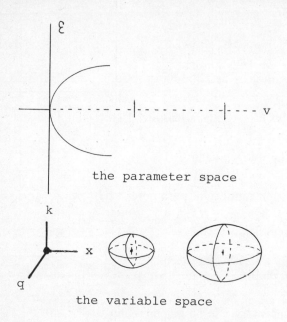

the parameter space

the variable space

Fig. 3.3.3. The Case of Supercritical Bifurcated Cycles

As shown in the proof of Theorem 3.3.6, whether the bifurcation is subcritical or supercritical depends on the higher order non-linear terms in the system. In the case of subcritical bifurcation, i.e., for a left neighborhood of $ß_0$, the economy will be locally stable around the equilibrium point. A large shock may throw the economy out or beyond the orbit, in which case it does not have a natural tendency to return to the stationary point.

For simplicity, we introduce: $K_0(t) = [k(t,\varepsilon) - k_0]/\varepsilon$, $X_0(t) = [x(t,\varepsilon) - x_0]/\varepsilon$, $Q_0(t) = [q(t,\varepsilon) - q_0]/\varepsilon$. Here, we note that $g_k > 0$, $g_q < 0$, and $g^* > 0$. If n is approximately equal to $sf'(k_0)$, then one has $G_2 < 0$ and approximately

$$M_0(t) = a'G_1K_0(t) + a''\sin[d(\varepsilon)t],$$

$$Q_0(t) = b'G_1K_0(t) + b''\sin[d(\varepsilon)t], \tag{3.3.21}$$

where a', a'', b' are positive constants, and b'' ($= Z_0/x_0 + nG_2/x_0$) is uncertain. Dynamic interactions among these three variables appear to be complicated. From (3.3.21) we see that an increase in the capital per capita may be associated with a decrease or increase in $M_0(t)$, which is determined by the "phase" of the system. We illustrate the dynamic interactions between $K_0(t)$ and $M_0(t)$ in Fig. 3.3.4.

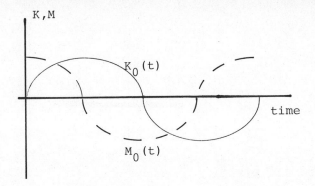

Fig. 3.3.4. The Dynamic Interactions When $G_1 > 0$

It is interesting to study the behavior of the other variables on the cycle. Firstly, the motion of price is given by

$$p(t) = L(t)x(t)/M(t)$$

$$= L(0)x(t)\exp[(n-z)t]/M(0) = cx(t)\exp(v^*t),$$

where c is constant and $v^* = n - z$. The behavior of price is described in Fig. 3.3.5.

In the long run prices will go towards infinity or zero if the labour growth rate is not equal to the money growth rate. As $K(t) = k(t)L(t)$, the motion of capital is shown in Fig. 3.3.6.

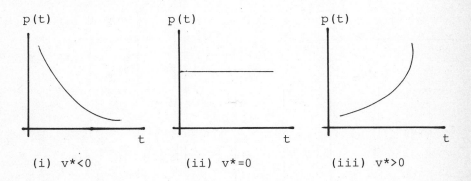

Fig. 3.3.5. Dynamics of Prices

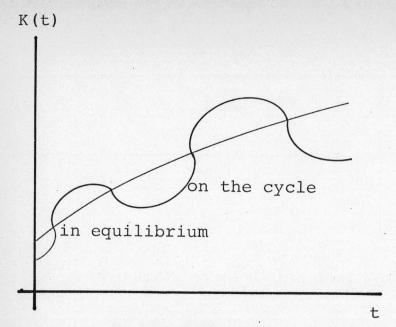

Fig. 3.3.6. Capital Growth

IV

PRICES, GROWTH RATES AND INTEREST RATES
IN THE DYNAMIC CONTEXT OF MULTISECTOR MODELS

1. Introduction

This chapter focusses upon interactions which occur among interest, growth and inflation rates, within the framework of multiple sector models. It can be argued that the study of the relations which occur between these variables has been one of the main areas of concern in economics (see, Morishima, 1964, Hicks, 1965, Andersson, 1968).

Our starting point is the Leontief dynamic input-output model with exogenous household behavior and neoclassical production functions. In Chapter VI, we will introduce Leontief technologies into the model. The basic difference between neoclassical and Leontief technologies is the manner in which the possibility of substitution of inputs is introduced - e.g, the choice of technique is altered in response to changing prices and rates of interest. We mainly concern ourselves with price fluctuations, the relations between the interest rate and the price structure, and interactions among rates of interest, expectation and growth.

This chapter is fundamentally limited to the Leontief input-output system, which has played a special role in economic growth theory and various applications of the theory. We shall provide a brief description of the extensive body of literature which concerns this system.

It may be claimed that the Leontief input-output model is the most fundamental applied economic system (Leontief, 1949, 1953, 1966), although the fundamental ideas of the system can also be perceived in the work of Quesnay, Karl Marx, and Walras. Quesnay's "Tableau Economique" provides an interactive solution to the structural interdependence in the economy, although Leontief was able to convert this formulation into a more general one, and in the process, expand capacities of the model. This is also the only economic model which has been used in the forecasting and planning of "capitalist" as well as "socialist" economies. Since Leontief published his celebrated work, the model has been extended in different ways. For instance, nonlinearized versions have been introduced (e.g., Morishima, 1964 and Nikaido, 1968). Leontief (1953), Isard (1953) and Johansson and Persson (1983) introduced the system to regional analysis. There is also a gravity version of the interregional model (Leontief and Strout, 1963). Kennedy (1966) has demonstrated the links between aggregate Keynesian analysis and input-output models.

Recently, an attempt has been made to link these models with some of the new developments in commodity flow modelling (see Batten, 1982). An applied equilibrium model with a spatially specified vintage technology and demand has been suggested by Westin (1987). And most recently, we have discussed the problems of decentralization and centralization (Andersson and Zhang, 1988a). The Leontief system has also been applied to environmental and energy problems, forestry economics and so on. In Andersson and Zhang (1988), we use a continuous 2-dimensional spatial input-output model to discuss the ways in which transportation flows can be distributed over space.

From Section 4.2 to Section 4.5, we are concerned with the determination of a short-run equilibrium of economic growth. The basic model accepted here is a dynamic Leontief system similar to the model presented in Morishima (1964), though we adhere to the original Leontief system in the sense that we do not differentiate between industries producing intermediary and capital goods.

There are a large amount of the literature on economic growth upon basis of different economic mechanisms (see, for instance, Hicks, 1965, Burmeister and Dobell, 1970, Takayama, 1985). From these studies, we know that the dynamics of quantitative and monetary variables are very different. For instance, in a Keynesian system, prices can - for institutional reasons - be assumed to be slow (almost fixed) variables, while outputs are fast variables. In neoclassical economics prices are fast variables, while outputs are slow variables in the sense that once outputs are decided, prices are determined by the market mechanism. In our short-run approach to economic equilibrium, the temporal behavior of the quantitative variables are treated as a genuine dynamics in the sense that once the output levels and the final demand for goods are given in period t, the system determines the output levels in period t+1. However, we suggest some mechanisms to determine the short-run equilibrium of the monetary variables.

Many factors have effects upon the dynamics of monetary variables. This gives a reason that there is no definite answer related to the role of monetary variables in economic growth. How monetary variables affect quantitative variables are dependent upon institutions and market structure and other factors. Real dynamics of price formation comes from forces such as speculation, bargaining in the markets, consumer preferences and conflicting expectations about an uncertain future. Innovation may also cause the price structure to change. All these factors imply that prices are subjected to changes, though it is difficult to anticipate from where the fluctuations will come. It is thus possible to introduce dynamics in different ways by only focussing attention to certain special sources of fluctuations. In this study, we are mainly concerned with the effects of the relative advantage of each industry and the structure of the market upon the determination of the monetary variables.

We differentiate between short-run, long-run time scales. It is really difficult to define precisely how long they endure. We define an equilibrium of the system which corresponds to each time scale. We introduce a concept called "short-run acceptable unit cost" for each sector in order to deal with short-run equilibrium problems. This concept can help us deal with, as Morishima called, weak and strong competition equilibrium problems in the Leontief dynamic system. As shown in the later contents, upon the basis of this concept it is also possible to treat the monopolistic equilibrium problems in the way that Nikaido did (1975).

It is assumed that in short term any industry will not carry out production as long as its unit cost of the production is greater than the acceptable unit cost. As an acceptable unit cost may be either greater or less than, or equal to the actual price, it is possible for the firms to obtain "marginal profit" in short terms. As shown later on, the concept of the acceptable unit cost is related to the concept of "marginal profit" defined in Morishima (1964). As we will discuss in Section 4.2, It is reasonable to define long-run and short-run equilibria in such a way that in a long equilibrium, the acceptable cost is equal to the actual price; and in a short-run equilibrium the acceptable unit cost may be different from the actual price.

In order to find relations between the technological coefficients and the monetary variables, we assume that the production structure is described by homogeneous production functions. To determine the coefficients, we assume that firms minimize the short-run production cost by adjusting the production structure.

Because of the special properties of the homogeneous functions, we can write the relations of the technological coefficients and the prices in very simple forms. It should be noted that if we adopt other forms of production functions, the relations between the coefficients and the prices may become very complicated.

The remainder of this chapter is organized as follows. Section 4.2 introduces the input coefficient matrix as functions of the prices under the assumptions that the technology is described by neo-classical production functions and the industries determine the input coefficients minimizing short-run unit costs. Section 4.3 defines the concept of acceptable unit costs and guarantees the existence of a short-run equilibrium, which determines the values of the prices and rate of interest, for the given acceptable unit cost functions. Section 4.4 examines the existence of a short-run equilibrium, which determines the prices and the "benefit rate", for a fixed rate of interest, and investigate the relations between the rate of interest and the benefit rate. In Section 4.5, we examine the relations between the rate of interest and the benefit rate when the investment matrix is dependent upon the rate of interest rate with a constant input matrix. Section 4.6 deals with relations among interest, inflation and growth rates within the framework of von-Neumann growth model.

2. The Input-Output System With Neoclassical Production Functions

The economic system consists of n competitive sectors or industries. We study the dynamics of the economy with discrete time series, $t = 0, 1, \ldots$ We are concerned with a typical dynamic Leontief system. The output of the ith sector is denoted by $X_i(t)$ $(i = 1, \ldots, n)$. Let a_{ij} $(i, j = 1, \ldots, n)$ be the current input per unit of output of the jth sector used by the ith sector (the current input or technological coefficient), and let b_{ij} $(i, j = 1, \ldots, n)$ be the quantity of good i invested in the jth sector in order to increase the output of that sector by one unit (the investment or capital coefficient). For the given coefficients, the basic balance equation is

$$X_i(t) = \sum_{j=1}^{n} a_{ij}X_j(t) + \sum_{j=1}^{n} b_{ij}[X_j(t+1) - X_j(t)] + c_i(t),$$

$$i = 1, \ldots , n, \hspace{5cm} (4.2.1)$$

where c_i $(i = 1, \ldots , n)$ stands for the final demand for good i at time t. In this study, we assume c to be exogenously given during the study period.

We may rewrite (4.2.1) as

$$X(t) = AX(t) + B[X(t+1) - X(t)] + c, \hspace{3cm} (4.2.2)$$

where $A = (a_{ij})$, $B = (b_{ij})$, $c = (c_i)$.

It should be noted that this quantitative system consists of simple accounting equations. By accounting equations we mean that the equations hold for any production system. As shown in Zhang (1989), different economic mechanisms can be introduced into this accounting system. In fact, it has been extended in different directions such as to treat the final demands as endogenous variables, to introduce production lags, the length of life of capital goods, accelerators, growth of final demand, structural changes due to technological innovation. These extensions make the coefficients of the input, investment, and final demand be related to the variables X and the monetary variables.

We now consider the "dual" problem of (4.2.2). Let $a_{n+1,i}$ $(i = 1, \ldots , n)$ be the labour input coefficient of the ith sector, P_i the price of good i, P_{n+1} the wage rate, and r the interest rate. In the long-run competitive equilibrium, the price must equal the long-run unit cost, which includes an interest change on the value of the unit capital requirements. The dual long-run equilibrium problem is defined as

$$P_i(t) = \sum_{j=1}^{n} a_{ji}P_j(t) + r(t) \sum_{j=1}^{n} b_{ji}P_j(t) + a_{n+1,i}P_{n+1}(t),$$

$$i = 1, \ldots , n,$$

which can be rewritten in terms of wage prices

$$p(t) = A^T p(t) + r(t)B^T p(t) + a_{n+1}, \hspace{3cm} (4.2.3)$$

where $p_i(t)$ $(= P_i(t)/P_{n+i}(t), i = 1, \ldots , n)$ are prices in terms of homogeneous labour. These equations contain n + 1 unknowns, i.e., n wage prices and the rate of interest at time t. Thus, there is one degree of freedom in the price system. It is well known that for an appropriate fixed value of the interest rate, there is a unique price vector which guarantees equilibrium. In what follows, we are concerned with short-run equilibrium problems under various added assumptions to the standard model (4.2.1) and (4.2.3).

Before developing short-run price dynamics, we will show that the technological coefficients are explicitly dependent upon prices. This is based upon microeconomic studies of the behavior of firms. In the original Leontief system it is usually assumed that the coefficients a_{ij} and b_{ij} are constants. Accordingly, in such a system changes in prices can only affect the output of goods by changing the final demand for goods. This is not a generally reasonable assumption as the price structure is known to influence production decisions of firms.

We assume constant returns to scale (in the form of homogeneous production functions of the first order). Let X_{ji} ($i = 1, ..., n, j = 1, ..., n + 1$) be the volume of input of the jth sector into the ith sector. The (n+1)th sector stands for labour which is a "primary" factor or a "nonproduced good". We consider the case that quantitative production is a rather fast adjustment process. That is, the production is always effectively completed for a given technology. This assumption permits us to describe the production process by a "static" production function of the ith sector as follows

$$X_i(t) = F_i(X_{1i}(t), ... , X_{ni}(t), X_{n+1,i}(t)),$$

$$i = 1, ... , n, \qquad\qquad\qquad (4.2.4)$$

where F_i ($i = 1, ... , n$) are assumed to be homogeneous of degree one. For simplicity, we assume that F_i takes on the Cobb-Douglas form as an approximation of the actual production function

$$F_i = d_i \prod_{j=1}^{n+1} X_{ji}^{h_{ji}}, \quad h_i > 0, \quad h_{ji} > 0,$$

$$i, j = 1, ... , n$$

$$h_{n+1,i} > 0, \quad \sum_{j=1}^{n+1} h_{ji} = 1, \quad i = 1, ... , n.$$

$$(4.2.5)$$

Since $a_{ji}(t) = X_{ji}(t)/X_i(t)$ ($i = 1, ... , n, j = 1, ... , n + 1$), (4.2.5) can be rewritten in terms of technological coefficients

$$d_i \prod_{j=1}^{n+1} a_{ji}^{h_{ji}} = 1, \quad i = 1, \dots, n. \tag{4.2.6}$$

It should be noted that the formula (4.2.6) do not involve the investment coefficients as in Morishima's model (1964, Chapter 3). The difference is due to our assumption that increased capacities of the production for the next period have no contributions to the production of the current period. The output is determined by the current inputs. In this initial stage, the investment coefficients are fixed during the study period. Obviously, this is a very strict requirement since the firms can change their investment coefficients to adjust the production structure. In section 4, we will suggest another economic mechanism to connect the investment coefficients with the interest rate.

As the neoclassical production functions hold at any point of time, we see that the input coefficients should be different under different conditions. In what follows, we suggest a possible mechanism to determine the coefficients as functions of the prices. We will show that how the inputs are combined by the firms are dependent upon the price structure.

As the firms can adjust production structure at a rather fast speed, it is acceptable to assume that the firms determine the input coefficients, a_{ji}, by minimizing the short-run unit cost of the production:

$$\sum_{j=1}^{n} a_{ji}P_j(t) + r(t) \sum_{j=1}^{n} b_{ji}P_j(t) + a_{n+1,i}P_{n+1}(t) ,$$

$$i = 1, \dots, n, \tag{4.2.7}$$

subject to (4.2.6).

The mechanism suggested here is different from that suggested by Morishima (1964) who assumes that the firms determine the coefficients by maximizing the long-run average cost. However, this assumption is not appropriate when short-run equilibrium is concerned. The long-run average cost is defined as

$$\sum_{j=1}^{n} a_{ji}P_j(t) + \sum_{j=1}^{n} b_{ji}P_j(t) + a_{n+1,i}P_{n+1}(t) .$$

From (4.2.7), we can see that the optimal solution for (4.2.7) should be identical to that for the long-run average cost.

From the works of, for instance, Morishima (1964), we know that as an optimal solution each technological coefficient is a non-negative and homogeneous function of zero degree in the prices $P_1(t), \dots, P_n(t), P_{n+1}(t)$, and at least one of $a_{1i}, \dots, a_{ni}, a_{n+1,i}$ $(i = 1, \dots, n)$ is strictly positive. If we fix the wage rate and use $p(t) = (p_1, \dots, p_n)^T$, then one has

$$a_{ji}(p(t)) > 0,$$

$$\sum_{j=1}^{n} a_{ji}(p(t)) + a_{n+1,i}(p(t)) > 0, \tag{4.2.8}$$

Now we determine a_{ji} when F_i takes the form of (4.2.5). In this case, the Lagrangian associated with the problem is defined by

$$L_i(a) = \sum_j (a_{ji} + b_{ji})P_j$$

$$+ a_{n+1,i}P_{n+1} - c_i(d_i \prod_j a_{ji}^{h_{ji}} - 1), \tag{4.2.9}$$

at time t. It is not difficult to show that the necessary conditions of the problem are

$$F_i = d_i \prod_{j=1}^{n+1} a_{ji}^{h_{ji}} = 1,$$

$$a_{ji}P_j = c_i h_{ji}F_i = c_i h_{ji}, \quad j = 1, \dots, n,$$

$$a_{n+1,i} = h_i h_{n+1,i}, \quad \text{for the ith sector.} \tag{4.2.10}$$

We thus have:

$$c_i = c_i' \prod_{j=1}^{n} p_j^{h_{ji}}, \quad c_i' = (\sum_j a_{ji}^{h_{ji}})^{-1} \tag{4.2.11}$$

Hence, we obtain:

$$a_{ji}(p(t)) = h_{ji}c_i(p(t))/p_j(t), \quad j = 1, \dots, n,$$

$$a_{n+1,i}(p(t)) = h_{n+1,i}c_i(p(t)),$$

for the ith sector. $\qquad\qquad$ (4.2.12)

From (4.2.12), we see that if the price of the jth sector increases, the input per unit from the jth sector to the ith sector falls down, while if the price of the ith sector (i and j being different) increases, the input per unit output from the jth sector to the ith sector becomes higher. Accordingly, there is substitution among all factors. Inserting (4.2.12) into (4.2.3), we obtain the nonlinear system of equations determining the prices

$$p(t) = A(p(t))^T p(t) + r(t)B^T p(t) + a_{n+1}, \qquad\qquad (4.2.13)$$

where $A(p) = (a_{ij}(p))$. It can be seen that we can also write the equilibrium conditions in terms of $P(t)$ since the system is homogeneous of degree one with respect to the arguments. Characteristics such as the existence and positiveness of the solution of (4.1.14) have been well investigated by Nikaido (1968) and Morishima (1964). The purpose of this section is to determine those possible price dynamics of this economic system in which dynamics will be introduced in a manner different from that described by Morishima.

As mentioned above, (4.2.13) determines a long-run equilibrium of the system. However, in short-terms this equation does not necessarily hold because many factors such as expectations, relative advantages of technology of some firms over others may disturb this equation. In terms of Morishima, as weak competition may dominate the market, some firms may get "marginal profit". It is necessary to investigate under what conditions such short-run equilibria may exist.

There are different approaches to the dynamics of the Leontief input-output system (e.g., Solow, 1957, and Morishima, 1958). Solow assumes that firms have perfect foresight and correctly forecast price changes. He is primarily concerned with logically consistent price movements. Morishima assumes that firms always expect prices to remain constant, although in fact they do change from time to time in order to clear markets. He is concerned with the set of constant prices and the interest rate which can actually be made to endure. In a sense, this study accepts Morishima's point of view. However, as we explicitly deal with short-run equilibrium, there are some differences between our model and the model developed by Morishima.

In order to deal with short-run problems, we introduce a concept called "acceptable unit cost" for an industry. "Acceptable" merely means that an industry will make a decision on production if the actual price structure is acceptable. According to this definition, an acceptable unit cost may be different from the current price, though in a long-run competitive equilibrium it is necessary for the acceptable cost and price to be equal. As it takes long time for a long-run competitive equilibrium to be realized, it is possible for the cost and price of unity product to be different. For instance, for a moment being if an industry is producing a rather newly innovated good and the new community has become popular among the consumers, it is highly possible for the industry to get "margin profit". That is, the industry's acceptable unit cost is less than the actual price. Surely, it is also possible that some industries think that for a short period production will be carried out even if they cannot get any benefits, or even lose, from the production. We are interested in whether it is possible for the economic system, for a short period, to be in equilibrium where some industries obtain margin profits, while others may not.

We denote the acceptable unit cost of the ith sector by Φ_i and the acceptable cost vector by $(\Phi, \Phi_{n+1})^T$. Instead of the long-run equilibrium (4.2.13), we write the short-run equilibrium for the dual system in the following way:

$$\Phi(t) = A(P(t))^T P(t) + r(t)B^T P(t) + a_{n+1}P_{n+1}(t). \tag{4.2.14}$$

where $P(t) = (P_1(t), \ldots , P_n(t))^T$.

We are interested in under what conditions we can guarantee the existence of the short-run equilibrium.

First, we have to specify how the acceptable cost are endogenously determined. It is reasonable to consider that an acceptable price is dependent upon the history and relative scale of the industry. Whether an industry is newly developed should have influences upon the expectations of the decision maker. A large relative scale of the industry may tend to make the maker decision to expect the industry to get more profits over others. Long-run expectations of production may make the decision maker to consider the production worthwhile even if the actual cost is higher than the current price. In order to be benefited in future, the industry may like to lose something in the present. All of these factors will play an important role in determining whether the system can actually be in equilibrium.

According to the discussions above, we may generally describe Φ_i as a function of $X_i(\mu)/\Sigma_j X_j(\mu)$, $a(P(\mu))$, $P(\mu)$, $P_{n+1}(\mu)$, $r(\mu)$ ($\mu = 0, 1, \ldots , t - 1$), $P(t)$, $P_{n+1}(t)$. As we are interested in short-run equilibrium for the given information, it is convenient to treat all of the information before t as a fixed parameter. We thus can write Φ as: $\Phi_i = \Phi_i(P_i(t),t)$, in which the functional forms of Φ are dependent upon the structure of the whole market. For simplicity, we consider the case of $\Phi_i = \Phi_i(P(t),P_{n+1}(t))$. The acceptable unit cost is a function of the current prices of all products. Moreover, the functional form of the acceptable cost is not necessarily unique for the whole economy. It depends on the characteristics of the industry.

We assume that Φ_i is positively continuous and increasing with respect to their positive arguments:

$$\Phi_i(P,P_{n+1}) > 0,$$

$$d\Phi_i/dP_j \geq 0, \quad \text{and if } i = j, \quad d\Phi_i/dP_i > 0,$$

$$\text{for } P > 0, \quad i, = 1, \dots, n, \quad j = 1, \dots, n, n + 1$$

$$\text{and} \quad \Phi_{n+1}(P,P_{n+1}) = P_{n+1}. \tag{4.2.15}$$

These requirements mean that the acceptable cost is necessarily positive. If the actual price increases, the acceptable cost should increase, too. The final equality, $\Phi_{n+1}(P(t),P_{n+1}(t)) = P_{n+1}(t)$, says that the acceptable wage rate is always equal to the actual one. Moreover, we require that the acceptable unit costs are homogeneous of degree one with respect to its arguments. This implies that if we increase the actual prices twice, then the acceptable costs will be doubled. As the actual cost functions are homogeneous of degree one, this requirement is obviously reasonable.

We thus can determine the actual prices at short-run equilibrium by following equations:

$$\phi(p) = A(p)^T p + rB^T p + a_{n+1}(p), \tag{4.2.16}$$

where $\phi_i(p) = \Phi_i(P,P_{n+1})/P_{n+1}$, r, p are defined at t.

As the functional forms of ϕ are given from the market structure, (4.2.16) consists of n equations with (n + 1) unknowns. Our question is under what conditions there are solutions to (4.2.16).

3. The Existence of Short-Run Equilibria with Endogenous Interest Rate

It is interesting to know whether there are variables P(t) and r(t) such that (4.2.16) are satisfied. As (4.2.16) consists of (n+1) equations, we have to add one condition on the system to guarantee the existence of equilibrium. We are interested in two cases.

First, we are interested in the case that:

$$\sum_{i=1}^{n} \phi_i(p(t)) = \sum_{i=1}^{n} p_i(t) = c ,$$

(4.3.1)

where c is a constant independent of time.

The constant c may be determined from the price structure of the period (t - 1). For instance, one may choose: $c = \sum_i p_i(t-1)$. As the price are defined in relative terms with respect to the wage rate, this requirement means that the sum of the prices of the material goods grow at the same speed as that of the wage rate over time. That is, the system as a whole has no margin profits. (4.3.1) implies that some industry will get positive marginal profit, while others get negative if ϕ_i is not identical to p_i for all i. If $\phi_i = p_i$ for all i, then the short-run equilibrium is identical to the long-run equilibrium.

We introduce: $z_i = \phi_i(p)$. As ϕ_i (i = 1, ... , n) are continuous, it is possible to add some constraints on ϕ_i such that the inverse functions of ϕ exist. We hence have: p = m(z) where m is a n-dimensional vector, and m(z) are continuous with respect to z. This requirement can be satisfied, for instance, if $D_p\phi$ has a bounded inverse. As ϕ are homogeneous of degree one with its arguments, so are m(z).

The problem is now reduced to solving:

$$z = A(m(z))^{\mathrm{T}}m(z) + r(z)B^{\mathrm{T}}m(z) + a_{n+1}(m(z)) = G(z),$$

(4.3.2)

in which

$$r(z) = [c - \sum_{i=1}^{n} \sum_{j=1}^{n} a_{ij}(m(z))m_i(z) - \sum_{j=1}^{n} a_{n+1,j}(m(z))]/g(z),$$

(4.3.3)

where

$$g(z) = \sum_{i=1}^{n} \sum_{j=1}^{n} b_{ij}m_i ,$$

which is not equal to zero. As $G_i(z)$ are continuous with respect to z and $\sum_i G_i(z) = c$, we see that G(z) is a transformation of the closed convex set S (defined by:

$S = \{z: \Sigma\, z_i = c, z_i \geq 0, \text{ for all } i\}$ into itself. According to the Brouwer fixed-point theorem, there exists at least one vector, z_0, such that (4.3.2) are satisfied. The short-run equilibrium actual price vector and the interest rate are given by:

$$p_0 = m(z_0), \qquad r_0 = r(z_0). \tag{4.3.4}$$

It can be seen that every component of p_0 (z_0) is positive.

As there are unique correspondence between p and z, to show the uniqueness of p_0 (z_0), it is sufficient to prove the uniqueness of z_0 (p_0). We show the uniqueness of r_0. If p_0 is uniquely determined, r_0 is unique, too.

Let there be two sets of equilibrium prices and interest rate, denoted by (p^1, r^1) and (p^2, r^2), respectively. Let p^1 be different from p^2 and $r^1 > r^2$ (the analysis for the case of $r^1 < r^2$ can be similarly carried out). As (4.3.1) holds for both p^1 and p^2 and p^1 and p^2 are strictly positive, we can find an index h such that:

$$z_h^1/z_h^2 = \min\{z_i^1/z_i^2, i = 1, \ldots, n\}. \tag{4.3.5}$$

According to this definition of h, we have: $z_h^1/z_h^2 < 1$ and

$$z_i^2/z_h^2 \leq z_i^1/z_h^1, \tag{4.3.6}$$

in which at least one inequality is strictly held. As

$$z_{hx} = \Sigma_i\, a_{ih}^x m_i^x + r^x \Sigma_i\, b_{ih} m_i^x + a_{n+1,h}^x,$$

where x = 1, 2, we have

$$0 = \Sigma_i\, [a_{ih}(m(z^1))m_i(z^1)/z_{h1} - a_{ih}(m(z^2)m_i(z^2)/z_{h2}] +$$

$$[r^1 \Sigma_i\, b_{ih}(m(z^1))m_i(z^1)/z_{h1} - r^2 \Sigma_i\, b_{ih}(m(z^2))m_i(z^2)/z_{h2}]$$

$$+ [a_{n+1,h}(m(z^1))/z_{h1} - a_{n+1,h}(m(z^2))/z_{h2}]. \tag{4.3.7}$$

As a_{ih} are homogeneous of degree zero, m are homogeneous of degree one, $a_{n+1,h}$ is homogeneous of degree one, we see that (4.3.7) can be expressed in terms of $Z_i = z_i/z_h$ as follows:

$$0 = \Sigma_i\, [a_{ih}(m(Z^1))m_i(Z_1) - a_{ih}(m(Z^2)m_i(Z^2)]$$

$$+ [r^1 \Sigma_i b_{ih}(m(Z^1))m_i^{-1}(Z^1) - r^2 \Sigma_i b_{ih}(m(Z^2))m_i(Z^2)]$$

$$+ [a_{n+1,h}(m(Z^1)) - a_{n+1,h}(m(Z^2))]. \tag{4.3.8}$$

As $Z^1 \geq Z^2$ which strictly holds at least for one component, $r_1 > r_2$, a_{ij} and m_i are increasing functions with respect to their arguments, we see that the right side of (4.3.8) is positive. Thus (4.3.8) cannot hold. This implies that $r^1 > r^2$ cannot hold, i.e., $r^1 \leq r^2$. Similarly we can prove that $r^1 < r^2$ cannot hold either. Accordingly, r is uniquely determined. From the properties of (4.3.8), we can also conclude that the vector Z is uniquely determined. Thus z is uniquely determined by using: $\Sigma z_i = c$. As $z = \phi(p)$, we see that p is uniquely determined.

Proposition 4.3.1.

For the given acceptable unit cost functions, there exists a unique short-run equilibrium, (p_0, r_0).

Although there exists a unique equilibrium under the given conditions, there are some problems to be solved. We are not sure whether the equilibrium interest rate is positive. As the equilibrium interest rate is related to the acceptable cost functions, it is highly possible that for some forms of the acceptable cost functions, the equilibrium interest rate is not positive. In a sense, this means non-existence of a reasonable equilibrium for the given acceptable cost structure. Another problem is that from an economic point of view it is more meaningful to investigate the existence of equilibrium for a fixed level of interest rate. The following section is concerned with this problem.

As $\Sigma \phi_i(p) = \Sigma p_i$ holds at the equilibrium, we see that if $\phi_i(p)$ is equal to p_i $(i = 1, \ldots , n)$, there is no "margin profit" for any industry. If $\phi_i(p)$ is not equal to p_i, then some industries must have positive margin profits while others get negative margin profits. For instance, if $\phi_i(p) < p_i$ which states that the actual unit cost of the ith industry is less than the equilibrium price, then the industry gets a positive margin profit $(= p_i - \phi_i(p))$. Obviously, such an equilibrium cannot be permanent in the long terms because relative advantages of each industry will be changed with time. It is important to examine how such series of short-run equilibria can be actually carried out in a long-run dynamic world.

4. The Existence of Equilibrium for a Fixed Interest Rate

In the preceding section, we examined the question that if the acceptable cost functions are given, whether there exist unique values of prices and interest rate such that the system is in a short-run equilibrium. As we assumed that at a short-run equilibrium the sum of the acceptable unit costs is equal to that of the actual prices, it is natural to expect that if an equilibrium exists, then some industries will get positive margin profits while others have negative ones. Such "inequality" to get profit is due to the assumed properties of the acceptable cost functions. It is natural to ask whether it is possible to have an equilibrium at which the margin profit rate is equal for all of the industries. It should be noted that similar results are proved in Morishima (1964), though we interpret the meanings of these results in a little different way.

We are still concerned with (4.2.16). However, we are interested in a special case of whether there exists a number v such that, $\phi_i(p) = (1 + v)p_i$, for a given fixed rate of interest. This case means that there is no relative advantage of one industry over another. Each sector gets the same (positive or negative) margin profit as the other sectors.

Substituting $\phi_i(p) = (1 + v)p_i$ into (4.2.16) yields:

$$(1 + v)p(t) = A(p(t))^T p(t) + r(t)B^T p(t) + a_{n+1}(p(t)). \tag{4.4.1}$$

In what follows, we call the negative of v (i.e., - v) the "benefit rate" of the production. The reason that (- v) is termed "benefit rate" is that as (- v) increases (i.e., v decreases), the margin rate of the production in terms of Morishima (1964) increases. It can be seen that if v is negative, the firms get positive margin profits; while if v is positive, the firms get negative margin profits.

There are (n + 2) unknowns (r, v and p) and n equations in our system. In order to guarantee the existence of a short-run equilibrium, it is necessary to add two constraints upon the system. We assume that the interest rate is fixed by the government at each point of time. Moreover, we add a constraint:

$$\sum_{i=1}^{n} P_i(t)/P_{n+1}(t) = \sum_{i=1}^{n} p_i(t) = c, \tag{4.4.2}$$

where c is a positive constant. The sum of the relative prices with respect to the wage rate is constant. (4.4.2) determines a convex set denoted by S. Our question is to examine whether there exist v and positive values of p such that (4.4.1) and (4.4.2) are satisfied. Although the proof of the existence is similar to the previous section, one should note that the economic mechanisms to reach an equilibrium are different. In the previous section, the acceptable costs are presumed to be given functions of prices and the problem is to examine the existence of equilibrium prices and rate of interest. In this section, the government fixes the rate of interest rate and the market determines the "benefit rate" (v) of the production and the price vector.

From (4.4.1), we can solve v as a function of the prices

$$v = \{ \sum_{i=1}^{n} \sum_{j=1}^{n} a_{ij}p_j + r \sum_{i=1}^{n} \sum_{j=1}^{n} b_{ji}p_j$$

$$\sum_{i=1}^{n} a_{n+1,i}\}/c - 1 = Q(p) . \tag{4.4.3}$$

Thus there is a correspondence between the price structure and "benefit rate". Once prices are determined, (4.4.1) gives a unique benefit rate. Substituting (4.4.3) into (4.4.1) yields:

$$p = F(p)\{A(p)^T p + rB^T p + a_{n+1}\} = G(p), \tag{4.4.4}$$

where $F(p) = 1/\{1 + Q(p)\}$. From the definition of $Q(p)$, we see that $F(p) > 0$ for a positive vector of prices. Let $G_i(p)$ denote the ith element of $G(p)$. From (4.4.3) and (4.4.4), we have

$$\sum_{i=1}^{n} G_i(p) = \sum_{i=1}^{n} p_i = c. \tag{4.4.5}$$

For $G_i(p) \geq 0$, $G(p)$ is a transformation of the closed convex set S into itself. Moreover, it is continuous. According to the Brouwer fixed-point theorem, there exists at least one p^0 carried into itself by this transformation. Thus p^0 is a solution to (4.4.1) and (4.4.2). We can thus obtain a solution of the problem. Moreover, p^0 are strictly positive. Because $v^0 = Q(p^0)$, v^0 may be positive, zero, or negative, though $1 + v^0$ is necessarily positive. Furthermore, if p^0 is uniquely determined, v^0 must also be uniform. We now prove the uniqueness of p^0.

Let us assume that there exist two sets of equilibrium prices which are denoted by p^1 and p^2, respectively. Corresponding to these prices, one has two "benefit rates" v^1 and v^2. It is assumed that

$$v^1 - v^2 > 0 \tag{4.4.6}$$

holds. To prove the uniqueness of the equilibrium price, it is sufficient to show that there do not exist p^1 and p^2 such that (4.4.6) holds. As both p^1 and p^2 satisfy (4.4.2), we have

$$\sum_{i=1}^{n} p_i^1 = \sum_{i=1}^{n} p_i^2. \tag{4.4.7}$$

Similarly as in the previous section, we define an index h such that

$$m_h = \text{Min}\{m_i, \; i = 1, \dots, n\}, \tag{4.4.8}$$

where $m_i = p_i^2/p_i^1$ ($i = 1, \dots, n$). Obviously, $m_h < 1$. From (4.4.8), one has, $q_i^1 < q_i^2$, $i = 1, \dots, n$, where $q_i^j = p_i^j/p_h^j$ (i, j = 1, 2, and h is fixed as in (4.4.8)). We note that both p_h^1 and p_h^2 satisfy

$$(1 + v)p_h = \sum_{j=1}^{n} a_{jh}(p)p_j + r \sum_{j=1}^{n} b_{jh}p_j$$

$$+ a_{n+1,h}(p). \tag{4.4.9}$$

As the technological coefficients are homogeneous of degree one with respect to prices, from (4.4.9) we have

$$1 + v^1 = \sum_{j=1}^{n} a_{jh}(q^1)q_j^1 + r \sum_{j=1}^{n} b_{jh}q_j^1$$

$$+ a_{n+1,h}(q^1) = W(q^1, r),$$

$$1 + v^2 = \sum_{j=1}^{n} a_{jh}(q^2)q_j^2 + r \sum_{j=1}^{n} b_{jh}q_j^2$$

$$+ a_{n+1,h}(q^2) = W(q^2, r), \tag{4.4.10}$$

where q^j (j = 1, 2) are vectors. It can be verified that W_i are non-negative (i = 1, ... , n) where W_i is the partial derivative of W with respect to q_i. W is a non-decreasing function of the corresponding variables. From (4.4.10), one has $v^2 - v^1 > 0$, which contradicts $v^1 - v^2 > 0$. This implies that $p^1 = p^2$. We have thus guaranteed the uniqueness of p and v.

Proposition 4.4.1.
Let the interest rate r be fixed. Then the prices and the benefit rate are uniquely determined. The prices at the equilibrium are strictly positive.

The proposition guarantees the existence of a unique equilibrium price. We will investigate relations between the "benefit rate" and the rate of interest.

First, let the interest rate r be fixed at r^1 and r^2, respectively. According to Proposition 4.4.1 for the given r^1 (r^2) the prices p^1 (p^2) and the inflation rate v^1 (v^2) are uniquely determined. Similarly to (4.4.8), we can define an index h. According to the definition of h, (4.4.8) also holds for p^1 and p^2. Like in (4.10), we can define functions $W(q^1, r^1)$ and $W(q^2, r^2)$. As W_i are non-negative and W_r is positive, W is a non-decreasing function of the variables. Accordingly, if $r^2 > r^1$, then

$$W(q^1, r^1) < W(q^2, r^2).$$

So, if $r^2 > r^1$, then $v^2 > v^1$.

Proposition 4.4.2.
Let (p^1, v^1) and (p^2, v^2) be the equilibrium solutions corresponding to the preassigned interest rates r^1 and r^2, respectively. If $r^2 > r^1$, then $v^2 > v^1$.

Proposition 4.4.2 implies that if the interest rate is increased, then the "benefit rate" decreases. Hence, for a short period of time the industries may get either positive or negative marginal profits according to the government policy. In other words, the industries may get positive margin profit only when the government fixes the interest rate at a low level.

As mentioned above, at the short-run equilibrium $(1 + v)$ is positive, i.e., $v > -1$. However, we are not sure about the sign of v. As proved by Morishima (1964), when $r = 0$ the corresponding equilibrium marginal profit rate is positive. This implies that $v^0 < 0$. As v increases with r and p_i are bounded, from (4.4.3) we see that there must a positive r,denoted by r^*, at which $v = 0$. Hence, if $r < r^*$, the actual unit cost for each industry is less than the current price; if $r > r^*$, the actual unit cost is larger than the current price.

5. The Interest Rate and Investment Coefficient Matrix

In the previous sections, we considered the technological matrices A as functions of prices. In this section we will discuss the case when the matrix A is constant and the matrix B is dependent on the rate of interest.

From Keynesian theory, we know that the interest rate has a role in affecting the investment behavior of entrepreneurs. In Keynes' approach investment demand explicitly depends upon a rate of interest which represents a "cost of capital". We are interested in how Keynes' theory of investment can be introduced into multiple sector models proposed in the previous sections. To analyse this problem, consider the price system defined in Section 4.4:

$$(1 + v)p = A^Tp + rB^Tp + a_{n+1}, \qquad (4.5.1)$$

where v represents a measurement of the common margin profit of the production. For simplicity, we assume the technological matrix A to be constant.

We propose that the investment matrix B is dependent on the interest rate r, $B = B(r)$, i.e.,

$$(1 + v)p = A^Tp + rB^T(r)p + a_{n+1}. \qquad (4.5.2)$$

According to the definition of the investment (or capital) matrix B, we know that its element b_{ij} $(i, j = 1, \dots , n)$ represents the quantity of good i invested in the jth sector in order to increase the output of that sector by one unit. It is proposed that the change rate of b_{ij} $(i, j = 1, \dots , n)$ is non-positive with respect to any increase in the interest rate. This assumption can be interpreted as follows. If the interest rate is increased, then it will cost more for the entrepreneurs to invest in increasing the capacity of production. In this case, the entrepreneurs will improve the technology by increasing the efficiency of investment, which will cause B to fall or at least not to increase.

Even if the technology is not improved, the entrepreneurs will be more careful about their investment behavior. As the model is highly aggregated, each coefficient b_{ij} represents a whole industrial sector. Thus, as a whole, the efficiency of investment may be improved since the entrepreneurs are more responsive in their investment behavior.

If we assume that (4.5.2) is subjected to the constraint: $p_1 + \dots + p_n = c$, where c is a positive constant, similarly to the proof of Proposition 4.4.2, we can guarantee the existence and uniqueness of the prices and the inflation rate for a fixed r. However, the comparative results of Proposition 4.4.2 will not hold for the system of this section.

For simplicity, first we discuss the case of a one sector model. The price equation for the one sector model can generally be described as

$$(1 + v)p = ap + rb(r)p. \tag{4.5.3}$$

Specifying $b(r) = mr^{-d}$ where m and d are positive constants, we have

$$(1 + v) = a + mr^{1-d}. \tag{4.5.4}$$

For a given interest rate, the equilibrium value of v is uniquely determined by (4.5.4). We have

$$dv/dr = (1 - d)m/r^d. \tag{4.5.5}$$

Thus, as the interest rate is increased, the benefit rate (- v) decreases if the parameter d is less than unity, and it becomes higher if d is greater than unity. Moreover, in the case of d = 1, there is no change in the benefit rate when the interest rate is shifted. Accordingly, we can conclude that the way in which benefit rate is affected by the interest rate depends upon how the entrepreneurs react to the changes in the interest rate. If the influence is strong (i.e., d > 1), the benefit rate may even increase after the interest rate is increased.

It should be emphasized that the result obtained above is qualitatively the same to that of Proposition 4.4.2 in Section 4.4 when d < 1, and contrary to it if d > 1. This is because we neglected the effects of the interest rate upon the investment matrix in the previous section.

We now examine the general case. As prices are also dependent on the interest rate, the comparative statics analysis with respect to r is not direct.

For convenience, introduce the matrix $C(r) = rB(r)$ where $c_{ij}(r) = rb_{ij}(r)$. Our main result regarding shifts of the interest rate is summarized in the following theorem.

Theorem 4.5.1.

Let (p^1, v^1) and (p^2, v^2) be the equilibrium solutions corresponding to the preassigned interest rates r^1 and r^2, respectively. Then we have
    (i) If $dc_{ij}/dr \geq 0$ (i, j = 1, ... , n) and $r_2 > r_1$, then $v_2 \geq v_1$; and
    (ii) If $dc_{ij}/dr \leq 0$ (i, j = 1, ... , n), and $r_2 > r_1$, then $v_2 \leq v_1$.

Proof:

As the prices at equilibrium are strictly positive, it is thus always possible to find indices h and d such that

$$m_h = Min\{m_i, \ i = 1, \ \dots \ , \ n\},$$

$$m_d = Max\{m_i, \ i = 1, \ \dots \ , \ n\}, \tag{4.5.5}$$

where $m_i = p_i^2/p_i^1$ (i = 1, ... , n). In what follows, h and d are fixed. Obviously, m_h < 1 and m_j > 1. And one has

$$q_i^1 < q_i^2, \quad i = 1, \ \dots \ , \ n, \tag{4.5.6}$$

$$g_i^1 > g_i^2, \quad i = 1, \ \dots \ , \ n, \tag{4.5.7}$$

where $q_i^j = p_i^j/p_h^j$, and $g_i^j = p_i^j/p_d^j$ (j = 1, ... , n). We note that p_h^1, p_h^2, p_d^1, and p_d^2 satisfy

$$(1 + v)p_h = \sum_{j=1}^{n} a_{jh}p_j + r \sum_{j=1}^{n} c_{jh}(r)p_j$$

$$+ \ a_{n+1,h}. \tag{4.5.8}$$

Thus we have

$$1 + v^k = \sum_{j=1}^{n} a_{jh}q_j^k + \sum_{j=1}^{n} c_{jh}(r^k)q_j^k$$

$$+ \ a_{n+1,h} = W(q^k, r^k), \quad k = 1, \ 2, \tag{4.5.9}$$

$$1 + v^k = \sum_{j=1}^{n} a_{jh}g_j^k + \sum_{j=1}^{n} c_{jh}(r)g_j^k$$

$$+ \ a_{n+1,h} = G(g^k, r^k), \quad k = 1, \ 2, \tag{4.5.10}$$

where q^j, g_j (j = 1, 2) are vectors.

If $dc_{ij}/dr \geq 0$ (i, j = 1, ... , n) and $r_2 > r_1$, using (5.9) we see that $W(q^2,r^2)$ $\geq W(q^1,r^1)$, i.e., $v_2 \geq v_1$.

If $dc_{ij}/dr \leq 0$ (i, j = 1, ... , n), and $r_2 > r_1$, using (5.10) we see that, $G(g^2,r^2)$ $\leq G(g^2,r^2)$, i.e., $v_2 \leq v_1$.

We have thus completed the proof.

It should be noted that the result we have obtained for the one sector model is a special case of this theorem.

It should be noted that in Sections 4.3 and 4.4 we discussed the behavior of the system when the input matrix is dependent on the prices and the investment matrix is constant. And we have just examined the case that the input matrix is constant and the investment matrix is dependent on the rate of interest. It is natural to combine these cases in a more general model as:

$$\phi(P) = A^T(P)P + rB^T(r)P + a_{n+1}P_{n+1},$$

where A and B are dependent on P and r, respectively. We may examine the existence and uniqueness of equilibrium and carry out comparative analysis similarly as in the previous sections.

6. The Relations Between Growth, Interest and Inflation Rates in the von Neumann Dynamic Model
- An extended concept of balanced growth

The previous sections excluded the possibility of joint production, although substitutions have been assumed. Furthermore, quantitative aspects were excluded when we discussed the interactions between interest and inflation rates. In this section, however, we follow von Neumann (1937) in assuming that each good may be produced jointly with other goods; viz., its joint products. We are still only interested in those interactions which occur among rates of inflation, interest and growth.

There are many discussions about and extensions of the von Neumann system in the literature. For example, Morishima (1960) explicitly introduced capitalists' and workers' consumption into the model, and subsequently he also took workers' savings into account (Morishima, 1969). Recently, Salvadori (1980), Bidard and E. Hosoda (1987) relaxed the assumption accepted by Morishima - that the demand for any good cannot be identical to zero. Although there are other generalized formalizations (e.g., Salvadori ,1988), we will not review the literature in greater detail here. Moreover, we are only concerned with the original von Neumann model, though the following discussion is extended to a generalized model.

The original work of von Neumann deals with the existence of a state of balanced growth in which prices are permanently fixed. It was proved that the growth rate and the rate of interest are uniquely determined and equal. In what follows, we try to extend the concept of balanced growth to allow prices to be changeable.

In the von Neumann model, capital goods at different stages of wear and tear are described as different goods. A production process is defined as an operation which converts one bundle of goods, including capital equipment left over from the preceding period - into another bundle of goods - including the capital goods which are carried forward for use in further production. Thus, the fixed capital equipment employed is included both in the bundle of inputs and again in the bundle of outputs. In the von Neumann model the "consumption" of goods is assumed to take place only through the process of production, which includes the necessities of life which are consumed by workers.

The model is defined as follows. There are n goods $(j = 1, ... , n)$ which can be produced by m processes with indexes running $i = 1, ... , m$. It is assumed that the ith process produces outputs of goods $b_{i1}, b_{i2}, ... , b_{in}$ by the end of a period by using as inputs the stocks of goods $a_{i1}, a_{i2}, ... , a_{in}$ existing at the beginning of the period (per unit of the activity levels). The technological coefficients (a_{ij}, b_{ij}) are assumed to satisfy the following conditions: (1) a_{ij} and b_{ij} $(i = 1, ..., m, j = 1, ... , m)$ being non-negative; (2) the necessity of inputs, $\Sigma_j\ a_{ij} > 0$ (for all i); and (3) in each process, any good appears as either an input or an output, i.e., $a_{ij} + b_{ij} > 0$ (for all i and j).

Let the activity level of the ith process in period t be $X_i(t)$ $(t = 1, 2, ... ,)$. Here, $X_i(t)$ $(i = 1, ... , m)$ is non-negative for any t. As the input of any good in period $t + 1$ cannot exceed its output in period t, the following inequalities hold

$$\sum_{i=1}^{m} a_{ij}X_i(t+1) < \sum_{i=1}^{m} b_{ij}X_i(t),$$

$$j = 1, ...n. \tag{4.6.1}$$

Let the price of the jth good in period t be denoted by $P_j(t)$ $(j = 1, ... , n, t = 1, 2, ...)$ where P_j is non-negative, and the homogeneous interest rate in period t is denoted by $r(t)$ $(t = 1, 2, ...)$. The unit cost of production of each process including interest payments, evaluated at the prices of period t, should be not less than the value of output evaluated at the prices of period $t + 1$. Hence one has

$$(1 + r(t)) \sum_{j=1}^{n} a_{ij}P_j(t) > \sum_{j=1}^{n} b_{ij}P_j(t+1),$$

$$i = 1, \dots, m. \tag{4.6.2}$$

The von Neumann model consists of (4.6.1) and (4.6.2).

We define the state of balanced growth in a manner which is different from that used by von Neumann. Rather than fixing prices, we allow them to change at a constant rate. It can be seen below that this is a rather natural extension of von Neumann's concept. We define the state of balanced growth as the proportional growth of the activity levels with constant inflation and interest rates:

$$X_i(t+1) = (1 + g)X_i(t), \quad i = 1, \dots, m,$$

$$P_j(t+1) = (1 + v)P_j(t), \quad j = 1, \dots, n,$$

$$r(t+1) = r(t) = r, \tag{4.6.3}$$

in which g is the growth rate and v is the inflation rate. If $v = 0$, our definition of balanced growth is identical to that of von Neumann.

Substituting (4.6.3) into (4.6.1) and (4.6.2), one has

$$(1 + g) \sum_{i=1}^{m} a_{ij}X_i(t) < \sum_{i=1}^{m} b_{ij}X_i(t),$$

$$j = 1, \dots, n, \tag{4.6.4}$$

$$(1 + r) \sum_{j=1}^{n} a_{ij}P_j(t) > \sum_{j=1}^{n} (1 + v) b_{ij}P_j(t),$$

$$i = 1, \dots, m. \tag{4.6.5}$$

Our task is reduced to establishing whether there exist appropriate values of P(t), X(t), r, g, and v such that (4.6.4) and (4.6.5) hold. To solve this problem, we add two subsidiary conditions: (1) the price of a free good is zero, i.e., if the jth inequality of (4.6.4) strictly holds, then $P_j(t) = 0$, (2) the activity level of a process with loss is zero, i.e., if the ith relation of (4.6.5) holds strictly, then $X_i(t) = 0$.

The system of (4.6.4) and (4.6.5) is identical to von Neumann's expanding economy if we interpret $(1 + r)/(1 + v)$ as "the interest factor" in the von Neumann model. Consequently, all the results of the standard von Neumann model are applicable to (4.6.4) and (4.6.5). From von Neumann (1937), we can obtain the following results: (1) The system of production actually used will have the greatest rate of expansion of all possible productive systems; (2) The "interest rate" factor (i.e., $(1 + r)/(1 + v)$), is equal to $1 + g$; and (3) The price system will have a possible "rate of interest" smaller than or as small as that of any other price system. Furthermore, the terms $(1 + r)/(1 + v)$ and $1 + g$ are uniquely determined and g is non-negative.

These results have very important economic implications. (1) and (3) state the existence of a maximum economic growth rate, and a minimum rate of interest, respectively. This section focusses upon an interpretation of (2), which determines a simple relation among inflation, interest and growth rates. We will show that this simple relation may provide some important information.

From (2) we have

$$(1 + r)/(1 + v) = 1 + g. \tag{4.6.6}$$

As $(1 + r)/(1 + v) = 1 + (r - v)/(1 + v)$, the term $(r - v)/(1 + v)$ is equal to the interest in the standard von Neumann model. This term is uniquely determined and non-negative since

$$(r - v)/(1 + v) = g, \tag{4.6.7}$$

where g is uniquely determined and non-negative. It should be noted that the inflation rate v may be negative (i.e., deflation).

Proposition 4.6.1.

In the state of balanced growth, the rate of interest rate is necessarily not less than the inflation rate.

Although $(r - v)/(1 + v)$ are uniquely determined, either the rate of interest r or the inflation rate has to be exogenously given. Otherwise, the inflation rate may be at any level in this automatic system. If von Neumann had not defined the state of balanced growth to have a zero inflation rate, the system could not be "automatically" determined.

Without any exogenous force, there are multiple solutions of $(r - v)/(r + v) = g$ for a given value of g. Consequently, in the von Neumann system only quantitative aspects can be uniquely determined, i.e., the activity levels and growth rate of the model. The monetary terms cannot be uniquely determined, unless we introduce some exogenous mechanism.

From the above discussion, we see that in the extended balanced growth state either the interest rate or the rate of inflation has to be exogenously fixed by the government or the banking system. It is reasonable to assume the interest rate to be exogenously fixed by the government.

Let us consider a case in which the government fixes the interest rate equal to the growth rate which is endogenously determined. From $(r - v)/(1 + v) = g$, one obtains $v = 0$. Hence, the inflation rate may only become zero if the government determines an appropriate level of the interest rate. When the rate of interest is equal to the growth rate it is termed the "natural interest rate", denoted by r^*.

Let us discuss some implications of the equality: $(r - v)/(1 + v) = g$. First, we analyse how the inflation rate is affected when the interest rate is shifted for a fixed g. It can be seen that an increase of the interest rate will always cause the rate of interest to become higher. If the rate of interest is fixed at a level below that of the natural interest rate, then we have deflation. Inflation takes place if the actual interest rate is higher than the natural one.

Next discuss the relation between inflation rates and growth rates for a fixed interest rate. As shown before, the growth rate is determined by the production structure of the system. Assume that the growth rate becomes higher due to technological changes. In this case, the inflation rate tends to be low as the interest rate is fixed. Moreover, if the growth rate is high enough, then deflation may take place. For a fixed interest rate, we call the rate of inflation "the natural growth rate". When the inflation rate is equal to zero, one has: $r = g^*$. It should be noted that although this equality also holds for the case of the natural interest rate, the mechanisms which allow this equality to be arrived are different in each case. If the growth rate is higher than the natural growth rate, we have deflation, while if the growth rate is lower than the natural growth rate, inflation is observed.

As in the previous section, it is possible to suggest a mechanism to describe the way in which the government determines the interest rate.

V

GROWTH RATE CONTROLLED AND ECONOMIC DYNAMICS IN A MULTISECTOR MODEL

The previous chapter investigated the relations between rates of inflation, interest and growth within the framework of input-output models with neoclassical production functions and von Neumann systems, respectively. The first two rates are related to monetary terms, while the growth rate is related to the quantitative aspect of the system. Although outputs and prices can be endogenously uniquely determined within the system for appropriately given rates of interest, inflation and growth, not all of the rates can be determined endogenously in either of these models. It is necessary to suggest some mechanism to determine them. As mentioned above, different mechanisms can be proposed because the way in which these rates are decided depends on the "type" of economy. In this chapter, we are especially concerned with centralization and decentralization in a "mixed" economy. The central government's behavior is assumed to be oriented towards the maximization of a social welfare function which depends on the economic growth rate. For detailed results see Andersson and Zhang (1988a).

1. Introduction

In this chapter we are concerned with the way in which the policy maker will control the economy under certain decentralized mechanisms. Most studies of the centralization and decentralization of decision making in economic systems have been performed within the framework of a basically static theory. The normal starting point is to construct a static model in which the structure of production and prices is determined as a static equilibrium solution. The question of stability is then analyzed with the help of a quasi-dynamical system, i.e., the system is assumed to have a dynamic search procedure for the equilibrium in the vicinity of the equilibrium point. One example of such a procedure is the well known tâtonnement process first proposed by Leon Walras (1874). According to this principle, the price of a commodity is assumed to increase if there exists a positive excess demand for the commodity, while it decrease in the case of excess supply. It can, under certain conditions, be shown that an economy based upon this adjustment principle can return to its equilibrium in finite time without any inference from a central policy making agent.

Roy Harrod was the first economist to properly address the problem of the stabilization of a dynamic economy. In his study "Towards a Dynamic Economics" in 1948 he conjectured that a growing economy based upon Keynesian assumptions, with investment determined by an accelerator, could not be automatically stabilized. Any equilibrium would lie on a "knife-edge" and any slight disturbance would throw the system into permanent divergence. Surprisingly enough, Harrod never addressed the Keynesian idea that there might be a need for central policy making in order to ensure the stabilization of the otherwise unstable economy. This chapter readdresses the problem of the existence, uniqueness and stability of dynamic models which are subjected to different types of economic policy regimes.

As in the preceding chapter, the present discussion is still limited to the framework of the input-output system. However, the systems in the previous chapter cannot endogenously and simultaneously determine the rates of interest, inflation and growth. One of the three rates is exogenously given. We relax this by assuming that the growth rate can be controlled by the central government.

This chapter proceeds as follows. Section 2 analyses the problem of equilibrium and the optimum properties of linear dynamic systems. Thereafter, the problem of stability in situations of completely decentralized policy making according to Marshallian and Walrasian adaption patterns is dealt with. Sections 5 and 6 examine what occurs when these basically decentralized reaction patterns are confronted with supplementary centralized policy making. It is then shown that an economy without the possibility of substitution between different inputs requires a combination of decentralized and centralized decision making if long term stable economic growth under conditions of equilibrium and optimality is to be achieved.

2. Economic Dynamics With Maximization of Welfare

We develop our model within the framework of the Leontief input-output system. As in the previous chapter, the production activities of the economy are classified into n sectors or industries (i = 1, ... , n). The output of the ith sector is written with X_i, or vector X. Outputs in these sectors are produced to be traded, consumed and invested. Each sector is assumed to produce one single kind of good, i.e., no joint production is permitted. This means that the system under consideration is a special case of the von Neumann model. The production of each sector involves the transformation of several kinds of goods in given quantities into a certain amount a single kind of good. The pattern of input-output relations is assumed to be stable, which is specified as constant input coefficients. Although we may relax this assumption for the convenience of the analysis, we accept this assumption throughout the chapter.

The economy is generally described by:

$$X = AX + H, \tag{5.2.1}$$

where H is an investment delivery vector with elements H_i (i = 1, ... , n). A constant element a_{ij} (i, j = 1, ... , n) is called an input coefficient of the technology matrix A. In order to produce one unit of the jth good, a_{ij} units (i = 1, ... , n) of the ith good are needed as inputs.

H_i consists of a sum:

$$H_i = \sum_{j=1}^{n} H_{ij}, \quad i = 1, ... , n, \tag{5.2.2}$$

where H_{ij} denotes the investment deliveries from sector i to sector j.

Similar to the coefficients a_{ij}, the coefficients b_{ij} (i, j = 1, ... , n) measure how much of the output from sector i is needed for investment in sector j to obtain an increase of one additional unit of capacity in terms of output. At this initial stage, let us assume b_{ij} to be constant, although they are really dependent upon the existing structure of the economy. With the definition of b_{ij}, one has

$$H_{ij} = b_{ij} dX_j/dt. \tag{5.2.3}$$

From (5.2.1) and (5.2.3) one obtains

$$X = AX + BdX/dt, \tag{5.2.4}$$

where $B = (b_{ij})_{nxn}$. The equation (5.2.4) is the fundamental system to be analyzed (see also Brody, 1970). Let us assume the existence of a long-run homogeneous growth rate g. Here, the homogeneous growth rate implies that all the sectors in the economy grow at the same rate g. Thus we have

$$dX_i/dt = gX_i. \tag{5.2.5}$$

Consequently, (5.2.4) can be re-written as

$$X = AX + gBX, \tag{5.2.6}$$

which can be written in a normalized form as

$$x = Ax + gBx,$$

where $x_i = X_i/\{\Sigma_j X_j\}$, $i = 1, \dots , n$. As product scale does not matter in the system, the normalization does not affect our analysis. However, we prefer to retain (5.2.6).

It should be noted that the assumption about the homogeneous growth rate can be relaxed. Consider the case in which the economy consists of no less than 2 sectors. If we denote g_i the growth rate of the ith sector ($i = 1, \dots , n$), then the economy is described by

$$X_i = \sum_{j=1}^{n} a_{ij}X_j + g_i \sum_{j=1}^{n} b_{ij}X_j.$$

We assume that in long-run the growth rates in different sectors are proportional during the study period. If we denote the growth rate of the first sector with g, then the ith sector growth rates can be expressed

$$g_i = gk_i,$$

where $k_1 = 1$, k_i ($i = 2, \dots , n$) are positive numbers. Substituting these equations into the system, one obtains

$$X_i = \sum_{j=1}^{n} a_{ij}X_j + g\sum_{j=1}^{n} k_i b_{ij}X_j, \quad i = 1, \dots, n.$$

With these equations, the system with proportional growth rates can be similarly described by (5.2.6), although the matrix B would have different implications for this case.

If we accept g as an endogenous variable in the system, it can immediately be seen that our system can be rewritten as a nonlinear system since (5.2.6) is nonlinear with respect to X and g.

The optimization problem accepted here is defined as follows

$$\max\{U(g)\}, \tag{5.2.7}$$

subject to (5.2.6). In (5.2.7), U is the welfare function of the society, which is dependent upon the growth rate. It is assumed that the social welfare function satisfies the following properties

$$U'(g) > 0, \quad U''(g) \le 0. \tag{5.2.8}$$

The first inequality simply implies that any increase in the growth rate improves the social welfare function. The second requirement means that the function may be not satisfactory with a very high growth rate. In other words, there could be disutility effects of economic growth. In this study, we use a simplified form of the welfare function as follows:

$$U(g) = ag^b, \tag{5.2.9}$$

where

$$a > 0, \quad 0 < b \le 1. \tag{5.2.10}$$

Obviously, (5.2.9) satisfies (5.2.8). When $b = 1$, no disutility effects exist in the growing economy. Now we show that the objective function in the system with proportional growth rates for different sectors can also be appropriately defined as in (5.2.9). For example, it is possible to propose a welfare function as follows

$$U = a \prod_{i=1}^{n} g_i^{b_i},$$

with $b_i > 0$, $0 < \Sigma b_i \leq 1$, where g_i is the growth rate of the ith sector. If we assume the same proportional growth rates as before, then the welfare function is reduced to the same form as (5.2.9) $U = ag^b$, where a and b are appropriate constants. The above discussion means that the system with proportional growth rates is mathematically identical to that with the homogeneous growth rate. Consequently, it is sufficient for us to study the system with the homogeneous growth rate.

The Lagrangian L of the problem is defined as

$$L = L(g,P,X)$$

$$= ag^b - P^T\{AX + gBX - X\},$$

where P is an n-dimensional vector. It is well known that an element P_i of P can be interpreted as the shadow price, simply referred to as the price of the output of the corresponding sector. The function L has explicit economic implications. We can call it "the economic potential" of the system. It may be also, in the very long term, be interpreted as a measure of the constrained welfare of the economic system. Clearly, it is better for the society if U(g) has a high value, as U(g) is defined to be the welfare of the economy. If we note that the vector X is supply, while the total term $\{AX + gBX\}$ is demand, then $\{AX + gBX - X\}$ is "excess demand" in the admittedly special case of a nonsubstitution economy. "Excess demand" represents the extent to which the requirements of demanders are not satisfied. Thus, the smaller that $\{AX + gBX - X\}$ is, the better it is for the society. The sectoral excess demand, multiplied by the respective price, is equal to the total value of excess demand. In what follows, we try to analyse the behavior of the problem by specifying the Kuhn-Tucker conditions.

If we only deal with the interior solution of the problem, the necessary conditions of the optimal solution can be written as

$$\partial L/\partial g = U'(g) - P^T BX = 0, \tag{5.2.12}$$

$$\partial L/\partial P_i = - \{AX + gBX - X\}_{(i)} = 0, \tag{5.2.13}$$

$$\partial L/\partial X_i = \{ \sum_{i=1}^{n} P_j(a_{ij} + gb_{ij}) - P_i \},$$

$$i = 1, \ldots ,n, \tag{5.2.14}$$

in which we use $_{(i)}$ to express the ith element of a vector. From (5.2.9), one has

$$U'(g) = abg^{b-1} \quad \text{if } b < 1, \tag{5.2.15}$$

$$U'(g) = a, \qquad \text{if } b = 1. \tag{5.2.16}$$

We separate the two cases $b < 1$ and $b = 1$, since the growth rate, as shown below, has different forms with respect to P and X in each case. From (5.2.12)-(5.2.14), we can thus obtain a solution of the problem. With comparative static analysis, it is not difficult to investigate how a shift in the structural coefficients can affect the optimal solution. Our main interest is, however, to develop a dynamic model with reference to the stationary solution of (5.2.12)-(5.2.14).

As we have mentioned before, the solution of (5.2.12)-(5.2.14) may be considered as a possible description of economic behavior in the long-run. As the economic system is always subjected to different perturbations, the actual development of the system may be distant from this equilibrium. That is to say, during a process of an actual evolution of the system it is possible for economic trajectories to be well-removed the long-run solution.

To find conditions for the system which are distant from the equilibrium, we have to develop a dynamic system to describe behavior if the economic system is perturbed. In what follows, we must try to define an adjustment of price and output dynamics. We consider that the dynamics of prices and outputs can be described, in relation to the short-term, with the following equations

$$dP_i/dt = - \partial L/\partial P_i = \sum_{j=1}^{n} (a_{kj} + gb_{kj})X_j - X_j,$$

$$i = 1, \ldots , n, \tag{5.2.17}$$

$$dX_i/dt = \partial L/\partial X_i = - \{ \sum_{j=1}^{n} (a_{ij} + gb_{ij})P_j - P_i \},$$

$$i = 1, \ldots , n, \hspace{4cm} (5.2.18)$$

subject to (5.2.12). This set of differential equations describes the dynamics of our economic system. It should be mentioned that (5.2.12) always holds along any trajectory of (5.2.17) and (5.2.18). A further analysis shows that the growth rate can be uniquely determined by the price and output at any time. This implicitly implies that the growth rate and interest rate are adjusted to their equilibrium very rapidly. Here, we assume that the cost of capital is decomposed into the price of capital and the interest rate r. In order for a full equilibrium to exist, g = r at the equilibrium point in our economy. For simplicity, we assume that g(t) = r(t) also holds when the system is outside of the equilibrium, though in the actual development process r and g may be different. We thus may interpret g(t) as the interest rate in our system. To explain an adjustment process of the growth rate, let us denote the optimal growth rate determined from (5.2.12) by $g^*(P,X)$. We can consider the dynamics of the actual growth rate to be governed by the following equation

$$dg/dt = s(g^*(P,X) - g), \hspace{3cm} (5.2.19)$$

where s is an adjustment parameter. (5.2.19) describes possible effects of central government controls on the interest rate. This adjustment equation simply implies that if the actual growth rate is above the optimal one, then the speed of growth should be decreased, and vice versa. We will explain the implications of (5.2.19) in greater detail later on. If the value of s is taken to be large, then g shall always be approximately equal to g^*. The behavior of the whole system can thus be understood from (5.2.17) and (5.2.18) under appropriate conditions. Further investigation of the cases where s takes other values is certainly worthwhile; this increases the complexity of the dynamics by introducing a new dimension into the system.

The task of this study is to investigate certain aspects of the dynamics just suggested. The system can be written in a vector form as

$$dP/dt = AX + gBX - X,$$

$$dX/dt = P - A^{T}P - gB^{T}P. \hspace{3cm} (5.2.20)$$

Now it is necessary to provide an economic interpretation of our dynamic system. Firstly, it should be mentioned that (5.2.17) simply means that if the demand for the ith good exceeds the supply of this good, then the price of the ith good should be increased, and vice versa. This equation takes account of the behavior of consumers in the system. Similarly, (5.2.18) implies that if the total cost per unit of the ith product is greater than the price of this good, then the ith sector should decrease its output in order to decrease its losses. To show this, it is necessary to interpret economic implications of different terms in the adjustment equations. As mentioned above, in (5.2.17) the terms on the right-hand side represent the excess demand for the ith good. Consequently, the price moves according to whether or not the demand of the users is satisfied. It is directly seen that the terms $(a_{ik}P_k)$ express the unit cost of production for the ith sector using the product of the kth sector as an input; (gP_jb_{ij}) is the unit rental cost of the ith sector in order to increase its capacity by the use of the kth good. Therefore

$$\Sigma_k P_k(a_{ik} + gb_{ik}),$$

is the total cost involved for the ith sector to produce one unit of output. As P_i is the revenue of the ith sector for one unit of the product, we see that the terms on the right-hand side of (5.2.18) are the profit of the ith sector in producing one unit of output. (5.2.18) implies that the direction of changes in output is controlled by profits (losses).

In our system, we have required (5.2.12) to hold at any point of time. This implies that in the short-term welfare is not explicitly influenced by a varying growth rate, though it is implicitly dependent upon it. A change in the welfare of the society is explicitly dependent upon price and output. As (5.2.12) holds at any time, we can reduce the dynamics by one dimension.

To solve g as a function of P and X from (5.2.12), we have to consider the two cases $b < 1$ and $b = 1$ separately. If $b < 1$, then from (5.2.12) and (5.2.15) one has

$$g = g^*(P,X) = (P^TBX/ab)^{1/(b-1)}. \tag{5.2.21}$$

Now, we consider the case of $b = 1$. Differentiating both sides of (5.2.12) with respect to time, we have

$$dP^T/dtBX + P^TBdX/dt = 0. \tag{5.2.22}$$

Substituting (5.2.20) into (5.2.22), one can find a solution for the growth rate g as follows

$$g = g^*(P,X) = f(P,X)\{(X^T - X^T A^T)BX + P^T B(I-A^T)P,$$

$$(5.2.23)$$

where $f(P,X)$ is a nonlinear function with respect to P and X determined as

$$f(P,X) = \{P^T BB^T P - X^T B^T BX\}^{-1}.$$
$$(5.2.24)$$

This form of $g^*(P,X)$ may be a very complicated nonlinear equation. We finally find that the economic system is described by the following set of nonlinear differential equations

$$dP/dt = AX + g^*(P,X)BX - X,$$

$$dX/dt = P - A^T P - g^*(P,X)B^T P.$$
$$(5.2.25)$$

In what follows, we study the properties of the model.

3. Economic Cycles in the Case of One Sector

For simplicity, let us consider the case of one sector model. Corresponding to (5.2.1), one has

$$X = a_1 X + b_1 dX/dt.$$
$$(5.3.1)$$

where X is a scalar variable. This system can be considered as the aggregate multiplier-accelerator model, where X is income, a_1 and b_1 are the propensity to consume and the incremental capital output, respectively. For simplicity, we specify the utility function as

$$U(g) = 2g^{1/2},$$
$$(5.3.2)$$

i.e., $a = 1$, $b = 1/2$ in (5.2.9). This functional form is obviously meaningful.

The corresponding Lagrangian for the one sector model is

$$L(g,P,X) = g^{1/2} - P(a_1 X + gb_1 X - X).$$
$$(5.3.3)$$

The dynamics corresponding to (5.3.3) can thus be written as

$$dP/dt = a_1X + b_1Xg^*(P,X) - X,$$

$$dX/dt = P - a_1P - b_1Pg^*(P,X), \tag{5.3.4}$$

in which g^* is given by

$$g = g^*(P,X) = 1/(bPX)^2. \tag{5.3.5}$$

The dynamics of the economic system consist of two nonlinear differential equations. Now we shall investigate the behavior of the system. First we show that any time-dependent solution of the system is periodic.

Proposition 5.3.1.
Any time-dependent solution of (5.3.4) is periodic.

Proof:
As (5.3.4) can be rewritten in the form of

$$dP/dX = - X/P, \tag{5.3.6}$$

we can find an invariance of the dynamic system

$$S(P,X) = P^2 + X^2 = c, \tag{5.3.7}$$

where c is a constant. (5.3.7) can be bound to an arbitrary trajectory of (5.3.4). The conclusion about the periodic solution is immediate from (5.3.7).

It should be noted, however, that this periodic solution is not a limit cycle, as any small perturbations of the initial conditions will destruct the existing cycle and produce a new one. Furthermore, the system is conservative, which is proved below.

From Proposition 5.3.1, it can be concluded that the model can be used to explain oscillatory phenomena in the economic system. It is important to know whether or not the solution is stable. If the solution is unstable, we have to be very careful in dealing with it as any small disturbance from the solution will be magnified, and the actual trajectory will be diverted from the unstable solution.

Before proving some properties of the system, it is necessary for us to define the concept of a conservative system. The fundamental property of a conservative system is the existence of a function of the variables of the system which is a constant of motion and plays the role of energy (Zhang, 1990).

Definition 5.3.1 (Conservative System)

For a dynamic system $dy/dt = f(y)$, where y is a vector variable, if there exists a function $H(y)$, known as a first integral, of the system such that

$$dH(y)/dt = \Sigma \partial H/\partial y_i \, dy_i/dt = 0,$$

then the system is called conservative.

One of conservative systems which is well known is the Lotka-Volterra system. Conservative systems often have oscillatory solutions, although they are structurally unstable, as we shall explain below.

Proposition 5.3.2.

The system (5.3.4) is conservative and the cycle in Proposition 5.3.1 is neither stable nor unstable.

Proof:

As we have already found an invariant amount S in the proof of Proposition 5.3.1, according to the definition of conservative system, we see that the proposition holds.

Now we shall show that the cycle cannot be stable. As S does not change as we move along a trajectory of the system, these trajectories are defined by the curves $S(P,X) = c$ for different values of the constant c. As this value is independent of time, we see that it can be determined by any point on a trajectory. In particular, it can be determined by given initial conditions. Consequently, two trajectories with different conditions can never intersect. It follows from this that the cycle cannot be stable. For if it were, then all trajectories in the neighborhood of it would tend towards it, and hence would have $S = c$, as S is a continuous function. This implies that any small perturbation of the initial conditions would result in different behavior of the system. Consequently, the system is not stable. The unstable case can be similarly explained. Actually, it is not difficult to see that all of the trajectories which start in the positive quadrant are bounded, so the phase plane must consist of closed trajectories, each with a different value of the energy function $S(P,X)$. We can illustrate the behavior as in Fig. 5.3.1.

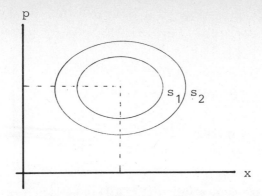

Fig. 5.3.1. Economic Cycles With Different Energies

From the discussion above, we know that the economic cycles are orbitally stable, although the system is not stable. Here, "orbitally stable" implies that two periodic solutions which start close together produce trajectories which remain close together all the time. However, it should be noted that although two cycles are very close, their speed of motion may be very different. A solution on one trajectory will complete a revolution more quickly or slowly than one on an adjacent trajectory and will increasingly gain or lag.

As mentioned previously, the model developed is only appropriate for the short-run as propositions 5.3.1 and 5.3.2 only hold effectively for that period. It may be said that any economic system is subjected to various exogenous perturbations. It is important to know whether the effects of such small perturbations remain in the system for ever. If they remain within the system, accumulative effects would exist in the long-run. It is clear that random perturbations will cause the solution to wander around the trajectories until it finally meets one of the axes P = 0 or X = 0. Such solutions are of no interest. Thus, the model cannot be considered adequate for describing the long-term oscillatory behavior of the economic system.

4. Properties of the Multiple Sector Model

In the preceding section, we have shown certain properties of a model with only one sector. It is also necessary to investigate the general case of a multiple sector model. In what follows, we show that we can find similar behavior to that in a one sector model.

We deal with the following system

$$dP/dt = AX + g^*(P,X)BX - X,$$

$$dX/dt = P - A^TP - g^*(P,X)B^TP, \qquad (5.4.1)$$

where the function g^* is given.

Proposition 5.4.1.

Any time-dependent solution of (5.4.1) is periodic.

Proof:

To identify periodic solutions, as in Section 5.3.1 we define a number $S(P,X)$ as

$$S(P,X) = P^TP + X^TX. \qquad (5.4.2)$$

Differentiating S with respect to t yields

$$dS/dt = 2(P^TdP/dt + X^TdX/dt). \qquad (5.4.3)$$

Substituting (5.4.1) into (5.4.3), one has

$$dS/dt = 2P^T\{(A + g^*B - I)X + 2X^T(I - A^T -$$

$$g^*B^T)P = 2P^T\{(A + g^*B - I)X + 2P^T(I - A^T -$$

$$g^*B^T)X = 0, \qquad (5.4.4)$$

which states that S is constant for any solution of (5.4.1). The invariant first integral on any trajectory can thus be obtained. As discussed in Proposition 5.3.1, the proposition is immediate.

Similarly to Proposition 5.4.1, one has:

Proposition 5.4.2.

The system (5.4.1) is conservative and the cycle in Proposition 5.4.1 is neither stable nor unstable.

Proof:

As we have already proved the existence of the first integral $S(P,X)$, the system is clearly conservative. Proof of stability can be completed similarly to the proof of Proposition 5.3.2.

5. Stabilization With Growth Rate Adjustment

In the previous sections, we have proved that the dynamic system emphasized in this study is unstable. However, it can be argued that the development in a dynamic model should be stabilized throughout most of the development processes of an actual economic system. In order to achieve this situation, we may add new terms to disturb the original system, which then results in a stable system. Otherwise, it is also possible to introduce new economically reasonable variables into the system to change the interactional relations among the variables, from which we can obtain a new stable system.

For simplicity, in this section we still focus our attention upon a system with one sector. However, we now consider a case in which the adjustment speed of the actual growth rate to the optimal one is not too fast. That is, the value of s in (5.2.19) is not too large. In this case, it is necessary to take (5.2.19) into account if we wish to understand the behavior of the whole system.

We take the welfare function to be of the form $U = 2g^{1/2}$. According to (5.3.5), the optimal growth rate is equal to $1/(bPX)^2$. The dynamics of the system are thus given by

$$dg/dt = s\{1/(bXP)^2 - g\}, \tag{5.5.1}$$

$$dP/dt = a_1X + b_1gX - X, \tag{5.5.2}$$

$$dX/dt = P - a_1P - gb_1X, \tag{5.5.3}$$

where the definitions of the variables and parameters are as given in Sections 5.2 and 5.3. Although the functional forms are specified, this will not influence our discussion about the dynamic characteristics of the system as all of the results below could even be obtained if we used general forms of the functions.

Firstly, we note that there still exists an invariant in this system. From (5.5.2) and (5.5.3), one obtains

$$S(P,X) = P^2 + X^2 = 1, \tag{5.5.4}$$

where we specify the integral constant with 1 as this does not affect our analysis. Consequently, the dimension of the dynamic system should be decreased by this constraint. Now, in order to rewrite the system in a simpler form, we introduce the following transformation:

$$Z = PX. \tag{5.5.5}$$

Obviously, Z can be interpreted as total value of the output. If X is capacity, then PX is the total value of the capacity. Taking derivatives of the two sides of (5.5.5) with respect to time, and then substituting (5.5.2) and (5.5.3) into the obtained equation, one obtains

$$dZ/dt = (X^2 - P^2)(1 - a_1 - b_1 X). \tag{5.5.6}$$

With (5.5.4) and (5.5.5), $(X^2 - P^2)$ can be reduced to a function of Z as

$$X^2 - P^2 = -1/2 \pm (1 - 4Z)^{1/2} = Q(Z), \tag{5.5.7}$$

in which we have to choose either + or - from ± to give a uniquely meaningful $Q(Z)$. $Q(Z)$ must be negative as Z has to be positive.

The problem is thus reduced into a two-dimensional system as

$$dg/dt = s\{1/(b_1 Z)^2 - g\},$$

$$dZ/dt = Q(Z)(1 - a_1 - b_1 g). \tag{5.5.8}$$

The reduced system thus describes the dynamic interactions between the growth rate and the welfare of the system.

In the first equation of (5.5.8), the optimal growth rate depends upon Z: the higher the value of Z, the lower the optimal growth rate. The economy is organized in such a way that it always tends to adjust its growth rate to the optimal growth rate. The second equation states that a change in the value of the capacity is related to the difference between the saving rate $1 - a_1$ and the "real" growth rate $b_1 g$. The function $Q(Z)$ can be interpreted as an adjustment parameter Z to its equilibrium.

The equilibrium of the system is determined by

$$s\{1/(b_1 Z)^2 - g\} = 0,$$

$$Q(Z)(1 - a_1 - b_1 g) = 0. \tag{5.5.9}$$

The equilibrium (Z_0, g_0) is

$$Z_0 = 1/b_1 g^2, \quad g_0 = (1 - a_1)/b_1. \tag{5.5.10}$$

The meaning of the equilibrium is easy to interpret. If the equilibrium is stable, we can perform a comparative analysis with respect to the parameters a_1 and b_1. If the propensity to consume is to be increased, then the growth rate must decrease, while the value of the capacity is increased at the equilibrium. Effects of a change in b_1 can also be similarly explained. The first condition in (5.5.10) corresponds to a "Wicksell equilibrium" condition, while the second corresponds to a "Harrod equilibrium" condition. As at the equilibrium, the interest rate and growth rates are equal. From the first equation of (5.5.10) we know that for a fixed b_1, if we have a higher level of the total value of capital at the equilibrium, the interest rate must be lower, and vice versa.

Now we can check the stability of the equilibrium. The Jacobian of the system is easily calculated as

$$J = \begin{bmatrix} -s & -2s/b_1^2 Z^3 \\ -b_1 Q(Z) & 0 \end{bmatrix},$$

in which Z is evaluated at the equilibrium. The eigenvalue k is determined as

$$k_{1,2} = -s/2 \pm (s^2/4 + 2sQ/b_1 Z^3)^{1/2}.$$

As Q is negative, the real part of k is always negative. Thus we obtain the following results.

Proposition 5.5.1.
The equilibrium is stable if there is a proper feed-back control of the interest rate.

This proposition is very significant if we note the difference between the systems in the preceding sections and (5.5.1)-(5.5.3). It may be concluded that the input-output dynamics defined in Section 5.2 are stabilized by introducing the growth rate dynamics. We can illustrate the local dynamics near the equilibrium by Fig. 5.5.2.

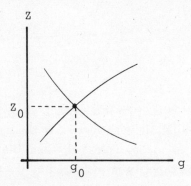

Fig. 5.5.2. Dynamics in (Z,g) Plane

6. Further Interpretations of the Dynamic System

We have introduced a possible dynamics of economy within the framework of the input-output system and have proved some properties of the system. Here, we would like to extend our model to take some of the more complicated factors in evolutionary processes into account and to explain some of the economic implications of our approach. It should be mentioned that further analysis based on this approach may be carried out. At this stage we only indicate some further directions for generalizing our approach with some interpretations of economic implications.

Until now, we have not differentiated between the adjustment speeds of prices and outputs towards their equilibria. It is often assumed that the adjustment speed of prices may be much lower than that of outputs. In some of the economic literature, this fact is recognized by "fixing" prices. It is not difficult to imagine that the dynamic behavior of economies with fixed prices and rapidly adjusting prices should be very dissimilar as variations in the adjustment speeds influence the stability of a dynamic system. Consequently, it may be valuable to investigate the behavior of our dynamic system according to different speeds of adjustment. We can generalize (5.2.17) and (5.2.18) a little as follows

$dP_i/dt = - u_i \partial L/\partial P_i$

$$= u_i \{ \sum_{j=1}^{n} (a_{kj} + gb_{kj})X_j - X_j \},$$

$$i = 1, \ldots , n, \tag{5.6.1}$$

$dX_i/dt = \partial L/\partial X_i$

$$= - v_i \{ \sum_{j=1}^{n} (a_{ij} + gb_{ij})P_j - P_i \},$$

$$i = 1, \ldots , n, \tag{5.6.2}$$

subject to

$$U'(g) - P^T B X^T = 0. \tag{5.6.3}$$

The parameters u_i and v_i ($i = 1, \ldots n$) are constant adjustment speeds for the corresponding prices and outputs, respectively. The adjustment speeds of prices and outputs should be different for other sectors. This system can be interpreted similarly as before. It may be noted that if the prices are fixed, i.e., $u_i = 0$ ($i = 1, \ldots , n$), then the dimension of the system can be largely reduced. Let all the adjustment speeds be not equal to zero.

Proposition 5.6.1.
The system (5.6.1)-(5.6.3) is conservative.

Proof:
Let us introduce a function S such that

$$S(P,X) = \sum_{i=1}^{n} (P_i^2/u_i + X_i^2/v_i).$$

It can easily be shown that $S(P,X)$ is the invariant first integral of the system. We have thus proved the proposition.

Consequently, we can similarly discuss the system as in Section 5.4.

In what follows, we show that different adjustments correspond to different economic mechanisms acting upon the system.

For convenience, we wish to write the system in a simpler form. We assume that the adjustment speeds of prices are of the same order of magnitude. That is, the differences among the adjustment speeds of prices are not too large. We also make similar assumptions for the adjustment speeds of outputs. We assume, however, that the difference between the adjustment speeds of prices and outputs may be very large. With these assumptions, after appropriate time scaling we may rewrite the system in the following form

$$dP_i/dt = \sum_{j=1}^{n} (a_{kj} + gb_{kj})X_j - X_j,$$

$$i = 1, \dots , n, \tag{5.6.4}$$

$$dX_i/dt = - v\{ \sum_{j=1}^{n} (a_{ij} + gb_{ij})P_j - P_i \},$$

$$i = 1, \dots , n, \tag{5.6.5}$$

where v is an appropriate "relative adjustment speed" parameter. It is required that $v > 0$. When the economy is governed by various mechanisms, v should take on different values.

Here, we consider the dynamics of the growth rate. As before, we assume the existence of a central government which influences the economy by controlling the growth rate. Let the optimal growth rate be denoted by $g^* = g^*(P,X)$. Then the dynamics of g are described by

$$dg/dt = s\{g^*(P,X) - g\}, \tag{5.6.6}$$

which corresponds to (5.2.19).

We further assume that the government does not directly control the prices. Thus it plays the role of an "auctioneer", influencing the dynamic process of prices which is determined by the disequilibrium of demand and supply. In this system the outputs of production are determined by the firms. The firms make their decisions according to prevailing profits in the market.

Now, we will show that it is possible for the parameter v to take a range of values from positive finite to infinite; the parameter s can take a range of values from zero to positive infinite. If v = a (= 1) where a is positive and finite, it implies that the firms adjust their products at the same speed as prices change. If v = + ∞, this implies that the market is perfectly competitive. s = 0 means that the growth rate is fixed by the central government. In this case, the system is reduced to a linear system. s = 1 implies that it takes some time before the actual growth rate arrives at the optimal rate. The case of s = + ∞ has been explained in Section 4.2. We have six different possible combinations of v and s, which correspond to various economic mechanisms. We list these combinations in Table 5.6.1.

Table 5.6.1.

The Possible Combinations of Adjustment Speeds

v	1	1	1	∞	∞	∞
s	0	1	∞	0	1	∞

Now, we interpret some implications of these combinations. Firstly, we note that if s = 0, the growth rate is fixed. In this case, the system becomes linear and structurally unstable. If the adjustment speed of the growth rate is infinite, the system is reduced to (5.4.1).

We also consider the case when both v and s are infinite. The corresponding dynamic system is reduced to (5.6.4). The dynamic behavior consists only of the adjustment processes of the prices. Actually, this means that once the price structure is determined, the product and the growth rate are soon determined. And the price structure is explicitly independent of product and growth rate, though the structure is implicitly dependent upon them. Obviously, this case corresponds to a purely competitive economy, which is both structurally and dynamically unstable.

In this special case, the process is reduced to the most popular means for modelling the price mechanism - the Walrasian adjustment process. There is an extensive body of literature about this process (Arrow and Hahn, 1971). It describes what is popularly referred to as "the law of demand and supply". If the prevailing market signals that there is a positive excess demand, the corresponding market price will rise, and if a negative excess demand is observed it will fall. Also, this process implies a state of perfect competition in which firms believe that they can trade whatever they wish to at current prices. As there is no possibility for any firm to change the prices, the auctioneer appears. This auctioneer may appear in the form of a "central government" in the system. The central government has perfect information about both the product and price structures so the actual growth rate can be brought rapidly towards the optimal level.

Let us consider the case when $v = h$ and $s = h^2$ where h is sufficiently small. After time is scaled, it can be shown that the system consists of (5.6.5) only. The adjustment speed of the growth rate is very low, while prices adjust very rapidly. Fast price adjustment suggests that the central government has perfect information about the price structure. Thus the firms can obtain information about the price structure very quickly. If more than one sector exist in the economic system, exchanges among the firms will take place as long as the firms can obtain mutual advantages by exchange. Adjustment processes without price adjustments have also been studied by various economists (e.g., Uzawa, 1962, Hahn, 1982).

If $v = s = 1$, then the dynamics consist of the adjustment processes of prices, outputs and growth rate. The firms are not perfectly competitive and the government has imperfect information. This is generally the case for a mixed economy.

7. Conclusions

This chapter has touched upon one of the most important issues in economics - the problem of the centralization and decentralization of decisions about quantities and prices of products and capital. This is discussed against the framework of a dynamic economic system based upon the Leontief input-output model with constant input, output and incremental capital output coefficients. Within this framework the problem of homogeneous economic growth in a model with n sectors is analyzed from the point of view of a "mixed" economy. It has been shown that this system can achieve an equilibrium in terms of long term welfare maximization. It can also be shown that a dynamic system of this type possesses a unique general equilibrium solution characterized by the same rate of growth in all n sectors.

VI

THE CHOICE OF TECHNIQUES

Until now, we concentrated primarily on the dynamics of quantities and prices and their relations in economic development - within the framework of multiple sector models. Technologies have been described by neoclassical production functions or by assuming constant input coefficients. Little emphasis has been placed upon the way in which techniques can be selected from amongst various alternatives within a given technology, and nothing has been said about the way in which technological change takes place and the impact which it may have upon economic growth. In the remainder of this study, we focus upon the dynamic relations between various forms of technology and economic development. In this chapter we restrict our attention to the problem of the "choice of (exogenously given) alternatives or techniques". Endogenous forms of technological change will be dealt with in Chapters VII and VIII.

In Section 6. 1 we explain how techniques can be chosen using a very simple equilibrium growth model. Sections 6.2 and 6.3 analyze the problem of the choice of alternatives or techniques within the framework of a multiple sector model with Leontief technology. Section 6.4 discusses the dynamic behavior of primal and dual systems. We demonstrate the impossibility of reswitching in a continuous substitution model in Section 6.5. The model presented in Section 6.1 can be found in Hicks (1965, Chapter XIII). The other models are referred to in detail in Chapter 8 of Burmeister and Dobell (1970), though the fundamental results can also be found in Morishima (1964).

1. The Choice of Techniques in a Simple Growth Model

We consider an economy which consists of two "industries" - a consumption good (corn) industry and a net investment good (tractor) industry. The same capital good is employed for production in both industries. As depreciation is omitted, the capital goods last for ever.

The population grows at a fixed rate (due to immigration). It is assumed that the supply of labour is perfectly elastic at some given wage. If this wage is maintained, the required number of workers will migrate into the system, but, if the wage level falls below that critical value, workers will leave the system. It is assumed that the wage is fixed in terms of corn. As corn-wages and the amount of labour employed are given, the share of the output for consumption which must be paid to labour is fixed in terms of corn; the share which is left over as profits is therefore also fixed in terms of corn. In equilibrium the earnings generated by making use of a tractor in tractor production must be the same as its earnings in corn production. Consequently, since the amount of labour and of tractors needed for tractor production are given, the cost of a new tractor is also fixed in terms of corn. If we define the rate of profit as the ratio of the earnings of a tractor to the cost of a tractor, then this rate is also fixed. Thus, even if we have no information about the growth rate of the economy, the whole of the relative price system is already determined.

To see precisely how the prices are determined, let us first introduce some notations:

w: wages;
q: the earnings (quasi-rent) of the capital good;
r: the rate of profit;
p_1 (p_2): the price of the consumption (capital) good;
a_1 (b_1): (fixed) production coefficients of capital
(labour) in consumption good production;
a_2 (b_2): (fixed) production coefficients of capital
(labour) in capital good production.

In equilibrium, since the earnings of the factors must be the same in both industries, we have

$$p_1 = a_1q + b_1w, \quad p_2 = a_2q + b_2w, \tag{6.1.1}$$

where $q = rp$ by definition. For given r, we thus have

$$q/w = rb/(1 - ra_2), \tag{6.1.2}$$

$$p_1/w = b_1 + ra_1b_2/(1 - ra_2). \tag{6.1.3}$$

(6.1.3) is termed as the "wage equation" by Hicks, though the same equation is also called the "factor-price" equation by Samuelson . It expresses a relation between the real wage and the rate of profit r. From the wage equation, we see that as r rises, the real wage w/p_1 falls.

From (6.1.2) and (6.1.3) relative prices are established independently of the savings rate. It should be mentioned that until now we have confined ourselves to the single technique represented by the set of coefficients (a_1,b_1,a_2,b_2). Along any particular constant proportional growth path, techniques cannot be changed. However, there is no reason why only one technique should exist. If multiple alternatives of techniques exist, the determination of the equilibrium state of the system may become a little more complicated.

It is assumed that the technology is given. That is, firms are faced with a given set of techniques from which a selection has to be made. A change from one technique of production to another involves changes in the chosen coefficients of production. It should be noted that here we only consider how the choice of techniques responses to changes of monetary terms.

We are still only concerned with the equilibrium state of the system. Let there be two techniques. As demonstrated above, there will be a certain rate of profit that can be obtained from each technique. If the first technique is chosen, when a higher rate of profit could have been obtained from the other technique, the economy cannot be in equilibrium. Thus, the equilibrium technique at given real wages is simply the technique which generates the higher rate of profit. If we fix p_1 at unity, the relation between the real wage (w) and the rate of profit (r) is given by the wage equation for a special given technique. The curve in the w-r plane described by the wage equation has to slope downward and it must cut the two axes. It is not difficult to see we should have various curves in the w-r plane that for different techniques (see Fig. 6.1.1). According to the optimality condition, at a given wage, it is the curve which is furthest out from these which will be selected. The curve which is actually followed will thus be the "outer frontier" or "outer envelope" of the technique curves.

From figure 6.1.1 we see that along the frontier the profit rate will fall more slowly than it would have done if the technique had not been variable. This means that the real wage can rise faster, for a given fall in the profit rate.

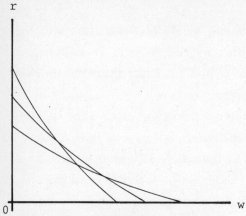

Fig. 6.1.1. Technique Curves

This wage frontier is the central concept in the theory of the choice of techniques in equilibrium. We will investigate its properties in a more general model which we describe in Sections 6.2 and 6.3.

Having simply illustrated the problem of the choice of techniques, we should also look at the quantitative aspects of the system. If we assume that quantitative variables are fast in comparison to relative prices, then we can investigate the behavior of the quantitative variables within the framework of a "fixed-price" system if the study is short-run. Let us introduce

c: the output of the consumption good;
x: the output of the capital good;
L: the labour employed;
K: the stock of capital:
g: the rate of growth.

In the above, the rate of growth is the ratio between the output of new capital and the stock of capital. In equilibrium, the stock of capital and the employment of labour must equal their corresponding desired levels, respectively. We thus have the following quantity equations

$$K = a_1c + a_2x, \quad L = b_1c + b_2x,$$

$$x = gK. \tag{6.1.4}$$

From (6.1.4), we have

$$K/c = a_1/(1-a_2g), \quad x/c = a_1g/(1-a_2g),$$

$$L/c = b_1 + a_1b_2g/(1-a_2g).$$

It should be emphasized that the price equations (6.1.1) and the quantity equations (6.1.4) cannot determine the whole system. A savings equation is proposed to close the system. Savings are assumed to be a fixed proportion s of total income, i.e., $p_2x = s(p_2x + p_1c)$, from which one has: $s/(1-s) = p_2x/p_1c$. In equilibrium, the growth rate is thus positively related to the propensity to save. Thus the system is completed. We can also introduce other mechanisms to complete the model.

2. The Basic Model of Leontief Technology and Some of Its Fundamental Properties With One Technique

In the preceding section, we have shown how the problem of the choice of techniques can be solved for a very simple model. We will now generalize the ideas to a multiple sector model.

We deal with a model in which the production functions are of a Leontief (or fixed proportions) form. It is assumed that there is a single primary factor - labour - growing at a fixed rate and that the labour force is homogeneous. Any joint production is excluded. We especially assume that there are n distinct capital goods and a single consumption good. The consumption good can never be used as an input in production. The economy consists of n + 1 production sectors, with the subscripts 1, ... , n designating the sectors producing the n capital goods, and the symbols X_i (i = 1, ... , n) denoting the stocks of these capital goods. The sector producing the consumption good is identified by the subscription 0. The services of each capital good and of labour may be used in each of the n + 1 sectors; X_{ij}

denotes the quantity of the ith capital good employed in the jth sector, and L_j denotes the quantity of labour employed in the jth sector (i = 1, ... , n, j = 0, 1, ... , n).

It is assumed that there are several methods of producing the same good. Here, we introduce an index v_j to denote the technology chosen by the jth sector. v_j may take any integral value from 1 to m_j where m_j is the number of alternative activity vectors for producing the jth good.

The Leontief technology is described by the following production functions

$$Y_j = \min[L_j/a_{0j}(v_j), X_{ij}/a_{ij}(v_j), i = 1, ..., n],$$

$$j = 0, 1, ... n, \qquad\qquad (6.2.1)$$

where $a_{ij}(v_j)$ (i, j = 0, 1, ... , n) are non-negative constant input coefficients for any choice of the index v_j. The vector $(a_{0j}, 0, a_{1j}, ... , a_{nj})$ is called an activity vector for producing the jth good.

If we assume static efficiency in production, then we always have

$$a_{0j}(v_j) = L_j/Y_j, \quad a_{ij}(v_j) = X_{ij}/Y_j,$$

$$i = 1, ... , n, j = 0, ... , n. \qquad\qquad (6.2.2)$$

An (n+2)x(n+1) matrix with activity vectors in the columns is called a technical matrix or a technique of production. As the activity vectors are selected independently, the number of possible combinations of the alternative technique matrices M is equal to $M = m_1...m_n$. The set of these M alternative techniques is the technology, or the economy's book of blueprints. It contains all the knowledge of production methods. We refer the matrices to as Technique u_1, Technique u_2 and so on.

Firstly, to investigate some fundamental properties of the system, we study the case when there is only one technique matrix available to the economy. We are only interested in steady states in which prices are constant over time. The interest rate is assumed to be exogenously given. The main concern is related to the viability of the economy. An economy is viable if it is productive enough to generate positive prices in competitive equilibrium.

As only one technique matrix is concerned, an input coefficient $a_{ij}(u)$ can be simply expressed by a_{ij} for Technique u. We assume full employment of the production factors

$$\sum_{j=0}^{n} X_{ij} = X_i, \qquad i = 1, \dots, n,$$

$$\sum_{j=1}^{n} L_j = L, \qquad\qquad\qquad\qquad\qquad\qquad (6.2.3)$$

which can be written in the form of

$$aY = X, \quad a_0 Y = L, \qquad\qquad\qquad\qquad\qquad (6.2.4)$$

where a is an $(n+1) \times (n+1)$ matrix whose jth column is: $(0, a_{1j}, \dots, a_{nj})^T$ $(j = 0, \dots, n)$ and

$$Y = (Y_0, \dots, Y_n)^T, \quad X = (0, X_1, \dots, X_n)^T,$$

$$a_0 = (a_{00}, \dots, a_{0n})^T. \qquad\qquad\qquad\qquad\qquad (6.2.5)$$

We use discrete time and assume that the inputs ($X_{ij}(t)$ and $X_j(t)$) may be employed during a production period t, the outputs produced from these inputs, denoted by $Y_j(t+1)$, are not available for use until the beginning of the next period $t + 1$. It should be mentioned that the beginning of the period $t + 1$ is the end of the period t. Obviously, one has

$$X_j(t+1) = Y_j(t+1) + (1-s_j)X_j(t), \qquad\qquad\qquad (6.2.6)$$

where s_j $(j = 1, \dots, n)$ is the depreciation rate of the jth sector during each production period.

An investor with one dollar at the beginning of period t can either invest in the ith capital good earning a profit equal to the net own rate of return $r_i(t)$ plus any net capital gains $[P_i(t+1) - P_i(t)]/P_i(t)$, or invest in some underlying financial asset at the money rate of interest $r_0(t)$. The competitive equilibrium implies

$$r_i(t) + [P_i(t+1) - P_i(t)]/P_i(t) = r_0(t),$$

$$i = 1, \dots , n. \tag{6.2.7}$$

Here, it should be mentioned that at a steady state: $P_i(t+1) = P_i(t)$, (6.2.7) is reduced to: $r_i(t) = r_0(t)$ for all i. If we introduce $W_i(t)$ as the gross rental rate for the ith capital at the end of period t and let the cost of maintaining machines be equal to $s_i P_i(t)$, then we have

$$r_i(t) = [W_i(t) - s_i P_i(t)]/P_i(t). \tag{6.2.8}$$

In competitive equilibrium, as the value of output must equal the cost of production, we have

$$P_j(t+1) = W_0(t)a_{0j} + \sum_{i=1}^{n} W_i(t)a_{ij}$$

$$= W_0(t)a_{0j} + \sum_{i=1}^{n} P_i(t)z_i(t)a_{ij},$$

$$j = 0, 1, \dots n, \tag{6.2.9}$$

where $z_i(t)$ $(= W_i(t)/P_i(t), i = 1, \dots , n)$ is the gross own-rate of return for the ith capital good. We have: $z_i(t) - s_i = r_i(t)$. In matrix notation (6.2.9) can be written as

$$P(t+1) = a_0 W_0(t) + P(t)z(t)a, \tag{6.2.10}$$

where $z(t) = \text{diag}[1, z_1(t), \dots , z_n(t)]$.

There appear to have been two independent conditions determining the prices $P(t+1)$ for the output of the t period. The first condition (6.2.9) relates to rentals for the use of the capital goods in production and determines the price as equal to the cost of production when rentals are given. The second condition, given by (6.2.7) and (6.2.8), relates to trading on asset markets among owners of the capital goods. In what follows, we investigate conditions which ensure that steady-state prices generated by (6.2.10) are positive when the vector z is given.

At a steady state

$$P_i(t) = P_i, \; W_i(t) = W_i,$$

$z_i(t) = z_i$, $r_i(t) = r_i$, for all t, i = 0, 1, ... , n.

Moreover, a competitive equilibrium requires that all the net own rates of return are equal to a common value called the interest or profit rate r_0, though we neglect this fact to avoid repetition. In view of the above discussions, (6.2.10) may be rewritten as

$$p = a_0 + pza, \tag{6.2.11}$$

where $p = (P_0/W_0, P_1/W_0, ... , P_n/W_0)^T$, is a vector of relative prices with the wage rate as numeraire. If the inverse of (I - za) exists, then we have

$$p = a_0 (I - za)^{-1}. \tag{6.2.12}$$

We seek the conditions under which (6.2.12) is economically meaningful (i.e., p > 0).

As the following results are well known in the literature (e.g., Dorfman, Samuelson, and Solow, 1958, Burmeister and Dobell, 1970, Nikaido, 1972), we shall only describe them briefly without providing the proofs. Firstly, we introduce some concepts and make certain assumptions.

Definition 6.2.1. (Viability)
A technical matrix is viable if the price vector (6.2.12) is strictly positive when $r_i = 0$, i = 1, ... , n.

Definition 6.2.2. (Feasibility)
The matrix z is called feasible if the price vector in (6.2.12) is strictly positive. We call r_0 feasible if z is feasible when $r_i = r_0$, i = 1, ..., n.

It can be shown that z is feasible if the matrix $[I - za]^{-1}$ is non-negative. Let k^* denote the dominant characteristic root of the matrix $a[I - sa]^{-1}$. If $s_i < z_i < 1/k^* + s_i$ (i = 1, ... , n), then z is feasible.

Assume: (A.1) Labour is required in producing every good; (A.2) At least one capital good is needed to produce every good, and every capital good is required to produce the consumption good; (A.3) The technology contains at least one viable technique matrix, Technique u. Let (n+1)x(n+1) matrix s = diag[1, s_1, ... , s_n]. Under these assumptions, the following theorems hold.

Theorem 6.2.1.

Let r^* ($\geq$) be a scalar. The matrix $[I - r^*a - sa]^{-1} \geq 0$ iff $r^* < 1/k^*$. Moreover, if $r^* = \max\{r_i, i = 1, \ldots , n\}$, then $[I - r^*a - sa]^{-1} \geq 0$ implies $[I - sa]^{-1} \geq 0$.

Theorem 6.2.2.

Let $z = r_0 + s$ be feasible where $r_i = r_0$, $i = 1, \ldots , n$. Then

$$dp_i/dr_0 > 0, \qquad i = 1, \ldots , n, \qquad (6.2.13)$$

$$dp_i/dz_j \geq 0, \quad i = 0, 1, \ldots, n$$

$$j = 1, \ldots , n, \qquad (6.2.14)$$

with inequality holding if the jth capital good is required, either directly or indirectly, for production of the ith good.

These results are similar to those proved in Chapter V.

Before investigating a model with many alternative techniques, we should look at the quantitative aspects of the system when only one technique is available to the economy. Let z be exogenously given and Technique u is employed. With the notations introduced previously, full employment of capital and labour implies that

$$a(u)Y(t+1) = X(t),$$

$$a_0(u)Y(t+1) = L(t). \qquad (6.2.15)$$

After appropriately rearranging the terms, we may rewrite (6.2.6) in the form of

$$Y(t+1) = X(t+1) - X(t) + sX(t) + C(t+1), \qquad (6.2.16)$$

where $Y_0(t+1)$ is consumption at the beginning of period $t+1$ and $C(t+1) = [Y_0(t+1), 0, \ldots , 0]^T$. Substituting (6.2.15) into (6.2.16) yields

$$Y(t+1) = a(u)[Y(t+2) - Y(t+1)] + sa(u)Y(t+1)$$

$$+ C(t+1). \qquad (6.2.17)$$

The growth of the labour is exogenously given by:

$$L(t+1) = (1 + g)L(t), \quad n > 0.$$

The equations (6.2.17) can thus be rewritten by

$$y(t+1) = a(u)[(1 + g)y(t+2) - y(t+1)] + sa(u)y(t+1)$$

$$+ c(t+1), \tag{6.2.18}$$

where $y_i(t+1) = Y_i(t+1)/L(t)$, $i = 0, 1, \ldots , n$. The system is in equilibrium if $y(t+1)$ $= y(t) = y$ for all t. From (6.2.18), the equilibrium is determined by

$$y = ga(u)y + sa(u)y + c. \tag{6.2.19}$$

Let k^{**} be the dominant characteristic root of the matrix $[I - sa(u)]^{-1}$. If $g < 1/k^{**}$, then $[I - (g+s)a(u)]^{-1}$ is non-negative and (6.2.19) can be solved for $y = [I - (g+s)a(u)]^{-1}c > 0$. As shown below, these quantitative aspects of the system do not affect the decision on the choice of techniques. Moreover, observe that the price system (6.2.10) and the quantitative system (6.2.18) are completely decoupled. There are no interactions between monetary variables and outputs. This feature reflects the issue raised by Dorfman, Samuelson, and Solow (1958): that this quantitative system is an illegitimate representation of allocation decisions that should properly depend on price considerations. In fact, from the structure of the model we see that no deep economic theories are involved in this system, because after all, the model is only a system consisting of simple accounting equations. No behavior mechanisms about firms or households are introduced in it.

3. The Model of Leontief Technology With Many Alternative Techniques

As mentioned in the preceding section, the jth good can be produced by any one of m_j alternative activities. This section will be concerned with the following questions: (1) For an exogenously given z, what technique matrix will be employed in steady-state price equilibrium? - the question of the "choice of technique; (2) How can the "switching point" be determined?

In relation to the first question, we are only interested in the case in which z is feasible for many alternative technique matrices. We determine the technique matrix (matrices) which minimize the cost of production. In what follows, when we mention Technique u_i, the given z is always assumed to be feasible.

Let Technique u_1 and Technique u_2 be identical except for the nth activity vector. For each technique, according to (6.2.12) prices are

$$p(u_k) = a_0(u_k)[I - za(u_k)]^{-1}, \quad k = 1, 2. \tag{6.3.1}$$

From (6.2.11), we also know that each price can be expressed as a linear combination of all the prices. Let the cost of producing the nth good with Technique u_2 be strictly less than that with u_1. In this case, as shown in Levhari (1965), we must have

$$p(u_2) \leq p(u_1), \tag{6.3.2}$$

where $p_i(u_2) < p_i(u_1)$ if either i = n or the nth good is required, directly or indirectly, for the production of the ith good. If we repeat the argument for all sets of alternative activity vectors, we conclude that there exists a matrix of activity vectors, say Technique u, such that: (i) The given z is feasible for Technique u, and (ii) The components of the equilibrium price vector are simultaneously minimized when the technique is employed. Moreover, it can be identified that the prices $p_i(u)$ are less than or equal to the equilibrium prices generated by any convex combination of matrices for which the given z is feasible (Levhari, 1965). Before representing an important theorem of the choice of technique, we define a set S_z as

$$Sz = \{u_k, \ k = 1, \ 2, \ \dots \ , \text{ the given } u_k \text{ is feasible}\}.$$

Theorem 6.3.1.

Let S_z be non-empty for a given z. Then among all the technique matrices belong to S_z there exists at least one technique, denoted by Technique u, such that the equilibrium prices $p_i(u)$ (i = 1, ... n) satisfy

$$p(u) \leq a_0(u_k) + p(u)za(u_k), \quad \text{for any } u_k \ \varepsilon \ S_z.$$

$$\tag{6.3.3}$$

We can find the theorem in Burmeister and Dobell (1970, p.240) or Morishima (1964, p.97).

As a lemma to Theorem 6.3.1, the following result is well known.

Theorem 6.3.2. (Nonsubstitution Theorem)

If the exogenously given r_0 is feasible, then in a competitive steady state the ratios of all prices are determined by r_0 alone and are independent of the quantities Y.

The theorem is referred to, for instance, in Dorfman, Samuelson, and Solow (1958), Samuelson (1961) and Burmeister and Dobell (1970).

Definition 6.3.1. (Optimality for z)

A technique matrix that satisfies the conditions stated in Theorem 6.3.1 is called optimal for the exogenous z.

We have fixed the matrix z. As in competitive equilibrium we have $z_i - s_i = r_i = r_0$ $(i = 1, ... , n)$, thus we may consider equilibrium prices as functions only of the exogenous profit or interest rate r_0. The choice of technique should be thus dependent upon the value of r_0. As the assumption (A.3) in the previous section holds for a Technique u_k, thus $z_i = s_i$ $(i = 1, ... , n)$ or r_0 is feasible for the technique. It should be mentioned that $1/p_i$ $(= W_0/P_i)$ is determined as a function of r_0. Moreover, according to Theorem 6.2.2, we have $d(W_0/P_i)/dr_0 < 0$ $(i = 0, 1, ... , n)$. It is thus possible to plot a graph in the r_0-W_0/P_i plane which is downward-sloping. The curve is termed "the factor-price curve for Technique u_k". Similarly, it is possible for us to obtain the factor-price curves for Techniques u_1, u_2, ... The shapes of these curves are generally not the same because the sign of d^2W_0/d^2P_i is different. The outer-envelope of these curves is called the economy's factor-price frontier - this term was originated by Samuelson (1957). For simplicity of illustration, let the economy have only three techniques u_i $(i = 1, 2, 3)$. The corresponding factor-price curves and the economy's factor price frontier are illustrated in Fig. 6.3.1.

Let the exogenously given profit or interest rate be fixed at $r_0 = 0$. We know that p_i will be minimized, or W_0/P_i will be maximized in competitive steady-state. From (6.3.1), we can conclude that Technique u_1 is optimal and will be employed. Moreover, it can be easily seen that Technique u_1 will be employed for $0 \leq r_0 < r_0'$. At $r_0 = r_0'$, Techniques u_1 and u_2 generate the same prices and both are optimal. When $r_0 > r_0'$, the economy "switches" from Technique u_1 to Technique u_2. The point r_0' is called a switching point. When r_0 researches $r_0^*(u_2)$, the real wage rate is equal to zero. Thus no interest rate is feasible if r_0 is not less than r_0'.

Moreover, Technique u_3 will never be employed. In the following, we will prove what has just been discussed.

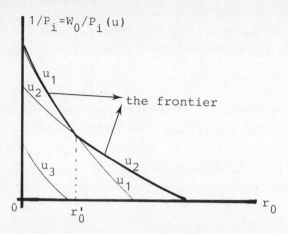

Fig. 6.3.1. Factor-price Curves and the Economy's Factor-Price Frontier for Techniques u_i (i=1, 2, 3)

Definition 6.3.2. (Switching Points)

An interest rate r_0' is a switching point between any two techniques, say Technique u_1 and u_2, if there exists $h > 0$ such that: (i) Only Technique u_1 is optimal for $r_0'-h < r_0 < r_0'$; (ii) Both Techniques u_1 and u_2 are optimal for $r_0 = r_0'$; and (iii) Only Technique u_2 is optimal for $r_0' < r_0 < r_0' + h$.

There may exist "multiple switching points" or reswitching points between two techniques (see Fig. 6.3.2).

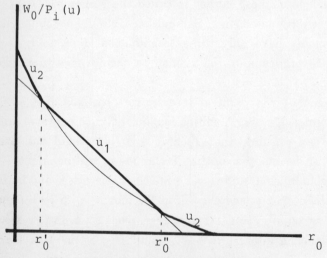

Fig. 6.3.2. Reswitching Points

Definition 6.3.3. (Reswitching of Techniques)

Consider a Technique u and three values of interest rates which satisfy the inequalities: $0 < r_0^1 < r_0^2 < r_0^3 < r_0^*(u)$. If: (i) Only Technique u is optimal for $r_0 = r_0^1$; (ii) Technique u is not optimal for $r_0 = r_0^2$; and (iii) Only Technique u is optimal for $r_0 = r_0^3$ - then the technology exhibits the reswitching of techniques and Technique u is said to recur.

The possibility of reswitching has been numerically proved (see "Paradoxes in Capital Theory: A Symposium", Q. J. E. LXXX, No. 4, 1966).

Consider an economy with a given technology in a steady state at a high rate of interest. Suppose this economy abstains from consumption for a period of time, therefore enabling it to accumulate capital. In the spirit of Jevons, Böhm-Bawerk and Wicksell, we would expect the economy to approach a new steady state with a lower interest rate. Moreover, we would expect that the new steady state would have more capital and that the technique employed would be more mechanised. However, imagine that the economy again abstains from consumption and that a third steady state with a still lower interest rate is attained. If reswitching has ocurred the technique matrix employed in the third steady state will be the same as that employed in the first. It is thus impossible to claim that an economy always (in a steady state) employs more mechanised technique matrices at lower interest rates. As reswitching contradicts the intuition of the authors just mentioned, it has been called paradoxical or perverse.

It may be interesting to consider consumption patterns under reswitching techniques. It is not difficult to establish that within an appropriate interval of values for r_0 (see Burmeister and Dobell, 1970): (i) consumption is a single-valued function of r_0, except at the switching points; (ii) At the switching points consumption may assume any one of an infinity of values depending on which articular convex combination of optimal techniques is employed; (iii) The consumption $c(r_0)$ attains a maximum when $r_0 = g$; and (iv) Under appropriate "well-behaved" requirements $c(r_0)$ is non-decreasing when r_0 is not larger than g, and non-increasing when r_0 is not less than g. It should be noted that (iv) does not always hold. Burmeister (1980) argues that the existence of reswitching reveals that lower steady state interest rates are not always associated with higher levels of steady state consumption.

It is important to discuss the choice of techniques within the framework of multiple sector model with a neoclassical production functions (see Chapter IV). We will show that reswitching techniques are impossible (i.e., $a_{ij}(r_0') = a_{ij}(r_0'')$) if the assumption of nonsubstitution is relaxed.

If we introduce inflation into the system, the choice of techniques will be affected. It is not difficult to investigate how inflation influences the choice of techniques if we note that the method for to introducing inflation has already been given in Chapter V. We may assume that the real interest rate is always equal to the growth rate which is determined from the quantitative aspects of the system. The technological coefficients can thus be determined as functions of the inflation rate. It is not difficult to see that the effects of the inflation rate should be opposite to those of the interest rate upon the choice of techniques just mentioned.

4. Dynamic Behavior of the Model With Many Alternative Techniques

In the preceding sections we have examined the behavior of a multiple sector model with Leontief technology. When the economy is faced with alternative techniques, the decision making about the choice of techniques is related to the profit rate. We also have discussed the switching debate. It can be seen that Jevons-Wicksell-Samuelson biotechnological determinism does not hold because of the existence of reswitching. However, all of these arguments are related to comparisons of one steady state with another. Although the possibility of reswitching does not affect the existence of equilibrium in the model, it is necessary to discuss the dynamic behavior of the system.

The dynamics of the quantitative aspects is given by (6.2.7)

$$Y(t) = a(u)[Y(t+1) - Y(t)] + sa(u)Y(t) + C(t),$$

which may be rewritten as

$$Y(t) = B[Y(t+1) - Y(t)] + AY(t) + C(t), \tag{6.4.1}$$

where $B = a(u)$ and $A = sa(u)$. A continuous version of (6.4.1) is given by

$$Y = BdY/dt + AY + C. \tag{6.4.2}$$

The mathematical structure of (6.4.2) is similar to that of the system studied in Section 4.1, though the matrices A and B are defined in different way. The matrix B in (6.4.1) is definitely singular because it has a row of zeros.

The system (6.4.1) can also be written in the form of

$$BY(t+1) = [I + B - A]Y(t) - C(t). \tag{6.4.3}$$

The characteristics of the system are well established. We know that a balanced growth path exists. An analysis of the growth path from specified initial conditions can show that the balanced growth path need not be stable. And if the system is not stable, it must depart from its balanced growth path until eventually some outputs are forced to become zero - if we add the constraints of the non-negative solutions to (6.4.3).

After substituting (6.2.7) into (6.2.10) the price dynamics is given by as follows

$$P(t+1)[I - A + B] = (1 + r_0)P(t)a + W_0a_0, \tag{6.4.4}$$

which is the dual system to (6.4.3). As investment and consumption are independent of the variables, the primal and dual problems are determined independently of each other.

There is a close link between the quantitative system and the price system, i.e., the dual stability exists. We can establish a similar result for the systems to that given in Theorem 3.4.1. Dual stability means that the system being studied cannot reflect reality because in the long terms either the quantitative system or the price system is destructed. However, the system can be stabilized by introducing some other mechanisms.

It should be mentioned that the reswitching problem becomes more complicated if we are concerned with dynamic processes, rather than steady states alone. If changes in techniques of the kind we have just discussed in comparing different steady states should occur along the actual growth path for given initial conditions, then the system ceases to be decoupled. As the technique matrix is related to prices, the whole system is connected. Evidently, it is very difficult to follow how the whole system behaves if it is not located in equilibrium.

5. The Impossibility of Reswitching in the Continuous Substitution Model

One important difference between models with fixed coefficients and continuous substitution models is that there is no reswitching in the continuous substitution case.

Consider a multiple sector production system similar to that in Section 4.1. The production functions of the n sectors have the form of

$$Y_j = F_j(L_j, X_{1j}, \dots, X_{nj}),$$

$$j = 0, 1, \dots, n. \tag{6.5.1}$$

Assuming the functions to be homogeneous of degree one, we may rewrite (6.5.1) as

$$1 = F_j(a_{0j}, a_{1j}, \dots, a_{nj}), \tag{6.5.2}$$

where $a_{01} = L_j/Y_j$, $a_{ij} = X_{ij}/Y_j$ ($i = 1, \dots, n$, $j = 0, 1, \dots, n$). The full employment of capital and labour are still assumed. That is, the equations (2.6.3) are satisfied. The price vector $p(t)$, the vector $z(t)$, and the input matrix are defined as in Section 6.2. The vector $w(t)$ of factor rental rates in terms of the wage rate as numeraire is defined as: $w(t) = (1, W_1/W_0, \dots, W_n/W_0)$. These variables are determined by the same functions as those in Section 6.2.

We assume that:

(A1): Labour is required, either directly or indirectly, to produce every good;

(A2): At least two factors are required to produce every good and every capital good is required directly or indirectly to produce the consumption good.

Let D denote the strictly positive orthant of R^n. We have

Theorem 6.5.1.

Let (A1)-(A2) hold. Then there is a nonempty set $D^* \, \varepsilon \, D$ such that a positive equilibrium price vector, $p = G(Z) > 0$ where $Z = (z_1, \dots, z_n) > 0$, is uniquely determined for all $Z \, \varepsilon \, D^*$. Moreover, if $z_i = z^*$ ($i = 1, \dots, n$), there exists an interval $(0, z^{**})$ such that $p = G(z^*)$ is uniquely determined for all $z^* \, \varepsilon \, (0, z^{**})$.

Corollary to Theorem 6.5.1.

Let the depreciation rates d_i all be positive and sufficiently small such that

$$r^* = z^{**} - \max_{\text{for all } i} d_i > 0. \tag{6.5.3}$$

Then for any $r_0 \, \varepsilon \, [0,r^*)$ a positive equilibrium price vector $p = g(r_0) > 0$ is uniquely determined.

Theorem 6.5.2.

Let $Z \, \varepsilon \, D^*$ be assigned. The activity vectors $(a_{0j}, 0, a_{1j}, \ldots , a_{nj})$, $j = 0, 1, \ldots$, n, are all uniquely determined. Similarly, for all $r^0 \, \varepsilon \, [0,r^*)$ all activity vectors are uniquely determined as functions of r_0.

Theorem 6.5.3.

Consider $Z \, \varepsilon \, D^*$ and define $B = [b_{ij}] = [I - za]^{-1}$. We have

$$(\partial p_0/\partial z_i, \partial p_1/\partial z_i, \ldots , \partial p_j/\partial z_i)$$

$$= (p_i a_{i0}, p_i a_{i1}, \ldots , p_i a_{in})B \geq 0,$$

with strict inequality holding iff the ith capital good is required, either directly or indirectly, for the production of good j.

Corollary to Theorem 6.5.3.

$$\partial p_0/\partial z_i > 0, \quad i = 11, \ldots , n,$$

$$dp/dr_0 = g'(r_0) > 0, \text{ for } r_0 \, \varepsilon \, (0,r^*),$$

$$w_i'(r_0) = p_i + (r_0 + d_i)dp_i/dr_0 > 0.$$

All of these results are similar to these in Section 6.2 and can be found in Morishima (1964) or in Burmeister and Dobell (1970). The following theorem is the main concern of this section.

Theorem 6.5.4

Under (A1)-(A2), reswitching of techniques is impossible.

Proof:

As (A1) and (A2) imply that there exist some indices i and j for which $a_{0j} > 0$ and $a_{ij} > 0$, for any such choice of indices, the equation

$$\frac{F_{ji}(a_{0j},a_{1j},\ldots,a_{nj})}{F_{j0}(a_{0j},a_{1j},\ldots,a_{nj})} = \frac{W_i/P_j}{W_0/P_j}$$

$$= W_i/W_0 = w_i(r_0), \tag{6.5.4}$$

must be satisfied. Reswitching means that two different levels of interest rates map onto the same input matrix, i.e., $a_{ij}(r_0') = a_{ij}(r_0'')$ (i, j = 0, ... , n) for some r_0' being not equal to r_0''. However, this is impossible because of $w_i'(r_0) > 0$.

VII

TECHNOLOGICAL POLICY AND ECONOMIC DEVELOPMENT
- A NEOCLASSICAL APPROACH

Having examined the problem of the choice of techniques in the preceding chapter, we will now deal with the way in which technological changes occur endogenously. Technology is not given to economic systems. There exist dynamic interactions between human knowledge and economic variables. There are numerous theories about the process of knowledge accumulation. A psychological approach may supply a "micro foundation" for an understanding of knowledge accumulation, although macro characteristics are not necessarily derived from any micro world. The interactions appear to be so complicated that we cannot hope to develop a perfect theory to explain all aspects of the actual process. We will employ a model to investigate what happens to human and physical capital accumulation and consumption under certain plausible conditions.

In this chapter, we return to the framework of the standard neoclassical growth model. In the next chapter, endogenously technological change will be treated within the framework of a multiple sector model. They will be analyzed from different points of view because each approach can only shed partial light on the problem.

1. Technological Change in Economic Development

Numerous studies in the 1950's, such as those by Solow (1957a) and Arrow (1962), indicated that technological progress was an extremely important determinant in the growth of output per capita, though little was said about how technological change is affected by economic development.

When discussing the role of technological change in an economy, we are usually confronted with at least four main questions. First, we are interested in how technological change affects different factors. Traditionally, some forms of technological change have been thought of as "labor saving", while some are considered to be "capital saving". To solve this question, different definitions of "neutral technological change" have been proposed (Zhang, 1989). Second, there is the problem of determining whether technological change is primarily "labour saving" or "capital saving". The third question is related to the determination of the technological change rate. At least two broad classes of theoretical models have been suggested. One focuses on technological change as a by-product of investment and production. This is reflected in Arrow's learning by doing approach. In the other model resources are explicitly allocated to research. The final question concerns the way in which technological change is introduced into the economy. This study focusses upon the last two questions.

This chapter analyzes various aspects of economic development. We will propose a model to explain the interactions between human and physical capital accumulation. The model is fundamentally related to the current Chinese economy. The issues that an economist emphasizes in his work are usually related to current economic problems. This applies to our case as well.

The role of intellectuals in economic development is still debated in China. We will try to shed some light on this problem. It is important to understand the interactions between human and physical capital because policy makers in developing countries such as China sometimes fail to recognize the importance of human capital in long-run economic growth.

There are some limitations to our study. First of all, we only discuss the problems within the framework of quantitative aspects of the economic growth. Dual or monetary aspects have been totally omitted. That is, we treat monetary terms as fast variables in economic growth.

The remainder of this chapter is organized as follows. Section 7.2 explains the characteristics of the economic system and defines the basic model. In Section 7.3 we guarantee the existence of a unique equilibrium and give the stability conditions. The effects of some parameters are analyzed in Section 7.4. In Section 7.5, bifurcation analysis with respect to the population growth policy is completed. It should be noted that this chapter is fundamentally based upon the work by Zhang (1990a).

2. The Model

We will develop our economic growth model within the framework of the neoclassical approach with knowledge as an endogenous variable, as in Uzawa's work. Although the standard Solow model has been extended to take account of endogenous technology (Zhang, 1989), we are more interested in the role of intellectuals in economic growth.

It is assumed that there is only one commodity which can be used both for consumption and capital. There is one production sector. The output of the sector can either be used as an investment in production or in the consumption of households. It is assumed that three inputs - (physical) capital, knowledge (human capital) and physical labour - are required in the production process.

The concept of knowledge has been used frequently in theoretical economics (e.g., Arrow, 1962, Uzawa, 1965, Robson, 1980, Andersson and Zhang, 1989, 1990). Obviously, in practice it is almost impossible to exactly measure human capital, though we know the existence and significance of knowledge. Knowledge can only be measured approximately. For instance, we can measure knowledge of the national economy by calculating how long times the population spends on education, and how much "capital" such as books the nation has. Surely, there are limitations in the measures.

The total labour force, denoted by L, is assumed to grow at a fixed rate n. Although it has been suggested that the growth rate of the population may depend on economic variables (e.g., Becker, 1975, 1981, 1988, Cigno, 1986, Cigno and Zhang, 1988), for simplicity we accept our own assumption, which may be not so strict for the case of the Chinese economy. There the government has used choice constraints in an attempt to control population growth. Because of the lack of religion and other such factors, the constraints have been very effective. Hence, if our study period is not too long, the assumption is quite acceptable.

It is assumed that the labour force is divided into knowledge workers (intellectuals) and physical workers, denoted by L_1 and L_2, respectively, where L_1 = $n_1 L$, $L_2 = n_2 L$, $n_1 + n_2 = 1$. We assume that n_1 and n_2 are constant. Accordingly, the intellectuals and physical workers are exogenously given to the system. In fact, we may consider the ratios as endogenous variables (Rodriguez, 1975, Zhang, 1988), though this will cause some analytical difficulties.

The physical workers take part in production, while the intellectuals indirectly influence production because they affect the knowledge accumulation of the society. At present in China, the ratio of the knowledge workers is not very high, though their role in the economy is becoming more significant. We distinguish between intellectuals and physical workers it is important to understand the impact of intellectuals upon economic growth.

It is assumed that the production can be described by the following production function

$$Y = F(G,L_2,K) = A(G)L_2^{\alpha}K^{\beta}, \tag{7.2.1}$$

where Y is the output, G is the knowledge (human capital), K the physical capital, and α and β are coefficients. A similar form of production function has been used in the literature (e.g., Uzawa, 1965, Robson, 1980, Andersson and Zhang, 1990).

It is assumed that $\alpha + \beta < 1$, which implies that for a fixed level of knowledge there are decreasing returns. In the case of fixed knowledge, doubling physical labour and capital cannot double output. It should be noted that we discuss this problem in relation to the whole society. If the discussion is only limited to a special industry, it is not necessary to assume the effects of decreasing returns to scale. If we do not increase knowledge, in the long term it is impossible to increase the efficiency of production if we are discussing the whole economy.

As the institutional structure is being reformed by the introduction of competitive mechanisms, the form of the production function may be changeable. As discussed in the final section of Chapter 2, the problem can be solved by assuming the following dynamics:

$$dY/dt = s_1\{F - Y\}, \tag{7.2.2}$$

where s_1 is an adjustment speed parameter. For simplicity, we assume s_1 to be sufficiently large.

It is assumed that the function $A(G)$ satisfies: $A'(G) > 0$. If knowledge is increased, production will become more effective because after the increase of knowledge we can obtain more output with the same inputs of physical labour and capital. Actually, we have little information about $A''(G)$. For convenience of analysis, we specify $A(G)$ as

$$A(G) = G^{\tau}, \qquad \tau > 0,$$

where τ is constant. Moreover, we require $\alpha + \beta + \tau = 1$.

This states that scale effects of production are neutral with respect to the inputs. If we double all the inputs, we can double output.

Now we will discuss the consumption levels of physical and knowledge workers. In contrast to some developing countries in which the consumption level of intellectuals is much higher than that of physical workers, in China it seems that for the moment there is little difference between the consumption of the workers on average. The distribution of consumption between intellectuals and physical workers is still the subject of debate. We do not know whether an intellectual consumes more or less than a physical worker. However, we will not discuss this distribution or how it should be determined as we are more interested in the effects of the given distribution.

The output per labour force is equal to Y/L. We assume that the consumption of the physical and knowledge workers is positively proportional to Y/L. The consumption level of a physical worker is given by $c_1 Y/L$, and that of an intellectual is given by $c_2 Y/L$, where c_1 and c_2 are constants. Actually c_2 may depend on the current economic situation because of the reform in which competitive mechanisms have been introduced to the Chinese economy. This means that c_2 is changeable. The parameter c_1 is heavily influenced by the government's policies.

Capital accumulation is given by

$$dK/dt = Y - c_1 L_1 Y/L - c_2 L_2 Y/L - \delta K, \qquad (7.2.3)$$

where δ is a given depreciation rate of capital. For the whole society the consumption rate is given by $(c_1 n_1 + c_2 n_2)$, while the savings rate is equal to $1 - (c_1 n_1 + c_2 n_2)$.

Now, we will discuss knowledge accumulation. It is assumed that knowledge accumulation is affected by the behavior of knowledge and physical workers. The knowledge workers affect knowledge accumulation through direct education and R&D activities, while the physical workers' impact is due to Arrow's "learning by doing" processes. This is a strict assumption. For instance, the physical workers can participate in R&D activities, while the knowledge workers may also take part in production activities.

A potential dynamics of knowledge is suggested as follows

$$dG/dt = pY + H(c_1 Y/L, L_1, G) - \mu G, \qquad (7.2.4)$$

where pY describes the "learning by doing" of the physical workers, H is the contribution function of the knowledge workers to knowledge growth, and μ is the depreciation rate of knowledge.

To ensure that the term pY in (7.2.4) expresses the "learning by doing" processes, let us consider the case in which "learning by doing" is the only source of knowledge accumulation. In this case, it is reasonable to assume that knowledge is a linear function of the total output produced from the initial starting point until the present. Here, we omit the "lag effects" on knowledge accumulation. One has

$$G = p \int_0^t Y \, dn + m, \qquad (7.2.5)$$

where m is a constant. From (7.2.5), we have $dG/dt = pY$. The parameter p describes the efficiency of the physical workers in relation to knowledge growth. If it is very small, the physical workers contribute little to knowledge growth, and vice versa.

We use the function $H(c_1 Y/L, L_1, G)$ to describe the efficiency of the knowledge workers' R&D activities. Here, $c_1 Y/L$ is the consumption level of a knowledge worker. In a developing country like China, the work efficiency of the intellectuals is obviously dependent on their level of consumption. A high consumption level will allow them much more time to do their scientific work. In fact, at certain consumption levels, there should be "scale effects" in the efficiency of the knowledge workers, though such "scale effects" may disappear once the consumption level becomes very high. Knowledge accumulation will depend on L_1 and G. This function should satisfy the following requirements

$$H_i > 0, \quad i = 1, 2, 3, \qquad (7.2.6)$$

in which H_i (i = 1, 2, 3) represent the partial derivatives of H with respect to $c_1 Y/L$, L_1, and G, respectively.

Knowledge accumulation also depends on additional factors. For instance, it may be related to how the Chinese intellectuals can communicate with foreign scientists. It is clear that the imitation of foreign technologies is playing a significant role in the economic development of China as it does in all developing countries. Such factors will influence the value of b and the functional form of H.

For simplicity of analysis, we specify H as

$$H = \frac{c_1 Y/L}{a_1 + c_1 Y/L} L_1^d G^\sigma, \quad d + \sigma = 1, \tag{7.2.7}$$

where a_1, d and σ are non-negative parameters. We interpret a_1 as a measure of the efficiency of the knowledge workers. If a_1 is equal to zero, then the consumption level will not affect knowledge accumulation. If it is infinitely large, then H becomes zero. That is, the knowledge workers cannot contribute anything to knowledge accumulation. Usually, we should have: $0 < a_1 < \infty$. From (7.2.7), we can see that if the consumption level $cc_1 Y/L$ is sufficiently high, then consumption will not affect knowledge accumulation. The function H is increasing with respect to L_1 and G, though it is "neutral" with regard to L_1 and G. This is a strict assumption because the evolution of knowledge may be more complicated than we have assumed.

The dynamics consists of the evolutionary equations (7.2.3) and (7.2.4). The system can be rewritten as

$$dk/dt = y - c_1 n_1 y - c_2 n_2 y - \delta k - nk,$$

$$dg/dt = py + H(y,g) - \mu g - ng, \tag{7.2.8}$$

where $k = K/L$, $g = G/L$, $y = n_2^\alpha g^\gamma k^\beta$, and

$$H(y,g) = \frac{n_1^d c_1 g^\sigma y}{a_1 + c_1 y}. \tag{7.2.9}$$

Now it is possible to investigate the properties of the system.

3. Equilibrium and Stability

First, we guarantee the existence of, at least, a locally unique equilibrium and find stability conditions of the equilibrium. An equilibrium is defined as a solution of

$$y - c_1 n_1 y - c_2 n_2 y - \delta k - nk = 0,$$

$$py + H(y,g) - \mu g - ng = 0. \tag{7.3.1}$$

From the first equation, we have

$$g = \{rk^{1-\beta}/n_2{}^\alpha\}^{1/\tau},$$

(7.3.2)

where $r = (\delta + n)/(1 - c_1 n_1 - c_2 n_2)$. Substituting (7.3.2) into the second equation of (7.3.1) yields

$$prk + n_1{}^d c_1 rk\{rk^{1-\beta}/n_2{}^\alpha\}^{\mu/\tau}/(a_1 + rc_1 k)$$

$$- (\sigma + n)\{rk^{1-\beta}/n_2 \alpha\}^{1/\tau} = 0.$$

(7.3.3)

To guarantee the existence of solutions of (7.3.3), let us define a function C as

$$C(k) = prk - (\sigma + n)\{rk^{1-\beta}/n_2{}^\alpha\}^{1/\tau}$$

$$+ n_1{}^d c_1 rk\{rk^{1-\beta}/n_2{}^\alpha\}^{\mu/\tau}/(a_1 + rc_1 k).$$

It can be identified that $C(0) = 0$, $C(\infty) = -\infty$, $C'(0) > 0$. Hence, the existence of the solutions may be identified as follows. Assume that there are multiple equilibria. From the properties of $C(k)$ we can see that if $C(k)$ has no unique solution, then $C(k)$ has at least three solutions, as illustrated in Fig. 7.3.1.

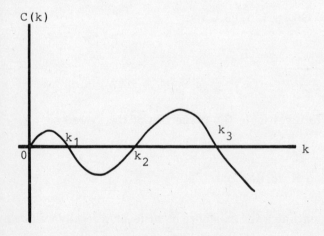

Fig. 7.3.1. The Case of Multiple Equilibria

We define $c(k) = (a_1 + c_1k)C(k)/k$. $c(k)$ also has at least three solutions. This implies that there is a positive value of k such that $c'' = 0$. On the other hand, it can be shown that if $\alpha/\tau - 1 > 0$, $(1 - ß)\sigma/\tau - 1 < 0$, c'' is always negative for any positive k. Therefore, a necessary condition for uniqueness is that $\alpha/\tau - 1 > 0$, $(1 - ß)\sigma/\tau - 1 < 0$. Here, uniqueness may be identified under more general conditions. The necessary condition holds if $\alpha > \tau > \sigma > 0$. That is, the parameter of capital in the production function is larger than that of knowledge, while the knowledge parameter of the production function is larger than that in the knowledge accumulation function. If this condition does not hold, we may have multiple equilibria. As we have little information about how knowledge can affect production and knowledge accumulation, in a system with endogenous knowledge it is difficult to get a unique conclusion. What we can do at this initial stage is to analyze what will happen under different conditions. Furthermore, for our analysis it is not necessary to require the uniqueness of equilibrium because all of our discussions are limited to local problems. What we need is a local uniqueness of the equilibrium.

To find stability conditions, let us denote the (at least, locally) unique equilibrium by (k_0, g_0). The Jacobian at the equilibrium is given by

$$J = \begin{bmatrix} n'ßy/k - (\delta+n) & n'\tau y/g \\ M(k,g) & N(k,g) \end{bmatrix} , \tag{7.3.4}$$

in which $n' = 1 - (n_1c_1 + n_2c_2)$, $M(k,g) = pßy/k + a_1ßH/k(a_1 + c_1y)$, $N(k,g) = p\tau y/g - (\mu + n) + \{\sigma + a_1\tau/(a_1 + c_1y)\}H/g$. It can be seen that n' and M are positive. As at the equilibrium $py/g + H(k,g)/g = \mu + n$, we have $N = py[\tau - 1]/g + [\sigma + a_1\tau/(a_1 + c_1y) - 1]H/g$, where $a_1\tau/(a_1 + c_1y) < 1$. Hence, if σ is sufficiently small, N is negative. If knowledge does not affect the knowledge accumulation function H (i.e., $\sigma = 0$), N is negative. On the other hand, in the case of $\sigma = 1$, $N = py[\tau - 1]/g + a_1c_1\tau y/(a_1 + c_1y)^2$. If there is no learning by doing process (i.e., $p = 0$), N is positive, while if the learning by doing process strongly affects the growth of knowledge, N may be negative.

The eigenvalues are given by

$$\Theta^2 + m_1\Theta + m_2 = 0, \tag{7.3.5}$$

where $m_1 = \delta + n - n'ßy/k - N(k,g)$, $m_2 = [n'ßy/k - (\delta + n)]N(k,g) - n'\tau yM(k,g)/g$, evaluated at the equilibrium. If $m_1 < 0$, the equilibrium is unstable. In the case of $m_1 > 0$, if $m_1 < 4m_2$, the system is stable. In the case of m_1^2 being greater than $4m_2$, if m_2 is positive, the system is stable, while if m_2 is negative, the system is unstable. When $m_2 = 0$, the system is neutral; the nonlinear terms cannot be neglected and complicated behavior may occur. From the above discussion we see that it is not easy to arrive at conclusions about stability because the expressions m_1 and m_2 are too complicated.

4. The Effects of Changes in Some Parameters

This section uses traditional comparative static analysis to analyse the effects of changes in some parameters. The discussion is limited to the domain of these parameters in which the system is stable. If the system is unstable, the traditional comparative static analysis fails (Zhang, 1990).

4-1. The effects of the knowledge workers' consumption

First, we analyse the effects of changes in c_1 upon economic growth. The parameter c_1 measures the percentage of the national output per capita that is distributed for the consumption of the intellectuals. This parameter does not give the actual level of consumption because an increase in c_1 may reduce production, which means that the consumption level is lowered as a whole.

In China, the consumption level of the intellectuals does not seem to be very high. It has been argued that low consumption directly affects the efficiency of the intellectuals. There are obviously other factors influencing their behavior, but we consider that the consumption level is one of the most important factors.

We will investigate how the equilibrium is shifted as the parameter is changed, for example, by the government. The effects of changes in c_1 are given by

$$\{n'\tau y/g\}dg/dc_1 + \{n'(\beta - 1)y/k\}dk/c_1 = n_1 y,$$

$$\{p(\tau - 1)ky + (\sigma + \tau - 1)kH - k\tau c_1 yH/(a_1 + $$

$$c_1 y)\}dg/dc_1 + \{p\beta gy + g\beta H - \beta c_1 gyH/(a_1 + c_1 y)\}dk/dc_1$$

$$= kyH/(a_1 + c_1 y) - kH/c_1. \tag{7.4.1}$$

First, we study the cases when $a_1 = 0$, and $a_1 = +\infty$, respectively. If the efficiency of the knowledge workers is not affected by the consumption level (i.e., $a_1 = 0$), we have

$$dk/dc_1 = zdg/dc_1,$$

$$n'y[\tau/g - (1 - \beta)z]dg/c_1 = n_1y, \qquad (7.4.2)$$

where $z = [p(1 - \tau)y + (1 - \sigma)H]/p\beta gy > 0$. It is worth noting that our conclusion for this case also holds for the physical workers' consumption, because c_1 and c_2 are symmetrical in the system.

From the first equation, we can conclude that if per capita knowledge is decreased, then per capita capital falls. The sign is primarily determined by $[\tau/g - (1 - \beta)z]$. It can be shown that this number is always negative. Hence, an increase in the consumption level will reduce both capital and knowledge. It should be emphasized that we obtain the result on the assumption that the consumption level does not affect H. It seems that it is not necessary to improve the living conditions of the intellectuals in order to increase economic growth if they work only for scientific curiosity or "pure devotion". If they really work for "pure devotion", an improvement in their living conditions should only result in a decrease in economic growth. The result is not surprising at all. However, the assumption that the scientists are "purely devoted" to their work cannot hold generally.

Let us consider the case of $a_1 = +\infty$. which means that the knowledge workers do not affect knowledge accumulation (e.g., $H = 0$). An increase in c_1 will result in decreases of k and g. If the intellectuals do not work at all, it is impossible to increase economic growth by improving their living conditions.

The above two cases are very strange because H should neither be zero nor be independent of c_1. However, if one considers how the intellectuals have been treated during "the Cultural Revolution" in China, one may agree that the existence of such functions might be imagined by some decision makers.

We will now discuss the general case. It is not difficult to see that one has

$$m_2dg/dc_1 = - n_1y\beta g\{py + a_1H/(a_1 + c_1y)\} +$$

$$a_1Hn'(1 - \beta)y/c_1(a_1 + c_1y),$$

$$m_2 dk/dc_1 = a_1 n'\tau y k H/c_1 g(a_1 + c_1 y) + n_1 y\{- p(1- \tau)ky$$

$$- (1 - \sigma)kH + a_1\tau kH/(a_1 + c_1 y)\}. \tag{7.4.3}$$

As stability is required, it is necessary to have $m_2 > 0$. As m_2 is dependent on the parameters, it is necessary to consider how m_2 is influenced when we shift the parameters. As the expression is extremely complicated, for simplicity, we only consider m_2 as a positive number.

First, we study the case in which there are no effects of "learning by doing" on knowledge accumulation, i.e., $p = 0$. The first equation in (7.4.3) is reduced to

$$m_2 dg/dc_1 = a_1 y H\{- n_1 \beta g + n'(1 - \beta)/c_1\}/(a_1 + c_1 y).$$

If β is appropriately small, an increase in c_1 will improve the knowledge level. The requirement of β being small means that in the production process physical capital inputs are not so important in relation to knowledge inputs.

From the second equation of (7.4.3), it is not difficult to see that if σ is sufficiently large, then dk/dc_1 is also positive. This requirement means that knowledge plays an important role in knowledge accumulation.

To understand this process, look at (7.2.8). From the first equation of (7.2.8), we see that an improvement in living conditions will reduce capital investment, which results in a lower output level, y. The direct effects of changes in c_1 upon knowledge accumulation are to increase the knowledge level, which will increase production. As we have a fast substitution between knowledge and capital, at the initial stage the impact upon y is uncertain. However, after the system arrives at the new equilibrium, as both k and g have been increased, production will also be increased. Consequently, in the long run the society should benefit, though the temporal effects may be uncertain.

If σ and β are appropriately large, an increase in the consumption of the knowledge workers may result in decreases of knowledge per capita, even though physical capital has been increased. In this case, the effects upon output are uncertain. This result states that if knowledge accumulation and the production function are strongly affected by human and physical capital, respectively, then improving knowledge workers' living conditions does not necessary increase social knowledge and production. In the long run the real knowledge income $c_1 Y/L_1$ may decrease because the level of production may fall. This is due to the assumption that knowledge does not influence productivity.

In the above discussion, we have neglected the effects of "learning by doing". Obviously, if p is large enough, then g and k will become smaller after c_1 is increased. As "learning by doing" strongly affects knowledge accumulation, it is not wise to invest in improving the living conditions of the knowledge workers. In this case, direct investment in production may improve all aspects of the society. It is easy to understand the reasons for this. If the "learning by doing" of the physical workers is fast enough and the intellectuals play no role in knowledge accumulation, then it might be reasonable to send the intellectuals to countryside to work with the peasants. This was done during "the Cultural Revolution", although it might not have been carried out for economic purposes. Due to this policy, it was possible to obtain a high economic growth rate because the intellectuals were transformed into physical workers who could contribute to knowledge accumulation through "learning by doing".

If p is not very large, it can be seen that the effects of c_1 upon economic growth are not easy to determine. The effects depend on the efficiency of knowledge workers and so on. That is, the problem is related to the whole structure of the system. Hence, to analyse actual problems, it is necessary to understand the characteristics of the parameters. Our discussions illustrate that in order to have a high economic growth rate, combined policies should be developed. If the living conditions of the knowledge workers are overemphasized or neglected it can be very dangerous for economic growth. Here, it seems necessary to emphasize again that we do not take account of morals and other social problems.

4-2. The effects of "learning by doing"

We have assumed two means of knowledge accumulation. The physical and knowledge workers can contribute to knowledge accumulation through different methods. It is important to understand how economic growth may be influenced if the characteristics of the behavior of workers are shifted. We now examine the effects of shifts of p upon economic growth. There are many factors which influence this value. Improvements in the organizational system may affect the "learning by doing" process. The introduction of competitive mechanisms may also increase p.

Taking the derivatives of (7.3.1) with respect to p yields

$$m_2 dg/dp = (\delta + n - n'\beta y/k)y,$$

$$m_2 dk/dp = y_2 \tau n'/g, \tag{7.4.4}$$

in which we require that $(n'\text{ß}y/k - \delta - n)$ is not equal to zero, and that m_2 is positive. As discussed above, m_2 being positive is a necessary condition for the equilibrium to be stable.

From the first equation one can conclude that if $\delta + n > n'\text{ß}y/k$, then an increase in p will improve knowledge per capita, and vice versa. However, it should be noted that the increased efficiency due to "learning by doing" does not necessarily imply an improvement in the level of knowledge. If $\delta + n < n'\text{ß}y/k$ which means that the marginal rate of the investment is larger than the "depreciation" rate with respect to k, the knowledge per capita becomes even lower. This case usually does not hold because the stability conditions may be not satisfied. To see this, let us assume that $N < 0$ at the equilibrium, i.e., . $py[\tau - 1]$ $+ [\sigma + a_1\tau/(a_1 + c_1y) - 1]H < 0$. This requirement holds if p is appropriately large. It is not difficult to see that m_2 is negative in this case (see (7.3.5)). Hence, the system becomes unstable and the traditional comparative static analysis cannot be done.

Although an increase in p may reduce g, a change in k is always non-negative. It is most important to understand how production is affected. It can be easily checked that

$$dy/dp = (\delta + n)cy_2/\text{ß}g > 0.$$

The output is always increased and so is the consumption. Hence, if the system is stable, the whole society should benefit. If we consider p to be influenced by the organizational system or any change in the level of responsibility of the physical workers, we can see that the society may benefit if reforms in China can motivate the physical workers, as well as leading to further investments in education.

4-3. The effects of change of intellectuals' efficiency

We study the effects of changes in a_1 in the knowledge accumulation function. An increase in this parameter means a reduction in the efficiency of the knowledge workers. If the intellectuals are purely devoted to the sciences, the parameter is equal to zero. If it is very large, the knowledge workers do not affect knowledge accumulation. Obviously, the two extreme cases are not realistic.

With regard to changes in a_1, one has

$$m_2 dg/da_1 = (n'\text{ß}y/k - \delta - n)H/(a_1 + cy),$$

$$m_2 dk/da_1 = - n'\tau y/g. \tag{7.4.5}$$

We require m_2 to be positive. As discussed in the previous section, if $(n'\text{ß}y/k - \delta - n)$ is positive, the equilibrium is potentially unstable. Hence, we will limit the discussion to the domain of $(n'\text{ß}y/k - \delta - n)$ being negative. From (7.4.5) one can conclude that if the efficiency of the intellectuals becomes low, the levels of knowledge and capital tend to be decreased. It is not difficult to see that the consumption of the workers and their level of production will be reduced. The society will benefit more if the knowledge workers work effectively.

4-4. The effects of population growth and population structures

We will now examine how economic growth can be affected if the population growth rate is shifted. The comparative static analysis with regard to n yields

$$m_2 dg/dn = - k\{\text{ß}py/k + a_1\text{ß}/k(a_1 + c_1y)\}$$

$$+ g(n'\text{ß}y/k - \delta - n),$$

$$m_2 dk/dn = - gn'\tau y/g + k\{p\tau y/g + \sigma H/g +$$

$$a_1\tau yH/(a_1 + c_1y) - \mu - n\}. \tag{7.4.6}$$

If the system is stable, an increase in the population growth rate will reduce knowledge per capita. This means that even if it is possible to improve material conditions by increasing the growth rate of the population, knowledge accumulation will always be decreased.

It is a little more complicated to analyse the impact upon physical capital. If p and a_1 are large enough, it is possible to increase capital per capita. That is, if the "learning by doing" of the physical workers is effective and the knowledge accumulation of the intellectuals is not effective enough, physical capital should be increased. However, it is a pity that neither of these parameters seems to be "appropriate" to make dk/dn positive in China. The "learning by doing" process, in particular, seems to have a very low efficiency rate there.

We have now analyzed the effects of population growth upon economic growth. It is also of significance to study effects of population structures upon economic growth. The population structure describes the way in which the population L is distributed between L_1 and L_2. It is described by n_1 and n_2. However, as $n_1 + n_2 = 1$ holds identically, an increase in n_1 must be associated with a decrease of n_2. Hence, it is sufficient to study one of the two parameters.

From the stationary equations (7.3.1), one obtains

$$m_2 dg/dn_1 = \text{ß}y(c_2 - c_1 - n'\alpha y/n_2)\{py + a_1 H/(a_1 + c_1 y)\}/k$$

$$- (\text{ß}yn'/k - \delta - n)(dH/n_1 - \alpha H/n_2 - \alpha py/n_2),$$

$$m_2 dk/dn_1 = (dH/n_1 - \alpha H/n_2 - \alpha py/n_2)\tau yn'/g - (dH/n_1 -$$

$$\alpha H/n_2 - \alpha py/n_2)\{p\tau y/g + \sigma H/g + a_1 \tau H/g(a_1 + c_1 y)$$

$$- \mu - n\}.$$

As before, let m_2 be positive.

It can generally be concluded that if the parameter α is small, and the parameter d is large, then g and k tend to increase after the knowledge workers' rate (i.e., n_1) is increased. We will not interpret the results in detail here. However, it should be noted that an increase in n_1 does not necessarily benefit the society. The conclusion depends upon the whole structure of the system.

5. Effects of Changes in the Population Growth Rate in the Case of Instability

From recent works in this field (e.g., Andersson, 1987, Zhang, 1990), we know that the instability of nonlinear systems cannot be treated as a temporal phenomenon because permanent economic oscillations can observed from potentially unstable systems. Instability and nonlinearity should be considered as sources of the complexity of dynamic systems rather than as problematic or unimportant (Haken, 1977, 1983, Prigogine, 1980, Prigogine and Stengers, 1984). However, other than in the literature on economic cycles, instability and nonlinearity have rarely been discussed in economics. We believe that it is valuable to examine the behavior of the system when it is unstable.

The arguments in the previous section were based upon the assumption that the equilibrium is stable. From the characteristic equation (7.3.5) one knows that this assumption is rather limited because, for example, m_2 may be not positive. The system is potentially unstable.

For convenience, we will rewrite the system in the local form near the equilibrium. Let

$$U_1 = k - k_0, \quad U_2 = g - g_0.$$

Then the system (7.2.8) can be rewritten in the form of

$$dU_1/dt = f^1, \quad dU_2/dt = f^2. \tag{7.5.1}$$

where

$$f^1(U,n) = r_1(n)U_1 + n'\tau y U_2/g + n'\beta(\beta - 1)yU_1^2/k^2 +$$

$$n'\beta \tau y U_1 U_2/kg + n'\tau(\tau - 1)yU_2^2/g^2 + O(|U|^3),$$

$$f^2(U,n) = MU_1 + N(n)U_2 + M_k U_1^2 + M_g U_1 U_2 +$$

$$N_g U_2^2 + O(|U|^3), \tag{7.5.2}$$

in which $U = (U_1,U_2)^T$, $r_1 = (n'\beta y/k - \delta - n)$, M_k, M_g, and N_g are the partial derivatives of M and N with regard to k and g, respectively. In (7.5.2), only r_1 and N are dependent on n. It can easily be checked that M_k and N_g are negative, while M_g is positive.

It is not difficult to identify that for appropriate parameter values we may have cases in which: (i) one eigenvalue is equal to zero, (ii) both eigenvalues are equal to zero with Reisz index two, (iii) both eigenvalues are equal to zero with index one. It is possible to observe bifurcations in each of these three cases. For simplicity, we are only concerned with case (i).

Let $m_2 = 0$ in (7.3.5). As m_2 may be either positive or negative, it is not necessary to assume the existence of appropriate parameters such that the equality holds. $m_2 = 0$ holds if $(n'\beta y/k - \delta - n)N = n'\tau y M/g$. As M is positive, if $(n'\beta y/k - \delta - n)$ is negative, N is negative too. We denote n_0 the value of n which keeps $m_2 = 0$ true. We choose n as a bifurcation parameter.

As $m_2 = 0$ and N is negative, $q_1(n_0) = 0$, $q_2(n_0) = - m_1 < 0$. As the equilibrium is at a critical state, it is impossible to analyse the effects of changes in n by traditional comparative statics so we will apply bifurcation theory to this problem. The following discussion is mathematically referred to Iooss and Joseph (Chapter V, 1980).

We will parameterize the bifurcating branches by

$$U_1 = h, \quad U_2 = hw(h), \quad n = n_0 + hz(h), \tag{7.5.3}$$

where h is the expansion amplitude parameter and $w(h)$ and $z(h)$ are continuous functions of h yet to be determined. We are especially interested in the behavior of U when $hz(h)$ is not equal to zero.

At $h = 0$, we have $f (= (f^1, f^2)^T) = 0$, and $m_2 = 0$. We will construct solutions of $f = 0$ for h not equal to zero.

Substituting (7.5.3) into (7.5.2) yields

$$f^1(U, n) = hm^1(w, z, h),$$

$$f^2(U, h) = hm^2(w, z, h), \tag{7.5.4}$$

where

$$m^1 = r_1 + n'\tau yw/g + h[- z + n'\beta(\beta - 1)y/k^2$$

$$+ n'\beta\tau yw/kg + n'\tau(\tau - 1)yw^2/g^2] + O(|h|^2),$$

$$m^2 = M + Nw + h[- z + M_k + wM_g + N_g w^2] + O(|h|^2).$$

$$\tag{7.5.5}$$

We wish to seek the steady bifurcating solutions of $m^i(w, z, h) = 0$ ($i = 1$, 2). We first require $m^1(w_0, z_0, 0) = 0$, $m^2(w_0, z_0, 0) = 0$, i.e., $r_1 + n'cyw_0/g = 0$, $M + Nw_0 = 0$. Since $m_2 = 0$, we can find a non-zero solution of the equation with respect to w_0 ($= - M/N = - gr_1/n'cy$). As N is negative, w_0 is positive.

Let $w(h) = w_0 + hw_1(h)$ and substitute this $w(h)$ into (7.5.5) to solve

$$m^i(w, z, h) = hs_i(w_1, z, h) = 0, \quad i = 1, 2, \tag{7.5.6}$$

where

$$s_1 = n'\tau yw_1/g - z + n'\beta(\beta - 1)y/k^2 + w_0 n'\beta\tau y/kg +$$

$$w_0^2 n'\tau(\tau - 1)y/g^2 + O(h),$$

$$s_2 = Nw_1 - z + M_k + w_0M_g + w_0{}^2N_g + O(h). \tag{7.5.7}$$

From $s_i(w_{i0},z_0,0) = 0$, we solve w_{10}, z_0 as

$$w_{10} = n''[n'\beta(1 - \beta)y/k^2 - w_0n'\beta\tau/kg +$$

$$w_0{}^2n'\tau(1 - \tau)y/g^2 + M_k + w_0M_g + w_0{}^2N_g],$$

$$z_0 = Nw_{10} + M_k + w_0M_g + w_0{}^2N_g,$$

in which n'' $(= 1/(n'\tau y/g - N)) > 0$. Hence, we have

$$n = n_0 + hz_0 + O(h^2), \; k = k_0 + h,$$

$$g = g_0 + hw_0 + h^2w_{10} + O(h^3), \tag{7.5.8}$$

in which all the parameters are explicitly given.

We will not discuss the stability of the new equilibrium because the expression is too complicated. However, we can determine the stability of the bifurcating solution by the standard linearization method with regard to the equilibrium (Iooss and Joseph, 1980).

First of all, it should be noted that dn/dh, dk/dh, and dg/dh are dependent upon the nonlinear terms of (7.5.2). The linearized terms cannot determine the effects of the parameter upon the variables.

As w_0 is positive, from (7.5.8) one can conclude that the effects of changes in the population growth rate depend upon the sign of z_0. If z_0 is positive, an increase in n will cause the level of capital and knowledge per capita to become higher, while if z_0 is negative, an increase in the growth rate will reduce the level of capital and knowledge. It is difficult to give a general conclusion about the effects of the population growth rate from the equation $z_0 = Nw_10 + M_k + w_0M_g + w_0{}^2N_g$ where Nw_{10} is uncertain, M_k and $w_0{}^2N_g$ are negative, and w_0M_g is positive.

We have analyzed this potentially unstable situation to illustrate the complexity of nonlinear systems. Further bifurcation analysis can be completed according to the method developed in Iooss and Joseph (1980).

6. Conclusions

We have introduced knowledge as an endogenous variable to the one-sector growth model. Knowledge is treated as the main cause of technological progress. It is assumed that physical workers and knowledge workers have different impacts upon the accumulation of knowledge: physical workers increase the level of knowledge by "learning by doing", while intellectuals increase it through their R&D activities. Our model consists of evolutionary equations of capital per capita and knowledge per capita. The existence of a unique equilibrium can be identified under very mild conditions. The equilibrium point may be either stable or unstable, depending on the forms of the "learning by doing" function, the knowledge accumulation function H, and the parameter values. Comparative static analysis is carried out under conditions of stability and instability, respectively. The results of our analysis are summarized below.

First, consider the case in which the system is assumed to be stable. Then,

1) with regard to living conditions of intellectuals:

(i) If the efficiency of the R&D activities of the intellectuals is not affected by level of consumption, any improvement in the living conditions will reduce the levels of capital and knowledge per capita.

(ii) If the knowledge workers have no impact upon knowledge accumulation, any improvement in their living conditions will reduce the level of capital and knowledge per capita.

(iii) If we neglect the effects of "learning by doing" on knowledge accumulation, any increase in the level of consumption of the intellectuals will increase both the level of knowledge and capital per capita.

(iv) If accumulated knowledge strongly influences the accumulation of further knowledge and capital input is very important in production, any increase in the level of consumption of the intellectuals will result in a decrease of the knowledge level and an increase of capital, though the effects on output are uncertain.

(v) If the impact of "learning by doing" is very strong, then improving the living conditions of intellectuals will reduce the level of knowledge and capital per capita.

(vi) If the impact of "learning by doing" is "appropriately" strong, the role of the policy of improving the living conditions of intellectuals is uncertain.

2) with regard to "learning by doing"

(i) If the marginal rate of investment is smaller than the "depreciation" rate of k, then any increase in the effects of "learning by doing" will increase the level of knowledge; if the marginal rate of investment is larger than the "depreciation" rate of k, then any increase in the effects of "learning by doing" will decrease the level of knowledge.

(ii) Any increase in the effects of "learning by doing" will always increase capital per capita.

(iii) Any increase in the effects of "learning by doing" will increase output and the levels of consumption of intellectuals and physical workers.

3) with respect to the efficiency of intellectuals:

(i) If the marginal rate of investment is smaller than the "depreciation" rate of k and the efficiency of intellectuals decreases, then the level of knowledge, capital per capita, output and the level of consumption will decrease.

4) with regard to the control policy of the population and the population structure:

(i) Any increase in the growth rate of the population will decrease the level of knowledge per capita;

(ii) If the effects of "learning by doing" are strong and the efficiency of the R&D activities is high, then any increase in the growth rate of the population increases capital per capita. Otherwise, capital per capita will decrease.

(iii) If the percentage of intellectuals of the population increase, then both the level of knowledge and capital will increase.

Next, we consider the case in which the system is unstable. As the traditional comparative statics analysis fails in this case, it is necessary to carry out a bifurcation analysis with respect to parameter changes. Moreover, as the system is unstable, nonlinear terms cannot be omitted, which makes the analysis very complicated. Even if we are able to obtain explicit results with the respect to the effects of the parameter shifts, as the results are expressed in such a complicated form it is generally very difficult to interpret them in economic terms. In this sense, the results obtained from bifurcation analysis appear "chaotic" to the analyst.

We have used the bifurcation method of Iooss and Joseph to analyze the effects of population growth on economic growth. The effects are dependent on the sign of the parameter z_0. If it is positive, then any increase in the population growth rate will reduce the level of capital and knowledge per capita. If it is negative, then any increase in the population growth rate will increase the level of capital and knowledge per capita. However, we are not clear about the economic implications of z_0.

VIII

TECHNOLOGICAL POLICY AND ECONOMIC DEVELOPMENT - MULTISECTOR APPROACH

We have introduced knowledge as an endogenous variable into a one-sector growth model. The interactions between knowledge and economic development have been emphasized. It is very natural to wonder how such ideas can be introduced into the framework of multiple sector models.

This chapter will explicitly introduce a new sector called the knowledge or non-material sector into the traditional input-output economic system. As in the preceding chapter, it is assumed that the growth of knowledge is the main source of technological change. Knowledge cannot be created as "manna from heaven". In order to increase knowledge we need "inputs" and investments just as we do to produce material capital.

The chapter is organized in the following manner. Section 8.1 defines the basic model, in which the K-set is explicitly introduced within the framework of input-output analysis. Section 8.2 investigates some properties of the model with a fixed form of technology. In Section 8.3, we develop the model of endogenous technological change according to the approach of learning by doing. Technological change related to investment in training is dealt with in Section 8.4. We develop the hybrid model of learning by doing and investment in training in Section 8.5. To conclude, we provide some comments on how monetary variables may affect the system in Section 8.6.

1. The Basic Model

It is assumed that the economy consists of different industrial sectors and knowledge (information or non-material) sectors. The outputs of the industrial sectors are materials or physical capital, such as machines, which can be used directly in the production process of the next period. The knowledge sectors exclude those activities whose outputs are related to physical capital in the normal sense. The output of the knowledge sectors is generally referred to as "human capital" - which is studied in life cycle analysis or human capital economics or "capital", such as books and library buildings.

The set including all of the material sectors is defined as the M-set. Similarly, the K-set includes all of the non-material sectors.

Let there be n material sectors and m non-material sectors, respectively. The output of the ith material sector is denoted by $X_{0i}(t)$ (i = 1, ... , n), while the output of the jth non-material sector is denoted by $X_{1j}(t)$ (j = 1, ... , m). In what follows, we omit time t in the variables. We introduce the following vectors

$$X_0 = (X_{01}, ... , X_{0n})^T, \quad X_1 = (X_{11}, ... , X_{1m})^T,$$

$$X = (X_{01}, ... , X_{0n}, X_{11}, ... , X_{1m})^T. \tag{8.1.1}$$

The production structure is assumed to be described within the framework of the input-output system. The output of the ith material sector is given by

$$X_{0i} = \sum_{k=1}^{n} a_{ik}X_{0k} + \sum_{k=1}^{n} b_{ik}dX_{0k}/dt$$

$$\sum_{q=1}^{m} c_{iq}X_{1q} + \sum_{q=1}^{m} d_{iq}dX_{1q}/dt + E_{0i},$$

$$i = 1, ... , n, \tag{8.1.2}$$

where E_{0i} (i = 1, ... , n) are the final demand of the ith material sector. It is assumed that the final demand is fixed in the study period. We term a_{ik} (i, k = 1, ... n) an internal input coefficient. This coefficient implies that in order to produce one unit of the kth good in the M-set, a_{ik} units of the ith good in the M-set are needed as inputs. Similarly, c_{iq} (i = 1, ... , n, q = 1, ... , m) is an external input coefficient; this states that c_{iq} units of the ith good in the M-set are required as inputs in order to "support" one unit of the qth good in the K-set. The coefficients, b_{ik} and d_{iq}, measure how much of the output from the ith sector of the M-set are needed for investment in the corresponding sector to obtain an increase of one additional unit capacity. We term b_{ik} and d_{iq} internal and external investment coefficients, respectively. (2.2) can be written in a vector form

$$X_0 = a_0X_0 + b_0dX_0/dt + c_0X_1 + d_0dX_1/dt + E_0, \tag{8.1.3}$$

in which

$$a_0 = (a_{ik})_{nxn}, \quad b_0 = (b_{ik})_{nxn},$$

$$c_0 = (c_{iq})_{mxn}, \qquad d_0 = (d_{ik})_{mxn}.$$

We describe the production process of the non-material sectors as follows

$$X_{1j} = \sum_{k=1}^{n} a_{jk}X_{0k} + \sum_{k=1}^{n} b_{jk}dX_{0k}/dt$$

$$\sum_{q=1}^{m} c_{jq}X_{1q} + \sum_{q=1}^{m} d_{jq}dX_{1q}/dt + E_{1j},$$

$$i = 1, \dots, n, \tag{8.1.4}$$

which can be rewritten as

$$X_1 = a_1X_0 + b_1dX_0/dt + c_1X_1 + d_1dX_1/dt + E_1, \tag{8.1.5}$$

in which

$$a_1 = (a_{jk})_{nxm}, \qquad b_1 = (b_{jk})_{nxm},$$

$$c_1 = (c_{jq})_{mxm}, \qquad d_1 = (d_{jk})_{mxm}.$$

The whole system is governed by

$$\begin{bmatrix} X_0 \\ X_1 \end{bmatrix} = \begin{bmatrix} a_0 & c_0 \\ a_1 & c_1 \end{bmatrix} \begin{bmatrix} X_0 \\ X_1 \end{bmatrix} + \begin{bmatrix} b_0 & d_0 \\ b_1 & d_1 \end{bmatrix} \begin{bmatrix} dX_0/dt \\ dX_1/dt \end{bmatrix}$$

$$+ \begin{bmatrix} E_0 \\ E_0 \end{bmatrix}, \tag{8.1.6}$$

or

$$X = AX + BdX/dt + E. \tag{8.1.7}$$

This is the fundamental relation among the economic variables. It should be noted that this system is composed of a number of "accounting" equations because no theories are introduced into the model.

Although the equations describing the material and non-material sectors are similar, the implications and characteristics of the coefficients in the two subsystems are different. Some coefficients may be almost equal to zero, while others may be dependent on the variables which are discussed below. The specification of different dynamics of the coefficients is the main concern of our study. It should be noted that Pasinetti (1979) explicitly introduced technological change into the multiple sector models. Technological change is also taken into account by shifts in the production coefficients. However, such shifts of technological changes are due to exogenous forces rather than being endogenously determined.

The properties of the system have been investigated thoroughly in the literature (e.g., Nikaido, 1968, Morishima, 1964) when the matrices are constant and the growth rate of all sectors is homogeneous.

By technological change (or progress) we mean a change in the relationships between the inputs and outputs. We assume that technological change is described by shifts in the technological coefficients. If these shifts are caused by exogenous factors, technological change is considered to be exogenous progress, but if the coefficients are explicitly (only) dependent on the variables of the system, technological change is endogenous. We are mainly concerned with endogenous change.

For simplicity we do not explicitly introduce any form of endogenous consumption. We are only concerned with a physically expanding economy. In the preceding chapter we have explicitly investigated the interactions between consumption and technological change.

2. Some Properties of the Basic System

Before introducing endogenous technological change, we will explain some of the fundamental properties of the system and discuss their relations to the standard input-output model which only consists of material sectors.

First, consider the case which there is no investment in the K-set. This means that d_0 and d_1 are equal to zero. Hence, from (8.1.5) one has

$$X_1 = (I - c_1)^{-1}[a_1X_0 + b_1dX_0/dt + E_1], \qquad (8.2.1)$$

in which I is the mxm unit matrix. In (8.2.1), we assume the existence of the inverse of $(I - c_1)$. This means that the demand for the knowledge from the production system is (uniquely) determined by product sales. If the production system is limited to a specific industry, this case may occur in reality as the industry may obtain its knowledge from society without making any investments in R&D and education. This is evidently invalid for a whole national economy because increases in knowledge cannot occur due to "manna from heaven".

Substituting (8.2.1) into (8.1.3) yields

$$X_0 = a_0^*X_0 + b_0^*dX_0/dt + E_0^*, \qquad (8.2.2)$$

where

$$a_0^* = a_0 + (I - c_1)^{-1}a_1, \quad b_0^* = (I - c_1)^{-1}b_1 + b_0,$$

$$E_0^* = E_0 + (I - c_1)^{-1}E_1.$$

The dynamics is thus reduced to (8.1.2), which only consists of material sectors. As soon as the structure of the M-set is determined, the demand for knowledge is uniquely given by (8.1.1).

In empirical studies we can directly estimate the parameters in (8.2.2). There is no need to explicitly introduce non-material sectors if our assumption about knowledge investment is valid. Even though we do not explicitly consider the K-set in the economic system, in the short-run we may analyze the dynamics of the M-set with an acceptable level of approximation since the demand for knowledge from the industry can be efficiently supplied by the society.

The system (8.2.2) is the standard dynamic Leontief input-output model. It can be analyzed in different ways. For instance, we can perform a comparative statics analysis to investigate the effects of shifts in the parameters. Let the matrix b_0^* be invertible. Then (8.2.2) may be rewritten as

$$dX_0/dt = a^*X_0 + E^*, \qquad (8.2.3)$$

where $a^* = (b_0^*)^{-1}(I - a_0^*)$, $E^* = - (b_0^*)^{-1}E_0^*$. We are interested in studying equilibria and their stability conditions. In an economic growth model, an equilibrium may be defined in two ways. It may be the state in which each sector grows at a unique growth rate. We have $dX_0/dt = gX_0$, where g is a positive homogeneous growth rate. The physical system is thus simply expanding. The other definition, which may be considered as a special case of the first, states that the equilibrium may be the static state in which the change rates of all sectors are set to zero. In the long-run it is important to study the case of an expanding economy, but in the short-run it may be sufficient to investigate the static state of zero growth rates.

In the static state, the problem is reduced to $X = AX + E$, if one has sufficient information about the K-set. The conditions for the existence and uniqueness of a positive solution of the system can be found in Nikaido (1968).

Let us consider at an expanding economy. (8.2.3) is reduced to

$$(gI - a^*)X_0 = E^*. \tag{8.2.4}$$

It can be seen that the Frobenius-Perron theorem (Nikaido, 1968) can be applied to (8.2.4) in order to identify the existence of a unique positive growth rate. However, as the matrices in (8.2.4) are related to the characteristics of the K-set, it is necessary to determine the conditions under which the system is soluble. Assume a^* and E^* to be non-negative and let r_i and s_j denote the row and column sums of the "combined" input coefficients a^*, respectively,

$$r_i = \Sigma_j a_{ij}^* , \quad s_j = \Sigma_i a_{ij}^* .$$

Proposition 8.2.1.
Either one of (i) or (ii) is sufficient for the workability of (3.4)
(i) $g > r_i$, for all i,
(ii) $g > s_j$, for all j.

The proof is referred to in Nikaido (1968, p.98). If we introduce the dual price system to (8.2.4), (i) or (ii) also implies the profitability of the production system. The following results guarantee the conditions for the existence of expanding equilibrium growth.

Proposition 8.2.2.
Let a^* be a nonnegative square matrix. Then one has
(i) a^* has a nonnegative eigenvalue. A nonnegative eigenvector is associated with the largest of all the eigenvalues, denoted by z;
(ii) $rI - a^*$ is nonnegatively invertible if and only if $g > z$;
(iii) If Ay is no less than z^*y for a real number z^* and a semipositive vector y, then z is no less than z^*.

We have investigated the case in which an industry can obtain all of the (fully supplied) knowledge it needs from the society. It is also important to deal with the case in which there is no direct investment in the M-set. It can be seen that an increase of knowledge will require inputs from the M-set to produce further new knowledge. In some sense the scale of the M-set should be uniquely determined by the K-set. We may thus neglect the M-set when analyzing the dynamic behavior of the system, though the coefficients of the M-set affect the properties of the K-set.

Finally, it is useful to study an economy in which there is investment in the material and knowledge sectors. The above conditions relating to the M- or K-economy are also valid for this general case.

In regard to the linear system, it is difficult to say whether there are qualitative differences between the standard input-output model and our system. In the rest of this paper, we discuss how the technology of the system is influenced by different sectors. The effects of the M-set and the K-set on technological progress are introduced.

3. Technological Change of "Learning by Doing"

This section is concerned with endogenous forms of technological change which are reflected in shifts of the coefficients of (8.1.7).

Due to the complicated characteristics involved, there are no unique solutions to describe how technological change takes place. Different authors have emphasized various aspects of technological change. For instance, various endogenous/exogenous and random/deterministic characteristics of technological progress have been proposed in the literature.

In this section, we assume that technological progress is caused by increases in human knowledge (capital). Three different formulations have been suggested in order to study how human capital is accumulated. According to the first view, utility-maximizing individuals accumulate human capital by choosing different jobs with different opportunities for training and learning (e.g., Rosen 1972, Blinder and Weiss, 1976). The second approach, being quite similar to the first, considers that each individual accumulates human capital by choosing the optimal time between working and training rather than the optimal job (e.g., Ghez and Becker, 1975, Heckmann, 1976). In the previous chapter we have already considered the third approach, called "learning by doing" or the "experience" model (e.g., Arrow, 1962, Eckaus, 1963, Andersson and Zhang, 1990). Recently, a theoretical synthesis of "learning by doing" and "investment in training" has been suggested by Killingsworth (1982) as an alternative from of human accumulation. We are interested in how these fundamental ideas can be introduced into the input-output model.

This section focusses upon Arrow's "learning by doing" approach.

First, we look at the subsystem which consists of the M-set. Within the framework of "learning by doing", we suggest a possible learning process as follows

$$da_{ik}/dt = A_{ik}(X_{0k}, a_{ik}),$$

$$db_{ik}/dt = B_{ik}(X_{0k}, b_{ik}), \quad i, k = 1, \ldots, n,$$

$$dc_{ik}/dt = C_{iq}(X_{11}, c_{iq}),$$

$$dd_{iq}/dt = D_{iq}(X_{1q}, d_{iq}), \quad j = 1, \ldots n, \tag{8.3.1}$$

in which A_{ik}, B_{ik}, C_{iq}, D_{iq}, are appropriate continuous functions to be discussed.

The exogenous technological change in Pasinetti's system may be considered as a special case of (8.3.1). To illustrate how technical change is treated by Pasinetti, we wish to provide an example. In Chapter IV (Pasinetti, 1979) Pasinetti assumes that technical progress is the same in all sectors of the economic system. This means that over time all of the technical coefficients of production decrease at a given percentage rate, i.e.,

$$a_{ij}(t) = a_{ij}(0)\exp(-ht),$$

where h is a positive constant. Evidently, this can be written as

$$da_{ij}/dt = - ha_{ij},$$

which is a special case of (8.3.1).

To explain how (8.3.1) can be used to describe a learning by doing process, we consider the case in which a coefficient a_{ik} is dependent on the accumulation of experiences of the workers engaged in various production activities. Obviously, the measurements of these experiences can be measured is not so simple. As in the previous chapter, we assume that the accumulated experience can be measured as a function of the total output that the industry has produced during the period it has been in operation up to the present. The total output is given by

$$\int_{t_0}^{t} X_{0k}(h)dh \ .$$

If we assume that the experiences are linearly related to the total output, and that the coefficients are negatively proportional to the experiences, we have

$$a_{ik}(t) = u_0 - u \int_{t_0}^{t} X_{0k}(h)dh \ ,$$

where u_0 and u are constant parameters. One thus has

$$da_{ik}/dt = - uX_{0k}, \qquad\qquad (8.3.2)$$

subject to appropriate initial conditions. This example illustrates how the experiences can affect the efficiency of the production process.

In general, we require that

$$A_{ik}^{1} \leq 0, \quad A_{ik}^{2} \leq 0, \qquad\qquad (8.3.3)$$

where A_{ik}^{1} and A_{ik}^{2} are the partial derivatives of A_{ik} with regard to X_{0k} and a_{ik}, respectively. The first inequality of (8.3.4) means that as the workers become more experienced, the efficiency of the production process should increase. Less inputs are needed to produce one unit of output. The second inequality is derived from an assumption that it is easy to improve the current production efficiency if the efficiency is very low. It should be noted that we do not specify the signs of the higher order derivatives of the learning functions. Generally, we have little information about them. Learning processes should be dominated by complicated nonlinearity. It seems that the second derivatives should be non-negative, at least during most of the period of the industrial development.

It is also assumed that the change rate of b_{ik} is dependent on the output as this coefficient is equal to the number of units of ith goods of the M-set needed to increase the M-set by one unit of kth goods. The current level of capital affects the efficiency of the investments. Similarly to (8.3.4), we assume $B_{ik}^{1} \leq 0, \quad B_{ik}^{2} \leq$ 0. The functions C_{iq} and D_{iq} can be interpreted similarly. Summarizing the above discussion, we can describe the dynamics of the M-set as follows

$$X_0 = a_0 X_0 + b_0 dX_0/dt + c_0 X_1 + d_0 dX_1/dt + E_0,$$

$$da_0/dt = A_0(X_0,a_0), \quad db_0/dt = B_0(X_0,b_0),$$

$$dc_0/dt = C_0(X_1,c_0), \quad dd_0/dt = D_0(X_1,d_0), \tag{8.3.5}$$

where the functional forms are determined from (8.3.1).

Similarly, we can build a model for the K-set. It should be noted that an increase of knowledge or (material) capital does not necessarily imply a decline in the value of the corresponding coefficient value. Complicated properties of knowledge accumulation may make the effects of investment in the knowledge sectors very difficult to understand.

The dynamics of the whole system is generally given by

$$X = AX + BdX/dt + E,$$

$$dA/dt = F(X,A), \quad dB/dt = G(X,B), \tag{8.3.6}$$

in which F and G are the corresponding evolutionary matrices of the coefficients.

It is possible to provide conditions for the existence of the solutions. As the problem is extremely complicated, we wish to discuss some special cases.

First, we assume that the adjustment speed of the technological coefficients is very slow in comparison to production in the material and knowledge sectors. To introduce this difference between the speeds, let us rewrite (8.3.5) in the form of

$$X = AX + BdX/dt + E, \tag{8.3.7}$$

$$dA/dt = sF(X,A), \quad dB/dt = sG(X,B), \tag{8.3.8}$$

in which s is a very small parameter. It should be noted that the matrix functions F and G in (8.3.6) and (8.3.7) are not the same. Furthermore, in practice, some elements of A or B may be fast variables in comparison to some elements of X.

Adjustment speeds are very difficult to identify. In a dynamic economic system a fast variable can be treated as a function of the slow variables in the long term. On the other hand, a slow variable becomes a constant in the short term. In a certain sense, in economic systems everything is changeable and all variables interact each other over time and space. This complexity makes any form of economic analysis very difficult. However, if we are aware of the dynamic characteristics of the economic variables and can be certain about the time scale of the study, the problem may become a little easier to handle.

Consider the problem in the short run. We assume that the functions F and G are bounded. If s is sufficiently small, sF and sG are almost equal to zero. Hence, the change rates of A and B are very small. This means that in the short run we may neglect (8.3.8) in the analysis. A and B may be treated as constant parameters. The system is thus reduced to (8.3.7) which has been discussed in the preceding section.

If we are concerned with long-run evolution, then the problem is reduced to (8.3.8). To see this, we make a time-scaled transformation $t^* = st$. Then we have

$$X = AX + sBdX/dt^* + E,$$

$$dA/dt^* = F(X,A), \quad dB/dt^* = G(X,B).$$

As s is sufficiently small, we may neglect the term $sBdX/dt^*$ in the first equation and have $(I - A)X = E$. If the inverse of $(I - A)$ exists, then one has

$$X = (I - A)^{-1}E. \qquad (8.3.9)$$

From (8.3.9), we see that the output is uniquely determined by the coefficient matrix A and the final demand. The output is independent of the investment coefficients. This results from our assumption that the investment coefficient sB can be omitted without affecting the qualitative behavior of the system.

Substituting (8.3.9) into the original equations yields

$$dA/dt^* = F[(I - A)^{-1}E,A] = F(A),$$

$$dB/dt^* = G[(I - A)^{-1}E,B] = G(A,B). \qquad (8.3.10)$$

The dynamics of the economic system is approximately specified by (8.3.10). The dynamics of A is independent of B, though B is explicitly related to A. To solve the problem, we can first solve A and then substitute the solution into the second equation of (8.3.10) to obtain B(t). Finally, from (8.3.9) we can determine the outputs.

The system can be reduced further. For instance, we may consider the case in which the adjustment speed of B is much slower than that of A. Consequently, the dynamics may consist of only dA/dt.

(8.3.10) is highly nonlinear. The system is potentially unstable. We know that very complicated behavior such as chaos can be observed from such a nonlinear dynamic system. We will not investigate the analytic properties because little insight into the problem can be obtained without sufficient simplifications.

In the discussion above, we assume that when s is sufficiently small, we can neglect the parts associated with s. The validity of such an approximation can generally be understood by studying the following system:

$$dx/dt = f(x,y), \quad dy/dt = sg(x,y) + p(x,y,s),$$

in which x and y are vectors and s is a small parameter. The relations between this system and the following one

$$dx/dt = f(x,y), \quad dy/dt = p(x,y,0),$$

have been examined in the recent mathematical literature. Applying these results, we can find the conditions for the validity of this approximation.

4. Technological Change due to Investment in Training

The previous model overlooks the (direct) effects of knowledge upon productivity. The influences of the K-set on the M-set occur due to changes in of the demand from the K-set. The technological coefficients of the K-set are not affected by the scales of the K-set. This is due to the fact that we only consider "learning by doing" as a source of technological progress. The productivity of an industry is not only changed by experiences; it should be also be affected by the introduction of new knowledge from other sources. These changes should cause the production structures to become more varied.

This section emphasizes "the public aspect" of the K-set. It is assumed that knowledge plays the role of a public good, although it may not be a pure public good because the use of human capital by one industry may exclude the accessibility of other industries. Certain specific knowledge may be useless for some sectors, while it may be necessary for others.

Similar to the investment in training model described in the literature, we suggest the following dynamics for the M-set

$$da_{ik}/dt = A_{ik}(X_1,a_{ik}),$$

$$db_{ik}/dt = B_{ik}(X_1,b_{ik}), \quad i, k = 1, \dots , n,$$

$$dc_{ik}/dt = C_{iq}(X_1,c_{iq}),$$

$$dd_{iq}/dt = D_{iq}(X_1,d_{iq}), \quad j = 1, \ldots n. \tag{8.4.1}$$

In (8.4.1), we assume that all of the technological coefficients are only dependent on the variables of the K-set. Technological changes in the M-set occur due to shifts of the variables in the K-set. We require

$$A_{ik}^1 \leq 0, \quad A_{ik}^2 \leq 0, \tag{8.4.2}$$

where A_{ik}^1 and A_{ik}^2 are the partial derivatives of A_{ik} with respect to X_{1j} and a_{ik}, respectively. The first inequality implies that an increase of knowledge will increase (or at least not decrease) the efficiency of the material production process. The second inequality can be similarly explained as in Section 8.3.

Corresponding to (8.3.6), we suggest the following investment in training model:

$$X = AX + BdX/dt + E, \quad dA/dt = sF(X_1,A),$$

$$dB/dt = sG(X_1,B), \tag{8.4.3}$$

in which F and G are the corresponding evolutionary matrices. The difference between (8.4.3) and the model in Section 3 is that F and G in this section are only dependent on X_1 and A, B, while the preceding model is related to all of the variables in the system. The adjustment speed parameter s is meaningful for any value in R^+.

This system is potentially so complicated that we can only hope to understand some aspects of its dynamics. From an analytical point of view, this model can be investigated in a number of different ways. Various mathematical methods can potentially be applied to the system. In what follows, we apply catastrophe theory (Zhang, 1990) to explain the structural changes in the system. We will use an acceptable case to illustrate the potential complexity of the system.

It is assumed that the K-set consists of a single (knowledge) sector. For simplicity, we denote knowledge (i.e., X_1 in (8.4.3)) by x. The equations for X are reduced to

$$X_0 = a_0X_0 + b_0dX_0/dt + c_0X_1 + d_0dX_1/dt + E_0,$$

$$x = a_1X_0 + b_1dX_0/dt + cx + ddx/dt + E_1,$$

in which we use c and d instead of c_1 and d_1. We are concerned with very short-run behavior of the system. It is assumed that the demand for knowledge from the M-set and the final demand of the K-set are fixed during the study period. That is, E is constant, where

$$E = a_1X_0 + b_1dX_0/dt + E_1. \qquad (8.4.5)$$

Hence, the dynamics of the knowledge sector is reduced to

$$dx/dt = x - cx - E. \qquad (8.4.6)$$

As c and d are only dependent on x, we have an "isolated" subsystem in this case. It would seem that this is only valid for a short-run period, because in our fundamental system the growth of knowledge and material production are strongly connected. As it is not easy to apply catastrophe theory to high dimensional problems, we have to simplify the model in order to obtain meaningful results. It is reasonable to obtain useful results by simplification as long as the process of simplifying a complicated problem are made explicitly.

We have to specify the dynamics of c and d. We suggest the following dynamics

$$dc/dt = -r_1x^2 - r_2c + r_3,$$

$$dd/dt = sf(x,d), \qquad (8.4.7)$$

where r_i are constant parameters, and s is a sufficiently small parameter. The dynamics of the K-set consists of (8.4.6) and (8.4.7).

In (8.4.7), it is assumed that the investment coefficient d is very slow in comparison to the input coefficients and knowledge. The first equation of (8.4.7) states that: (i) If human capital is increased, then the input coefficient tends to fall; and (ii) If x is high, c tends to decrease. Obviously, this equation can only hold for certain values of x and c. An equilibrium point of the knowledge dynamics is given by

$$x - cx - E = 0,$$

$$- r_1x^2 - r_2c + r_3 = 0. \tag{8.4.8}$$

Substituting the first equation into the second equation yields

$$x^3 - rx - q = 0, \tag{8.4.9}$$

where $r = (r_3 - r_2)/r_1$, $q = r_2E/r_1$. x is different for various values of the parameters. It is interesting to see how the equilibrium point is shifted with the parameters. However, this equation is none other than the canonical cusp catastrophe surface with "normal factor" q and "splitting factor" r (Zeeman, 1977). The cusp catastrophe is illustrated in the (q,r,x)-space in Fig. 8.4.1.

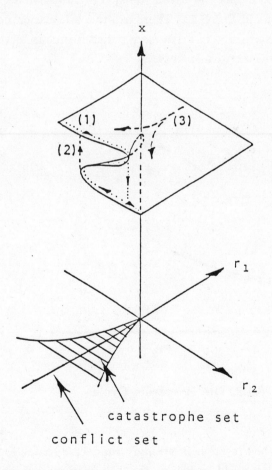

Fig. 8.4.1. Cusp Catastrophe of Knowledge Growth

The equation (8.4.9) describes a catastrophe dynamics for the variable x, making the upper and lower sheets (given by $3x^2 > r$) into "attractors", and the middle sheet (given by $3x^2 < r$) into a "repeller". This dynamics has three characteristics: (i) it rapidly carries any point on to the attracting surface; (ii) it holds the point on the attracting surface for as long as possible; and (iii) when this becomes no longer possible, for example, when the point crosses one of the fold curves (given by $3x^2 = r$) bounding the attracting surface, then the dynamics causes a catastrophic jump on to the other attracting sheet.

In comparison to r and q, the variable x changes more slowly. Once x lies on the surface, then $dx/dt = 0$, and so slow parameters control the direction of any change in x. As the parameter is shifted, there is a hystersis cycle in the system. To illustrate this cycle, fix the parameter q. Then the behaviour can be described in the (r,x)-plane as in Fig. 8.4.2. There are two bifurcation points - r_1 and r_2 - at which structural changes occur. We have a discontinuous increase (or decrease) of knowledge near these critical points.

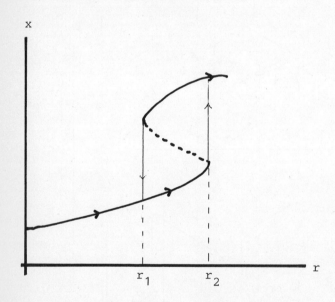

Fig. 8.4.2. The Hystersis Cycle

As the whole system is strongly connected, catastrophic changes in the level of knowledge should influence the behavior of the other variables in the system. We can examine the reactions of the other variables to these catastrophe changes by studying the dynamics of (8.4.3).

The model can be applied realistically to the computer industry. A group of science and engineering students have a joint level of knowledge at the outset. In the short term, the exogenous demand for the knowledge may be assumed to be fixed. Some "trivial" creative ideas, which shift the parameters in the system, may result in a sudden increase in the joint level of knowledge of the group. Evidently, such a change can bring about improvements in the productivity of the industry.

We have explained the events which may lead to a cusp catastrophe. It is also possible to observe other kinds of bifurcations in the system. Look at the dynamics again

$$dx/dt = x/d - cx/d - E/d,$$

$$dc/dt = - r_1 x^2 - r_2 c + r_3. \tag{8.4.10}$$

Let there exist a locally isolated equilibrium denoted by (x_0, c_0). The Jacobian evaluated at the equilibrium is given by

$$J = \begin{bmatrix} (1-c_0)/d & - c_0/d \\ - 2r_1 x_0 & - r_2 \end{bmatrix}. \tag{8.4.11}$$

The two eigenvalues are given from

$$z^2 - \{(1-c_0)/d - r_2\}z - r_2(1-c_0)/d + 2r_1 c_0 x_0/d = 0. \tag{8.4.12}$$

We are interested in the existence of limit cycles in the system. According to the Hopf bifurcation theorem, if the system has a pair of purely imaginary eigenvalues and the loss of stability can be guaranteed, then there exists a limit cycle near the equilibrium. It can be identified that the Hopf bifurcation theorem holds if

$$(1 - c_0)/d = r_2, \quad r_2(1 - c_0)/d > 2r_1 c_0 x_0/d,$$

are satisfied and the bifurcation is subcritical. We do not need to find the expression and stability conditions of the cycles as it can easily be done by some well known methods. We illustrate the limit cycle in Fig. 8.4.3.

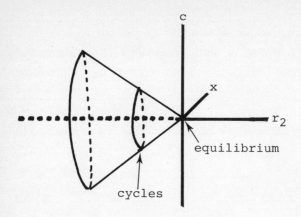

Fig. 8.4.3. Subcritical Hopf Bifurcation

There are periodic interactions between human capital and the input coefficients. The behavior is created from the nonlinear interactions between x and c. It should be noted that as the input coefficient is usually a slow variable in comparison to knowledge, it may be difficult to observe such a cyclical interaction in practice.

5. A Growth Model of "Hybrid" Technological Change

We have introduced technological progress as a result of learning by doing and investment in training to the input-output dynamic system. However, these two kinds of changes may take place simultaneously. Thus, a "hybrid" approach is necessary to take account of these two sources.

After considering the models in the preceding two sections, we suggest the following dynamics for the M-set

$$da_{ik}/dt = A_{ik}(X_{0k},X_1,a_{ik}),$$

$$db_{ik}/dt = B_{ik}(X_{0k},X_1,b_{ik}), \quad i, k = 1, \dots , n,$$

$$dc_{ik}/dt = C_{iq}(X_1,c_{iq}),$$

$$dd_{iq}/dt = D_{iq}(X_1, d_{iq}), \quad j = 1, \ldots n. \tag{8.5.1}$$

These equations take learning by doing and investment in training into account. As the previous two sections, we can add some constraints on these functions.

Omitting derivation in detail, we may describe the dynamics of the whole system as follows

$$X = AX + BdX/dt + E, \quad dA/dt = sF(X,A),$$

$$dB/dt = sG(X,B). \tag{8.5.2}$$

For simplicity, in (8.5.2) we assume that the adjustment speeds of A and B are on the same scale.

We call (8.5.2) the "hybrid" model of technological change. Although the system is formally the same as (8.3.6), the functions F and G in the two systems are different. Here we are mainly concerned with the existence of a long-run equilibrium.

An equilibrium is defined as a state at which the variables X grow at a homogeneous growth rate g, and the change rates of the input coefficients are equal to zero. An equilibrium point is determined by

$$X = AX + gBX + E, \quad F(X,A) = 0, \quad G(X,B) = 0. \tag{8.5.3}$$

It is assumed that from $F(X,A) = 0$ and $G(X,B) = 0$, we can uniquely determine A and B as functions of X. This assumption does not always hold as was shown in the previous sections. Let the implicit function theorem (e.g., Takayama, 1985) be valid for $F(X,A) = 0$ and $G(X,B) = 0$. Then we have $A = A(X)$ and $B = B(X)$.

Theorem 8.5.1.
Let $F(X,A)$ and $G(X,B)$ be continuously differentiable in a neighborhood of (X,A) and (X,B), respectively. If both $\det(F_A)$ and $\det(G_B)$, in which F_A and G_B express the partial derivatives of F and G with regard to A and B, respectively, are not equal to zero, then near a neighborhood of X we have that:
(i) there exist two unique mappings $A(X)$ and $B(X)$ such that: $A = A(X)$ and $B = B(X)$;
(ii) $A(X)$ and $B(X)$ are continuously differentiable in a local sense.

The theorem can be proved by directly applying the implicit function theorem. It is locally valid. If the theorem is held, then the problem is reduced to solving

$$X = A(X)X + gB(X)X + E = H(X), \qquad (8.5.4)$$

in which the nonlinear functions H are continuously differentiable with respect to X. We are interested in whether it is possible to find a solution of (8.5.4) for fixed g and E. As the convexity of the functions cannot be generally guaranteed because of the characteristics of technological change, it is not easy to establish the existence and uniqueness of the equilibrium. If H is convex, the problem can be solved by applying the Brouwer fixed-point theorem. However, even if we can identify the existence of a unique equilibrium, it is more difficult to guarantee the stability of the equilibrium.

It should be mentioned that the assumption of fixed final demand can be relaxed by considering the final demand as a function of the present outputs in the M-set and the K-set. The analytic work is not carried out in detail here because of the complexity of the problems. Non-convexity, non-linearity and instability dominate the system. Without sufficient simplifications, any analysis of such problems with traditional (mathematical) methods in economics is hopeless.

6. Some Comments

In the preceding sections we were concerned with the way in which technological change can be introduced into the multiple sector growth model. Different mechanisms which influence the growth of knowledge have been studied. However, monetary variables have been completely neglected. Now we will discuss the possibility that monetary variables may affect this process.

First, consider the case in which the quantitative system is given by (8.5.2). i.e.,

$$X = AX + BdX/dt + E,$$

$$dA/dt = sF(X,A), \quad dB/dt = sG(X,B). \qquad (8.6.1)$$

The dual system to the first equation is described by

$$P = A^T P + rB^T P, \qquad (8.6.2)$$

where P is the price vector and r is the rate of interest.

Although the quantitative system is independent of the price system, the latter is determined after the former is known. The technological progress connects the two systems.

There is another way for the input coefficients to be changed. For instance, we may assume that the production structure of each industry is described by the neoclassical production function. It can be seen that the introduction of this relation does not essentially affect our arguments in the previous sections.

It is assumed that the coefficient a_{ji} are determined by the condition that the long-run average cost is at a minimum. It should be noted that here we implicitly assume that the cost of R&D activities is not included in this average cost. It is not difficult to see that in this case the matrix is a function of P, i.e.,

$$A = U(P), \tag{8.6.3}$$

holds at any point of time. Therefore, the input coefficients are changed by two sources. The first source is R&D activities and the effects of learning by doing. The second factor which causes firms to adjust their production structures is information about prices. The first source is a slow process in comparison to the second one.

The dynamics of the whole system is given by

$$X = AX + BdX/dt + E,$$

$$P = A^T P + rB^T P, \quad A = U(P),$$

$$dA/dt = sF(X,A), \quad dB/dt = sG(X,B). \tag{8.6.4}$$

As prices affect the input matrix, we see that the quantitative system is not independent of the price system. On the other hand, if s is zero, the system is identical to that developed in Section 4.1.

Our system is not closed in the sense given in Section 3.5. We can use different theories to close the model. However, as our system is already complicated enough, the introduction of more realistic assumptions to the system will only make the problem even more complicated. Little insight into the behavior of the system can be obtained.

CONCLUSION AND PROSPECTS FOR FURTHER RESEARCH

The development theory proposed in this study emphasizes different aspects of economic development. Various aspects of the theory, including the choice of indicators in economic analysis, fast and slow variables, the time scale of the study period, business cycles, the role of monetary variables in economic evolution, inflation, economic controls and technological change, have been studied. Analytically, in contrast to traditional economic growth theory, we treat nonlinearity and instability as sources of order in economic development. We have argued that complicated economic behavior can be explained by introducing nonlinearity and instability into economic analysis. In what follows, we summarize the results of our study and outline some problems which remain to be solved.

1. Summary

In Chapter I, we discussed various aspects of development and provided a simple review of economic growth theory. We also explained the rationale for the choice of development indicators and discussed the concepts of equilibrium, non-equilibrium, stability, and instability. In particular, we examined the various roles of fast and slow variables in dynamic economic analysis. We showed that their roles are dependent on the time-scale of the study period. The explicit emphasis on the adjustment speeds of economic variables helped us to distinguish between various economic theories.

In Chapter II, we focusses on a review of some quantitative economic growth theories. We re-examined the dynamic behavior of the growth model with exhaustible resources and endogenous population growth and showed that the standard neoclassical growth model may become unstable if resources and endogenous population growth are taken into account. The existence of economic cycles was identified in the model and the implications of the assumption of the existence of production functions in dynamic analysis were also examined.

Chapter III reviewed how monetary variables can be introduced into neoclassical growth theory. Some elementary issues of money theory in economic development were investigated in this chapter. We made a new contribution to the field by identifying the existence of business cycles in the generalized Tobin model, via applications of the bifurcation method by Iooss and Joseph.

We examined the dynamics of prices in the context of dynamic multiple sector models in Chapter IV. We mainly confined ourselves to the interactions among interest, growth and inflation rates within the framework of multiple sector models.

In Chapter V, we studied a "mixed" economy with centralization and decentralization in which the central government is assumed to maximize a social welfare function which depends on the economic growth rate. This chapter is also based upon the joint work between Andersson and Zhang (1988a). We readdressed the problem of the existence, uniqueness and stability of dynamic models when subjected to different types of economic policy regimes. We re-examined the problem of stability in situations of completely decentralized policy making in relation to Marshallian and Walrasian adaption patterns. It was demonstrated that an economy without the possibility of substitution between different inputs requires a combination of decentralized and centralized decision making if long term stable economic growth under conditions of equilibrium and optimality are to be achieved.

In Chapter VI, we reviewed the literature on the problem of the "choice of (exogenously given) alternatives or techniques".

A growth model with endogenous technological change is presented. The model of this chapter was developed by Zhang (1989a). It was built upon a development problem currently existing in the economy of China and thus it particularly emphasized the dynamic interactions between human knowledge and economic variables. Above all, the way in which the consumption level of knowledge workers and the "learning by doing" process of physical workers can affect economic development was analyzed. When the system is stable, we applied the traditional comparative static analysis to examine the effects of different parameters on economic development. However, as the system was potentially unstable, the traditional comparative static analysis may be invalid. Bifurcation analysis was applied to study the effects of changes in the population growth rate when the system was unstable.

Chapter VIII explicitly introduced a new sector called the knowledge or non-material sector into the traditional input-output economic system (Andersson and Zhang, 1989). The fundamental ideas here are similar to those developed in Chapter VII. We attempted to develop our models upon the basis of the human capital theories of economics. As the system is extremely complicated, we only discussed some of behavior which can be observed from the system.

2. How To Close Dynamic Models - The neoclassical, neo-Marxian and neo-Keynesian approaches

Some of the models reviewed and developed in this study are not closed in the sense that either one or more of the elements - investment, consumption, wages, interest rates, growth rates, the labour force or technology - are exogenously fixed. It seems clear that not all of these elements are given to any economic growth process, at least not in any long-run analysis. There are interactions between these elements and other economic variables as some economists are well aware. However, for logical reasons we have to fix something in order to build a "believable" theory. In a "purely flowing world", no scientific analysis can be carried out. Economists choose different constraints to place upon their theories. In some sense, from a "purely" economic point of view, the way in which the fixed parameters have been chosen characterizes the theory. In what follows, we provide an example in order to explain the differences between neoclassical, neo-Marxian and the neo-Keynesian approaches to economic growth. The explanation is oversimplified, but it provides suggestions for further developments and improvements of our models. The following model is given by Marglin (1984).

Consider a simple product system which includes most of the fundamental variables involved in economic growth theory. Production is characterized by a one-commodity model in which corn is produced by means of a fixed coefficient technology in which the only inputs are seed corn and labour. The production relationship is

$$X = C + a_1 X_{+1},$$
(9.2.1)

where X represents the current corn output, C consumption from this year's harvest, X_{+1} output in the following year, and a_1 the requirements of seed corn per unit of corn harvest. It is assumed that wages W are paid at harvest time and that no profit accrues on this portion of the costs. The price formation equation is

$$P = Wa_0 + (1 + r)Pa_1, \tag{9.2.2}$$

where P is the price of this year's corn, r the rate of interest and a_0 is the labour requirement per bushel of corn output. This is obviously the simplest case of the systems presented in Section 3.4.

There are six unknowns in this system. Here, we are only interested in balanced growth paths where the rate of output growth, prices, wage rates and profit rates are all constant. We have: $X_+ = (1 + g)X$ where g is the rate of corn output growth. Treating C as consumption per worker rather than consumption in the aggregate and normalizing the system by $a_0 X = 1$ (where $a_0 = L/X$, L is employment) and $P = 1$, the system is reduced to

$$1 = a_0 C + a_1(1 + g), \quad 1 = Wa_0 + (1 + r)a_1. \tag{9.2.3}$$

The first equation represents a "growth-consumption frontier", while the second represents a dual "factor-price frontier" as shown in Fig. 9.2.1.

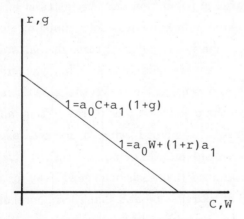

Fig. 9.2.1.

Growth-Consumption and Factor-Price Frontiers

However, this model is incomplete since the production equation and the price equation contain two unknowns, C and g, W and r, respectively. It can be seen that one of the two unknowns - the profit rate or the wage rate and the consumption rate or the growth rate - must be determined from outside this production model. In this sense, we consider eqs. (9.2.3) as accounting relationships rather than theories of distribution and growth. We have to add two independent relationships to complete the model. We now close the model according to the neoclassical, neo-Marxian, and neo-Keynesian approaches, respectively. In an oversimplified sense, we may say that in order to complete the model by specifying additional relationships (i) the neoclassical approach first determines g and C, and then r and W; (ii) the neo-Marxian approach determines W and C, and then r and g; and (iii) the neo-Keynesian approach determines r and g, and then W and C.

(a) The neoclassical approach

We are already aware of some characteristics of neoclassical theory from the standard neoclassical growth model in Section 2.1. In this model the desired accumulation of capital is determined by the lifetime utility maximization of households. The number of households is assumed to grow at a constant rate. The demand for employment is determined by accumulation and technology, while the supply is determined by the level of population and the tastes of households with respect to leisure and goods. Actual employment is determined by the interplay of demand and supply. The labour market is adjusted through real wages in such a way that full employment is always guaranteed. The economy arrives in equilibrium only when profit and wage rates make the growth rate of capital desired by households equal to the population growth rate. Thus, an exogenously given rate of population growth combined with household psychology and production technology determines the distribution of income.

For simplicity, it is assumed that each household lives for two periods - a period of work and a period of retirement - and that each household comes into the world naked and leaves the same way. All households are assumed to be identical in composition and preferences and each is assumed to allocate its corn wage ($P = 1$) between consumption in the two periods of its economic life (C_1 and

C_2). It is assumed that households maximize a "life-cycle" utility function of the form

$$U(C_1,C_2), \tag{9.2.4}$$

subject to the life-cycle budget constraint

$$C_1 + C_2/(1 + r) = W. \tag{9.2.5}$$

As W is also dependent on r as determined from (9.2.3), we thus can rewrite (9.2.5) as $C_1 + C_2/(1 + r) = W(r)$. The optimal solution defines the household's demand as a function of r alone, $(C_1(r), C_2(r))$.

The aggregate consumption demand in any one year is the sum of demands of overlapping generations of working households and retired households. If there is at present only one worker and production grows at the rate g, there must have been $1/(1 + g)$ workers in the last period. Accordingly, there must be $1/(1 + g)$ retired households today. Hence, the aggregate consumption demand is

$$C(r,g) = C_1(r) + C_2(r)/(1 + g). \tag{9.2.6}$$

On the other hand, the supply function determined from (9.2.3) is given by

$$C(g) = (1 - a_1)/a_0 - a_1 g/a_0. \tag{9.2.7}$$

From (9.2.3), (9.2.6) and (9.2.7), it can be easily shown that equality of consumption demand and supply $C(r,g) = C(g)$ is equivalent to

$$(r - g)C_2(r)/(1 + r)(1 + g) = (r - g)a_1/a_0,$$

or

$$r = g, \tag{9.2.8}$$

$$C_2(r)/(1 + r)(1 + g) = a_1/a_0. \tag{9.2.9}$$

We thus have two equilibrium conditions (9.2.8) and (9.2.9). We show that only (9.2.9) guarantees the balance of savings = investment.

Desired gross savings $S(r,g)$ is defined as the difference between perceived income Y and desired consumption $C(r,g)$: $S(r,g) = Y - C(r,g)$. Gross investment is the difference between gross output and consumption: $I(g) = X - C(g)$. Thus $C(r,g) = C(g)$ and $X = Y$ together imply that $S(r,g) = I(g)$. The problem is that X and Y are not necessarily equal. $X = 1/a_0$ and Y is the sum of perceived wages ($W(r) = (1-a_1)/a_0 - ra_1/a_0$) and perceived profits ($= C_2(r)/(1+r)$). We thus have that Y is equal to X iff (9.2.9) holds. This implies that (9.2.8) is not in general compatible with a savings = investment equilibrium.

(9.2.9) provides only one of the two relationships required to close the model. The other relationship is provided by the neoclassical theory of employment. According to the neoclassical approach, competitive labour markets guarantee full employment. As our focus is on an equilibrium path, full employment requires that the rate of the growth of output and employment g be equal to the rate of expansion of the labour force, which in neoclassical theory is an exogenously given population growth rate n, i.e.,

$$g = n. \tag{9.2.10}$$

There are four unknowns and four equations (9.2.3), (9.2.9) and (9.2.10). Thus the system is closed. Surely, the existence of equilibrium can be guaranteed only for a subset of possible technologies and utility functions. However, we will not investigate these conditions in detail here. The mechanism for determining neoclassical equilibrium is given in Fig. 9.2.2 in which $s(r)$ is defined as the net savings per bushel of seed corn: $s(r) = a_0 C_2(r)/a_1(1+r) - 1$, and r^* is the equilibrium value of r.

It should be noted that the only difference between the model reviewed here and the standard neoclassical growth model in Section 2.1 is that in this case we assume constant technology coefficients, while in the standard model continuous substitution is accepted. A model with continuous substitution may have substantially different behaviour from one with fixed coefficients, even though the models are based upon similar economic mechanisms. It can be shown that the neoclassical model reviewed here is unstable, while the standard model is globally stable. As we are only interested in the structures of different approaches, we will not analyse each theory in detail.

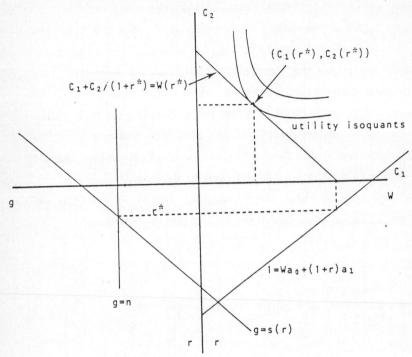

$$C_1 + C_2 / (1 + r^*) = W(r^*)$$

$(C_1(r^*), C_2(r^*))$

utility isoquants

C_1

W

g

c^*

$1 = W a_0 + (1 + r) a_1$

$g = n$

$g = s(r)$

r

Fig. 9.2.2.

Determination of Neoclassical Equilibrium

(b) The neo-Marxian approach

Next, we study the neo-Marxian approach. First, we must recognize that no mathematical economic model can explain all aspects of Marx's system. Moreover, if we only use the equilibrium approach to "explain" the system, it is potentially misleading since the approach is really dynamic. Nevertheless, one can formalize Marx's views on the determination of growth, distribution and prices in a capitalist system in terms of a steady-state model without doing substantial violence to the approach. We can also find an interpretation of Marx's system in terms of modern economic analysis in Morishima (1973).

The neo-Marxian theory classifies the population into capitalists and workers. It is assumed that capitalists have a higher saving propensity than do workers. Class power, technology and customs, determine the real wage rate and profit rate. The profit rate and capitalists' saving propensity normally determine the rate of growth. Thus, the class division is central to the determination of the real wage rate and capital accumulation. It is noted that the consumption preferences only determine the composition of output. In the neo-Marxian view, causality runs from distribution to growth, while in the neoclassical theory for a given natural rate of growth the distribution of income is accordingly determined. However, in the neo-Marxian theory the key assumption that allows the rate of growth to be determined within the model is that the labour supply is endogenous: the reserve army adjusts the supply of labour to demand.

Now, we consider how the incomplete system (9.2.3) can be closed. Subtracting one equation from the other in (9.2.3) directly yields

$$(W - C) = (g - r)a_1/a_0. \tag{9.2.11}$$

If all wages are consumed and all profits are saved, then

$$W = C. \tag{9.2.12}$$

We also have

$$g = s(r) = r, \tag{9.2.13}$$

where g and r belong to $[-1, r_m]$ and r_m is solved by setting $W = 0$ in (9.2.3).

In the neo-Marxian theory, the rate of profit or the rate of exploitation emerges from the labour theory of value. According to Marglin (1984, p. 57) exploitation is defined to occur whenever (i) a worker's annual production of corn exceeds the quantity of corn required for the replenishment of seed and his own subsistence, and (ii) workers do not exercise control over the disposition of surplus production. The labour theory of value assigns to every commodity a value defined by its "cost", measured by the labour time embodied in its production. The surplus value is thus defined as the difference between the value of a unit commodity and the value of the embodied labour power. The rate of exploitation is the rate of surplus value - i.e., the ratio of surplus value per worker to the value of the embodied labour power.

The concept of embodied labour power is very subtle. The labour power represented by a bushel of corn includes (i) the time spent its direct (living) labour content (e.g., planting, weeding and harvesting), (ii) the time spent producing the seed for this year's crop, and (iii) the time required last year for this year's seed, and the time required two years back to grow the seed for last year's seed and so forth. According to the definitions, we see that the labour time required this year is a_0, that required last year was a_0a_1, ... and t years back it was $a_0a_1^t$ (t = 0, 1, 2, ...). The sum of direct and indirect labor time is thus

$$a_0 + a_0a_1 + ... + a_0a_1^t + ...,$$

which for $a_0 < 1$ equals

$$T = a_0/(1 - a_1). \tag{9.2.14}$$

The value of one man-year of labor power, denoted by V_m, is measured by the amount of labour time required directly and indirectly to provide a single worker with the corn that makes up the subsistence wage W, i.e.,

$$V_m = TW. \tag{9.2.15}$$

The labour-time value of seed corn V_s is similarly given: a_1 bushels of corn embody

$$V_s = Ta_1, \tag{9.2.16}$$

man-years of labour time. The difference between the value of the corn a worker produces and the value of his maintenance and the seed he uses during one year is the surplus value per worker S:

$$S = T/a_0 - V_m - V_s/a_0, \tag{9.2.17}$$

where $1/a_0$ is the gross output per worker per year. From the price equation (9.2.3) and (9.2.15) to (9.2.17) one has

$$S = a_1 r/(1 - a_1), \tag{9.2.18}$$

which says that the surplus value per worker is equal to the capital:output ratio multiplied by the rate of profit. (9.2.18) also means that a positive surplus value and a positive profit go together. We can rewrite (9.2.18) as $r = S/c$ where c (= $a_1/(1-a_1)$) is constant capital per unit of output. It should be noted that the standard Marxian formula is $S/(c + V_m) = r$. The departure is due to the assumption that wages are paid at harvest time and hence do not form part of the "capital". The rate of exploitation is defined by

$$S_e = S/V_m = ra_1/Wa_0. \tag{9.2.19}$$

So the rate of exploitation is equal to the ratio of net profits to wages.

For Marx, a given rate of exploitation is the starting point from which the price equation is solved. For a given level of subsistence W^*, V_m and S are determined from (9.2.15) and (9.2.17), respectively. Substituting (9.2.19) into the price equation yields

$$r^* a_1/(1 - a_1) = S_e^*/(1 + S_e^*), \tag{9.2.20}$$

which determines the value of r. From (9.2.20) we can see that the labour theory of value becomes a theory of the profit share. As $g = r$, it is a theory of growth as well.

To see how the equilibrium is determined, the labour theory of value may be bypassed altogether since the whole system consists of

$$W = W^*, \quad g = s(r) = r, \quad 1 = a_0 C + a_1(1 + r),$$

$$1 = Wa_0 = (1 + r)a_1. \tag{9.2.21}$$

The system is closed. How the equilibrium can be determined is illustrated in Fig. 9.2.3.

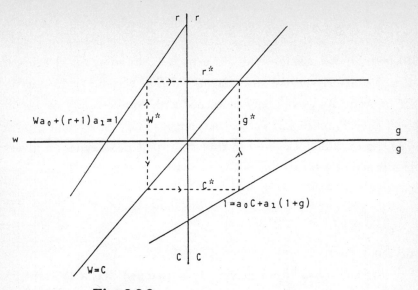

Fig. 9.2.3.

Determination of Neo-Marxian Equilibrium

(c) The neo-Keynesian approach

Some of the characteristics of the neo-Keynesian view are reflected in the Tobin model analyzed in Sections 9.2 and 9.3. The neo-Keynesian theory introduces investment demand, which is not dealt with in the neoclassical and neo-Marxian approaches. Investment demand is assumed to be positively related to the profitability of investment. Investment demand and the saving propensity of capitalist determine the equilibrium rates of profit and growth. The rate of profit, along with technology, determines the real wage. The rate of growth and the distribution of income are simultaneously determined.

The neo-Keynesian model is closed by an investment function interacting with a savings function. In the neo-Keynesian model the independent variable on which investment demand explicitly depends is neither a rate of interest representing a "cost of capital" (as for Keynes) nor the intensity of capital utilization (as for Harrod). It is the expected rate of profit - the prospective "quasi-rent" per unit of capital. Here, the expected rate of profit is to be understood as the probability distribution of outcomes. It is related to the degree of risk aversion of the business community. Thus, investment behavior depends on the psychology of the business community, its state of confidence or "animal spirits".

However, if we assume that the expected rate of profit is equal to the current rate, the neo-Keynesian investment function becomes a function of the current rate of profit. As we are only concerned with equilibrium, this assumption is quite acceptable. From (9.2.3) we see that output and employment grow at the same rate as the capital stock. We can thus represent neo-Keynesian investment demand as a function relating the rate of growth g to the rate of profit as

$$g = i(r), \qquad (9.2.22)$$

where $di/dr > 0$.

Now, we specify savings behavior. It is assumed that a constant fraction of aggregate output is saved. On a per worker basis savings are equal to $s(1 - a_1)/a_0$, where s is the fraction of income saved and $(1 - a_1)/a_0$ is the net output per worker. If savings intentions are realized, we should have savings = investment, i.e., $s(1-a_1)/a_0$
$= ga_1/a_0$, or

$$g = s(1 - a_1)/a_1. \qquad (9.2.23)$$

Thus the system is completed as follows

$$1 = a_0C + a_1(1 + g), \quad 1 = Wa_0 + (1 + r)a_1,$$

$$g = i(r), \quad g = s(1 - a_1)/a_1. \qquad (9.2.24)$$

Thus for exogenously given a_0, a_1, $g = i(r)$, the four unknowns g, r, W and c are determined (see Fig. 9.2.4).

(d) Some comments

We have introduced the mechanisms proposed by the neo-classical, neo-Marxian, and neo-keynesian approaches for closing the simple production model or the accounting equations (9.2.3). The review is oversimplified and it is limited to the one sector model. Different generalizations of the models just reviewed and various approaches to multiple sector models can also be found in Marglin (1984). In particular, the neo-Marxian theory is also investigated by Morishima (1973, 1977, 1989).

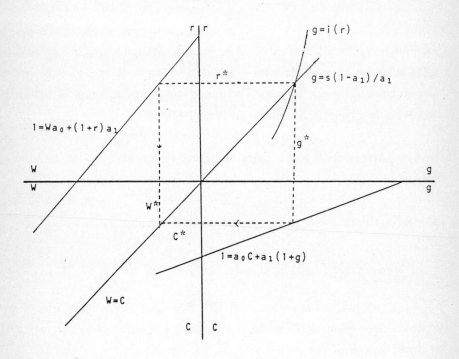

Fig. 9.2.4.
Determination of Neo-Keynesian Equilibrium

The theories described above can be appropriately introduced the models we reviewed and developed in the previous chapters. For instance, it is possible to introduce these mechanisms to close the model developed in Chapter 8.

APPENDIX
NONLINEAR DYNAMIC SYSTEM THEORY

Many important concepts and theorems in nonlinear dynamic theory are not to be found in standard textbooks of economics. Without striving for rigour, this appendix provides some of those most relevant to the matters under discussion in the present work. The reader may find many other applications of nonlinear dynamic analysis to dynamic economics in Zhang (1990).

A.1. Ordinary Differential Equations and Existence of Solutions

Consider the following ordinary differential equations

$$dx/dt = f(x,t), \quad (x,t) \; \varepsilon \; R^n x R^1, \tag{A.1.1}$$

where $f: U \dashrightarrow R^n$ with U an open set in $R^n x R^1$. Eqs. (A.1.1) are often referred as a **vector field**. The space of dependent variables x is often referred to as the **phase or state space** of the system (A.1.1).

The most essential problem is whether the equations have solutions for the given initial conditions. A mathematical model is meaningless if it has no solution under any conditions. In what follows we provide some conditions under which the existence of solutions can be guaranteed.

Suppose that f is C^r in U (note: by C^r, $r \geq 1$, we mean that f has r derivatives which are continuous at each point of U; C^0 means that f is continuous at each point of U) and for some $\delta_1, \delta_2 > 0$ let $I_1 = \{t \; \varepsilon \; R \; | \; t_0 - \delta_1 < t < t_0 + \delta_1\}$ and $I_2 = \{t \; \varepsilon \; R \; | \; t_0 - \delta_2 < t < t_0 + \delta_2\}$; then we have the following theorem.

Theorem A.1.1.
Let (x_0, t_0) be a point in U. Then for δ_1 sufficiently small there exists a solution of (A.1.1), $\phi_1: I_1 \dashrightarrow R^n$, satisfying $\phi_1(t_0) = x_0$. Moreover, if f is C^r in U, r $\geq$

1, and ϕ_2: $I_2 \longrightarrow R^n$ is also a solution of (A.1.1) satisfying $\phi_2(t_0) = x_0$, then $\phi_1(t) = \phi_2(t)$ for all $t \, \varepsilon \, I_3 = \{t \, \varepsilon \, R \mid t_0\text{-}\delta_3 < t < t_0\text{+}\delta_3\}$ where $\delta_3 = \min\{\delta_1,\delta_2\}$.

It should be mentioned that for a solution of (A.1.1) to exist, only continuity of f is required; however, in this case the solution passing through a given point in U may not be unique.

Theorem A.1.2.
If $f(x,t)$ is C^r in U, then the solution of (A.1.1), denoted by $\phi(t,t_0,x_0))$, (x_0,t_0) ε U, is also a C^r function of t, t_0 and x_0.

This theorem justifies the procedure of computing the Taylor series expansion of a solution of (A.1.1) about a given initial condition. This also enables one to determine the nature of solutions near a particular solution.

Theorem A.1.3.
Suppose $f(x,t)$ is C^r, $r \geq 1$, in U and let $\phi(t,t_0,x_0)$, (x_0,t_0) ε U, be a solution of (A.1.1). Then the nxn matrix $D_{x_0}\phi$ is the solution of the following linear ordinary differential equation

$$dZ/dt = D_x f(\phi(t)),t)Z, \quad Z(t_0) = I_{nxn}, \tag{A.1.2}$$

where Z is an nxn matrix.

Equation (A.1.2) is often referred to as the first variational equation.

We now consider the case that the dynamics of the economic variables are dependent upon some exogenous parameters such as tax policy and development of public infrastructures. That is, we consider f in (A.1.1) to be dependent on parameters

$$dx/dt = f(x,t,\delta), \quad (x,t,\delta) \, \varepsilon \, R^n x R^1 x R^p, \tag{A.1.3}$$

where f: U $\longrightarrow$ R^n with U an open set in $R^n x R^1 x R^p$. It is significant to know in what way the economic variables are dependent upon the initial conditions and exogenous parameters. The following theorem gives an answer.

Theorem A.1.4.

Suppose $f(x,t,\delta)$ is C^r in U. Then the solution of (A.1.3) $\phi(t,t_0,x_0,\delta)$ (t_0,x_0,δ) ϵ U, is a C^r function of δ.

A.2. Stability

It may be said that the concept of stability is the most essential concept in our approach to dynamic economics. In a sense, the most important contribution of this work is to explore dynamic behavior of economic systems which lose their stabilities when the systems are subjected to some exogenous influences. Traditional economics mainly deals with such economic phenomena which exhibit permanent stabilities. In this sense, we only extend the scope of traditional economics by allowing possibility of various instabilities.

We are still concerned with ordinary differential equations

$$dx_i/dt = f_i(x_1, x_2, ..., x_n,t),$$

or

$$dx/dt = f(x,t),$$ (A.2.1)

where $x = (x_1, ... , x_n)$, $f = (f_1, ... , f_n)$.

First, we define some common terminology that applies to solutions of the equations.

A solution $\phi(t,t_0,x_0)$ of (A.2.1) may also be called the **trajectory**, **phase curve** or **motion** through the point x_0.

The graph of the solution $\phi(t,t_0,x_0)$, i.e., $\{(x,t) \ \epsilon \ R^n x R^1 \ | \ x = \phi(t,t_0,x_0), t \ \epsilon \ I\}$ where I is some interval in R^1, is called an **integral curve**.

Definition A.2.1. (Lyapunov Stability)

(i) The point x_0 is called an **equilibrium point**, a **steady state**, or a **singular point** of (2.2.1) iff $f(x_0,t) = 0$ for all $t \geq 0$;

(ii) The equilibrium point $x_0 = 0$ is called **stable** iff small changes in the initial conditions lead only to small changes in the solutions. More precisely, for every $\varepsilon > 0$ there exists an $\delta(\varepsilon) > 0$ such that whenever $||x(0)|| < \delta(\varepsilon)$, then there exists exactly one solution $x(x(0),t)$ for (A.2.1) for all $t \geq 0$ and $||x(x(0),t)|| < \varepsilon$ for all $t \geq 0$;

(iii) The equilibrium point $x_0 = 0$ is **asymptotically stable** iff it is stable and there exists a number $\mu > 0$ such that $||x(0)||$ implies $x(x(0),t) \rightarrow 0$ as $t \rightarrow \infty$.

(iv) Let $y_0(t)$ be a solution of $dy/dt = g(y,t)$ for all $t \geq 0$. The stability of $y_0(t)$ is defined as follows. Set $y(t) = y_0(t) + x(t)$ where $x(0) = 0$. Then we get:

$$dx/dt = f(x,t), \tag{A.2.2}$$

where $f(x,t) = g(y_0 + x,t) - g(y_0,t)$ with $x_0 = 0$ an equilibrium point. We call $y_0(t)$ **stable** or **asymptotically stable** iff x_0 has this property with respect to the modified equation (A.2.2).

Consider the case that the function f is explicitly independent of time t. That is

$$dx/dt = f(x). \tag{A.2.3}$$

Assume that we can identify one or several steady-state points, x^*. The **Jacobian** of $f(x)$ at x^* is defined by:

$$J = [\partial f(x^*)/\partial x]_{nxn},$$

where the i-j element of the nxn matrix is defined as $\&f_i/\&x_j$. Eigenvalues σ of this matrix now satisfy

$$\det (J - \sigma I). \tag{A.2.4}$$

Hence, σ must satisfy a characteristic equation

$$\sigma^n + a_1 \sigma^{n-1} + ... + a_n = 0, \tag{A.2.5}$$

where a_i $(i = 1, ... , n)$ are real numbers determined from (A.2.4). Suppose that σ_i

are all known eigenvalues of the linearized system dX/dt = JX. We know that if one or more eigenvalues have positive real parts, the steady state x* will be unstable. It should be noted that fixed points of vector fields which have the property that the eigenvalues of the matrix associated with the linearization of the vector filed about the fixed point have nonzero real parts are called **hyperbolic** fixed points.

To guarantee that the steady state is stable, we need to ensure that all of eigenvalues have negative real parts. The following Routh-Hurwitz criteria provide the conditions of stability upon basis of the information involved in (A.2.5).

The Routh-Hurwitz Criteria

Given the characteristic equation (A.2.5), we define n matrices as follows:

$$H_1 = (a_1), \quad H_2 = \begin{bmatrix} a_1 & 1 \\ a_3 & a_2 \end{bmatrix} \qquad H_3 = \begin{bmatrix} a_1 & 1 & 0 \\ a_3 & a_2 & a_1 \\ a_5 & a_4 & a_3 \end{bmatrix}$$

$$H_j = \begin{bmatrix} a_1 & 1 & 0 & 0 & \dots & 0 \\ a_3 & a_2 & a_1 & 1 & \dots & 0 \\ \cdot & \cdot & \cdot & \cdot & \dots & \cdot \\ a_{2j-1} & a_{2j-2} & a_{2j-3} & a_{2j-4} & \dots & a_j \end{bmatrix}$$

$$\dots$$

$$H_n = \begin{bmatrix} a_1 & 1 & 0 & \dots & 0 \\ a_3 & a_2 & a_1 & \dots & 0 \\ \cdot & \cdot & \cdot & \dots & \cdot \\ 0 & 0 & 0 & \dots & a_n \end{bmatrix}$$

$$(A.2.7)$$

where the (p,q) term in the matrix H_j is

$$a_{2p-q} \quad \text{for } 0 < 2p - q < n, \quad 1 \text{ for } 2p = n,$$

$$0 \quad \text{for } 2p < q \quad \text{or} \quad 2p > n + p. \tag{A.2.8}$$

Then all eigenvalues have negative real parts; that is, the steady state x* is stable iff the determinants of all Hurwitz matrixes are positive:

$$\det H_j > 0, \quad j = 1, 2, \dots, n. \tag{A.2.9}$$

For instance, for $n = 2, 3, 4$, the Routh-Hurwitz criteria are given as:

$$n = 2, \quad a_1 > 0, \quad a_2 > 0; \tag{A.2.10}$$

$$n = 3, \quad a_1 > 0, \quad a_3 > 0, \quad a_1 a_2 > a_3; \tag{A.2.11}$$

$$n = 4, \quad a_1 > 0, \quad a_3 > 0, \quad a_4 > 0, \quad a_1 a_2 a_3 > a_3^2 + a_1^2 a_4. \tag{A.2.12}$$

We now consider another important theorem about stability of differential equations.

Consider a set of differential equations

$$dx/dt = Ax + f(x,t), \tag{A.2.13}$$

where f contains the terms about first order in x, and A is an $n \times n$ time-independent matrix.

Lyapunov Stability Theorem

Suppose that (i) All the eigenvalues of A have real parts; and (ii) The map $f: R^* x R \to R^n$ is locally Lipschit-continuous with respect to x and continuous with respect to t. If $f(0,t) = 0$ for all $t \geq 0$, then the equilibrium point $x = 0$ of (A.2.13) will be asymptotically stable whenever:

$$||f(x,t)|| / ||x|| \to 0, \quad \text{uniformly as } x \to 0 \text{ for all } t \geq 0.$$

It can be further proved that if the hypotheses (i) and (ii) in the Lyapunov stability theorem are satisfied, and suppose further that

$$||f(x,t)|| / ||x|| \to 0, \quad \text{uniformly as} \quad ||x|| \to \infty \quad \text{for all } t \geq 0,$$

and that f is p-periodic, i.e., $f(x,t+p) = f(x,t)$ for all (x,t), then (A.2.13) has a p-periodic solution.

The proofs of these results are given in Zeidler (1986, pp.87-91).

A.3. Linearization Principle and Its Valid Domain

Our key question is as follows. When do the solutions of the nonlinear system $dx/dt = Ax + F(x)$ $(F(0) = 0)$ and of the linearized system $dx/dt = Ax$ have the same qualitative behavior in a neighborhood of $x = 0$.

For simplicity, let us limit our discussion to a two-dimensional problem, i.e., $x \, \varepsilon \, R^2$. Let the eigenvalues of A be σ_1 and σ_2, respectively. We will call the point $x = 0$ **hyperbolic** iff the real parts of both σ_1 and σ_2 are not equal to zero.

As summarized in Zeidler (1986), we have the following answers to the question just made.

(i) If $Re(\sigma_1) < 0$ and $Re(\sigma_2) < 0$, the nonlinear system has the same asymptotic behavior at $x = 0$ as the linearized system.

(ii) If $x = 0$ is hyperbolic, then the solution curves of the nonlinear and the linearzied systems have the same qualitative behavior in a neighborhood of $x = 0$. Surely, (i) is a special case of the conclusion (ii).

(iii) Difficulties arise when $x = 0$ is nonhyperbolic points. In this case, a perturbation of the linear differential equation can fundamentally alter the qualitative behavior of the solutions. A centre, for instance, can develop into a stable or an unstable spiral point. Which of these cases occur depends on the nonlinear terms. Here the linearization principle fails. In Zhang (1990), I provide some examples of dynamic economic systems to show what may happen when a steady state is nonhyperbolic.

A.4. Limit Cycles in Two Dimension
- The Poincaré-Bendixson theory

Before presenting the main contents of the section, we explain some useful terms. Let us consider an ordinary differential equation

$$dx/dt = f(x), \quad x \, \varepsilon \, R^n. \tag{A.4.1}$$

A **periodic solution**, $\phi(t)$, of the equation (A.4.1) is a solution which is periodic in time, i.e., $\phi(t) = \phi(t+T)$ for some fixed positive T. T is called the **period** of $\phi(t)$. A **periodic orbit** of an ordinary differential equation is the orbit of any point through which a periodic solution passes.

Definition A.4.1.

A function

h: R^1 --> R^m

  t --> h(t)

is called **quasiperiodic** if it can be represented in the form

$$h(t) = H(w_1 t,...,w_m t), \qquad\qquad (A.4.2)$$

where $H(x_1,...,x_m)$ is a function of period 2π in x_1, ... , x_m. The real numbers w_1, ..., w_m are called the **basic frequencies**.

A **quasiperiodic solution**, $\phi(t)$, of the ordinary differential equation (A.4.1) is a solution which is quasiperiodic in time. A **quasiperiodic orbit** is the orbit of any point through which $\phi(t)$ passes. A quasiperiodic orbit may be interpreted geometrically as lying on an n dimensional torus. This can be seen as follows. Consider the equation: $y = H(x_1, ..., x_m)$. Then, if $n \geq m$ and $D_x H$ has rank for all $x = (x_1, ..., x_m)$, then this equation can be viewed as an embedding of an m-torus in n-space with x_1, ..., x_m serving as coordinates on the torus. Now, viewing h(t) as a solution of an ordinary differential equation, since $x_i = w_i t$, $i = 1$, ... , m, h(t) can be viewed as tracing a curve on the n-torus as t varies.

Periodic solutions are important for describing economic behavior since observed economic data exhibit time-dependent behavior. However, it is necessary for us to find more suitable descriptions of stable economic cycles since unstable cycles are impossible to be observed. We use the term of limit cycles, which in phase-plane plots are any simple oriented closed curve trajectories that do not contain steady points, to describe such economic oscillations. A limit cycle is closed so that a point moving along the curve will return to its starting position at fixed time intervals and thus execute periodic motion.

The distinction between a limit cycle and the cycles around a neutral centre is that the limit cycle represents the limiting behavior of adjacent trajectories; points nearby will approach the limit cycle either for t --> + ∞ or for t --> ∞. If the former case holds, the limit cycle is stable. Otherwise it is unstable.

In this section, we are only concerned with the existence of limit cycles in two dimension dynamic systems which can be written in the following form:

$$dx/dt = F(x,y), \quad dy/dt = G(x,y),$$ (A.4.3)

where F and G are continuous functions with continuous partial derivatives with respect to x and y so that a unique solution to (A.4.3) will exist for a given set of initial values (x_0, y_0).

The Poincaré-Bendixon theory is a cornerstone on which much of the theory of two-dimensional limit cycles rests. The theory consists of a few of important theorems as follows.

Theorem A.4.1. The Poincaré-Bendixson Theorem

For (A.4.3), if for t ≥ t_0 (t ≤ t_0) a trajectory is bounded and does not approach any singular point, then it is either a closed periodic orbit or approaches a closed periodic orbit for t --> ∞ (t --> - ∞).

The following theorems outline properties of a phase plane that are essentially equivalent to the Poincaré-Bendixon theorem and that serve equally well discovering periodic orbits.

Theorem A.4.2.

Suppose the direction field of the system of (A.4.3) has the following properties:

(a) There is a bounded region in the plane that contains a single repelling steady state and into which flow enters but from which it does not exit.

(b) There is a bounded region A in the plane into which flow enters but from which flow does not exit, and A contains no steady states of (A.4.3).

Then the system possesses a periodic solution.

Theorem A.4.3.

(a) If either of the regions described in theorem A.4.2 contains only a single periodic solution, that solution is a stable limit cycle.

(b) If L_1 and L_2 are two periodic orbits such that L_2 is in the interior of the region bounded by L_1 and no periodic orbits or critical points lie between L_1 and L_2, then one of the orbits must be unstable on the side facing the other orbit.

From those theorems, we see that if one can find a region in the x-y plane containing a single repelling steady state (i.e., unstable node or spiral) and show that the arrows along the boundary of the region never point outward, one may conclude that there must be at least one closed periodic trajectory inside the region.

The Poincaré-Bendixon theory prescribes the existence of a limit cycle in two equivalent cases: (a) Flow cannot leave some region D that contains an unstable node or focus; and (b) Flow is trapped inside an annular region A in the x-y plane.

According to Green's theorem, it can be easily shown that: (a) If D is a simply connected region of the plane, $\partial F/\partial x + \partial G/\partial y$ is not identically zero and does not change sign in D, then there are no closed orbits in this region; and (b) If D is a simply connected region in the plane and there exists a function of $B(x,y)$, continuously differentiable on D, such that the expression $\partial(BF)/\partial x + \partial(BG)/\partial y$ is not identically zero and does not change sign in D, then there are no closed orbits in this region. These results are useful in ruling out the presence of a limit cycle in the region D.

The result (a) just mentioned has an important implication. We may conclude that if (A.4.2) are linear in x and y, then the only possible oscillations are the neutrally stable ones. Hence, we cannot use linear systems to explain limit cycles. To understand this, let $F = ax + by$, $G = cx + dy$. Then, $F_x + G_y = a + d$. This is a constant and has a fixed sign. Thus only when $a + d = 0$ one may have oscillations. In this case, the equations would be $dx/dt = by$ and $dy/dt = dx$. Such equations have neutral cycles (not limit cycles), provided that b and d have opposite signs.

A.5. Bifurcations

The term bifurcation is broadly used to describe significant qualitative changes that occur in the orbit structure of a dynamic system as the parameters of the system are changed.

Consider a dynamic system

$$dx/dt = F(x,\mu) \tag{A.5.1}$$

where x and μ are vectors. An equilibrium of (A.5.1) is determined as a solution of

$$F(x,\mu) = 0. \tag{A.5.2}$$

If $F(x_0,\mu_0) = 0$, $F_x(x_0,\mu_0) =/ 0$, and F is a C^1-map in a neighborhood of (x_0,μ_0), then by the implicit function theorem (see, Takayama, 1985), the equation $F(x,\mu)$ can be solved uniquely for x in a neighborhood of (x_0,μ_0). On the other hand, if $F_x(x_0,\mu_0) = 0$, then it is possible that there is a bifurcation at (x_0,μ_0).

Bifurcation phenomenon play an important role in economics. They are closely connected to changes in the qualitative behavior of systems, and to changes in stability behavior. This concept is precisely defined as follows.

Definition A.5.1.

Let X belong to R^n. The point (x_0,μ_0) is called a **bifurcation point** of (A.5.2) iff

(i) $F(x_0,\mu_0) = 0$; and

(ii) for n = 1, 2, ... there are two sequences, $\{(x_n,\mu_n)\}$ and $\{(y_n,\mu_n)\}$, of solutions of (A.5.2), which converge to (x_0,μ_0) as n --> ∞. These are distinct sequences, i.e., $x_n =/y_n$ for all n.

The following result follows immediately from the implicit function theorem.

Proposition A.5.1. (Necessary Bifurcation Condition)

Let X and Y belong to R^n, and let F: $U(x_0,\mu_0)$ @ $R^n xR$
--> R^n be a C^1-map in a neighborhood of (x_0,μ_0). If (x_0,μ_0) is a bifurcation point of (A.5.2), then the inverse operator $F_x(x_0,\mu_0)^{-1}$ does not exist as a continuous linear operator on Y.

We now provide a few examples about bifurcations. First, consider **the fold bifurcation (or fold catastrophe or saddle-node bifurcation)**, in which a saddle-node pair of fixed points appear simultaneously as a single control parameter passes a threshold. The "normal form" of the bifurcation is given by

$$dx/dt = \mu - x^2. \tag{A.5.3}$$

For $\mu < 0$ all solutions diverge to x --> $-\infty$ as t --> ∞, while for $\mu > 0$ a pair of equilibria exist, one attracting and the other unstable. The unstable equilibrium is a repellor in the one-dimensional centre manifold, or a saddle if the full multi-dimensional phase space is considered. Decreasing μ from positive values, these two equilibria approach and annihilate each other at $\mu = 0$. Increasing μ from negative values, the saddle-node pair suddenly materialize "out of the blue".

The **transcritical bifurcation** occurs in the system

$$dx/dt = \mu x - x^2. \tag{A.5.4}$$

In this case, the μx term is of higher order than the simpler μ dependence of (A.5.3). Adding a term $- \delta$ to (A.5.4) will change the bifurcation from transcritical to fold, no matter how small δ is. This implies that the system is not structurally stable. In fact, the transcritical bifurcation is structurally stable within a restricted universe of dynamic systems in which fold catastrophes are prohibited by replacing the lowest-order transversality condition (non-zero coefficient of μ) with a higher-order condition (non-zero coefficient of μx).

A.6. Limit Cycles - The Hopf bifurcation theorem

Another important tool for establishing the existence of a limit-cycle trajectory is the Hopf bifurcation theorem. This theorem has been widely used in natural sciences and economics (e.g., Haken, 1977, 1983, Zhang, 1990).

The theorem predicts the appearance of a limit cycle about any steady state that undergoes a transition from a stable to an unstable focus as some parameter is varied. The result is local in the following sense: (i) It only holds for parameter values close to the bifurcation value; and (ii) the predicted limit cycle is close to the steady state.

Theorem A.6.1. (n = 2)
Consider a system of two equations that contains a parameter r:

$$dx/dt = f(x,y,r),$$

$$dy/dt = g(x,y,r), \tag{A.6.1}$$

where f and g are continuous functions with continuous partial derivatives with respect to x, y, and r. Suppose that for each value of r the equations admit a steady state whose value may depend on r, that is, $(x^*(r),y^*(r))$. Let the eigenvalues of the Jacobian at the steady state be $\sigma = a(r) \pm b(r)$. Also suppose that there is a value r^*, called the bifurcation value, such that $a(r^*) = 0$, $b(r^*) =/ 0$, and as r is varied through r^*, the real parts of the eigenvalues change sign ($da/dr =/ 0$ at $r = r^*$). Given these hypotheses, the following possibilities arise:

(i) At $r = r^*$ a centre is created at the steady state, and thus infinitely many neutrally stable concentric closed orbits surround the point (x^*,y^*);

(ii) There is a range of r values such that $r^* < r < c$ for which a single closed orbit surrounds (x^*, y^*). As r is varied, the diameter of the limit cycle changes in proportion to $|r - r^*|^{1/2}$. Since the limit cycle exists for r values above r^*, this phenomenon is known as a **supercritical bifurcation**.

(iii) There is a range of values such that $d < r < r^*$ for which a conclusion similar to case 2 holds. And this is termed as a **subcritical bifurcation**.

The following theorem provides conditions of stability of the bifurcated cycles in two-dimensional system.

Theorem A.6.2. (Conditions of Stability)

For (A.6.1), it may assumed that for $r = r^*$ the Jacobian matrix is of the form:

$$J = \begin{bmatrix} 0 & 1 \\ -b & 0 \end{bmatrix}$$

In this case the eigenvalues at the critical point are $\sigma_1 = bi$ and $\sigma_2 = -bi$. Let us define a real number V as:

$$V''' = 3\pi(f_{xxx} + f_{xyy} + g_{xxy} + g_{yyy})/4b$$

$$+ 3\pi[f_{xy}(f_{xx} + f_{yy}) + g_{xy}(g_{xx} + g_{yy}) + f_{xx}g_{xx} - f_{yy}g_{yy}].$$

Then one has: (i) If $V''' < 0$, then the limit cycle occurs for $r > r^*$ and is stable; (ii) If $V''' > 0$, the limit cycle occurs for $r < r^*$ and is unstable; and (iii) If $V''' = 0$, the test is inconclusive.

The two theorems and the following example can be found in Marsden and McCracken (1976).

Consider the system of equations:

$$dx/dt = y = f(x,y,r),$$

$$dy/dt = -y^3 + ry - x = g(x,y,r). \tag{A.6.2}$$

The only steady state occurs when $x = y = 0$. The eigenvalues at this point are:

$$\sigma = r/2 \pm (r^2 - 4)^{1/2}/2. \tag{A.6.3}$$

The bifurcation value is thus given by $r = 0$ at which $\sigma = \pm i$ and $da/dr =/ 0$. The Hopf bifurcation theorem therefore applies. There is a limit cycle in the system. As

$$V''' = - 9\pi/2 < 0,$$

the limit cycle is supercritical and stable.

It should be noted that for the case of $n > 2$ the Hopf Bifurcation Theorem is still valid. Consider a system of n equations in n variables

$$dx/dt = F(x,r), \tag{A.6.4}$$

where $x = (x_1, ... , x_n)$, $F = (F_1(x,r), ... , F_n(x,r))$ with the appropriate smoothness assumptions on F_i which are functions of the variables and a parameter r. If x_0 is a steady state of this system and linearization about this point yields n eigenvalues

$$\sigma_1, ... , \sigma_{n-2}, a + bi, a - bi, \tag{A.6.5}$$

where eigenvalues σ_i ($i = 1, ... , n - 2$) have negative real parts and σ_{n-1} and σ_n (precisely these two) are complex conjugates that cross the imaginary axis when r varies through some critical value, then the theorem still predicts limit cycles.

A.7. Maps

We are now concerned with a discrete time system or map.

A **C^r map** of some open set U @/ R^n into R^n is denoted as follows

$$f: U \longrightarrow R^n$$
$$x \longrightarrow f(x), \quad x \, \varepsilon \, U, \tag{A.7.1}$$

with $f \, \varepsilon \, C^r$ in U. The dynamics of f means the nature of the iterates of points in U under d. For a point $x \, \varepsilon \, U$, equivalent notations for the nth iterate of x under f are

$$f(f(...(f(x))...)) \equiv f^n(x). \tag{A.7.2}$$

By the **orbit of x under f** we mean the following bi-infinite sequence if f is invertible

$$\{..., f^n, ... , f^1, x, f(x), ..., f^n(x), ...\}$$

and the following infinite sequence if f is noninvertible

$$\{x, f(x), ... , f^n(x), ... \}.$$

It should be noted that orbits of ordinary differential equations are curves and orbits of maps are discrete sets of points.

Definition A.7.1.

A point x^* in the phase space of a map $x \longrightarrow f(x)$ is called a **fixed point** (**equilibrium point, stationary point, steady point, rest point, singular point,** or **critical point**) if $x^* = f(x^*)$.

A period k point, x^*, of a map is a point such that $f^k(x^*) = x^*$. The **orbit of a period k** point is a sequence of k distinct points $\{x^*, f(x^*), ..., f^{k-1}\}$ and the orbit is called **a periodic orbit of period k.**

Definition A.7.2.

A point x (ε U) is said to be Lyapunov stable, or **stable**, if given $\delta > 0$ we can find a $\mu = \mu(\delta) > 0$ such that for any other y (ε U) with $|x - y| < \mu$ then we have $|f^n(x) - f^n(y)| < \delta$ for $n > 0$. If x is not stable then it is said to be **unstable**.

A point x is said to be asymptotically stable if it is Lyapunov stable and there exists $\delta^* > 0$ such that if $|x - y| < \delta^*$, then $\lim |f^n(x) - f^n(y)| = 0$ as $n \longrightarrow \infty$.

Let p be a period k point of f, i.e., the orbit of p under f is given by

$$O(p) =$$

$$\{p, p_1 \equiv f(p), ... , p_{k-1} \equiv f^{k-1}(p), p_k \equiv f^k(p) = p\}.$$

We ask whether or not $O(p)$ is stable. As p_i ($i = 1, ... , k$) is a fixed point for $f^k(x)$

and $Df^k(x) = Df(f^{k-1}(x))Df(f^{k-2}(x)) \ldots Df(x)$, stability of $O(p)$ is reduced to the question of the stability of a fixed point p_i for any $i = 1, \ldots, k$ of $f^k(x)$.

Consider the map

$$x \longrightarrow f^k(x), \quad x \in R^n, \tag{A.7.3}$$

which has fixed points of p_i, $i = 1, \ldots, k$. Following an argument similar to that given for ordinary differential equations we consider the associated linear map

$$y \longrightarrow Df^k(p_i)y, \quad y \in R^n, \quad i = 1, \ldots, k, \tag{A.7.4}$$

which has a fixed point at $y = 0$. We have the following result.

Theorem A.7.1.

Suppose that p be a period k point for (A.7.3) and Df^k has no eigenvalues of modulus one. Then asymptotic stability (or instability) of the fixed point $y = 0$ of (A.7.3) corresponds to asymptotic stability (or instability) of $O(p)$.

The proof can be found, for instance, in Hartman (1964).

A.8. Chaos

The discovery of chaos in a relatively simple dynamic system shows us how much we have missed by traditional dynamic analysis. Chaos theory has been stimulated and sustained by important and exciting new applications that have multiplied throughout the biological, ecological, social and economic sciences, not to say the traditional fields of mechanics, physics, and chemistry. Chaos theory has indeed deepened our thinking about evolution of the Nature and society.

There are a large amount of literature on chaos. Mathematicians have recently made great efforts to exploring the complexity of dynamic systems which may exhibit chaotic behavior. It may be said that almost all advanced mathematics are involved in chaos literature. As chaos theory involves too many sophisticated mathematical techniques and concepts, it is beyond scope of this book to explore the theory in detail. Hence, we only explore some aspects of chaos theory.

In this study the word of chaos in its technical sense refers to irregular motion that is generated by nonlinear systems whose dynamic laws uniquely determine the time evolution of a state of the system from a knowledge of its previous history. We are especially concerned with chaos which occur in deterministic nonlinear systems. Here, by "deterministic motion" we mean that there exists a prescription, either in terms of differential or difference equations, for calculating its future behavior from given initial conditions.

It should be emphasized that there is no generally accepted definition of chaos and in the literature chaos is often referred in the context of dissipative system as the phenomena related to the occurrence of randomness and unpredictability in completely deterministic systems, which have been called "dynamical stochasticity", "deterministic chaos", "self-generated noise", "intrinsic stochasticity, "Hamiltonian stochasticity".

We refer to chaos as irregular motion stemming from deterministic equations. A difficulty rests in how to measure "irregular motion".It is desirable to develop criteria to distinguish regular such as quasiperiodic motion from chaos. The next section will introduce some measures to detect existence of chaotic behavior.

There are different kinds of time-dependent behavior, such as periodic solutions and quasi-periodic motion, in dynamic systems. Irrespective of their complicated appearance, these behavior are "regular" in the sense that there are some fixed patterns for the system to follow. Chaos would be really "irregular" according to its definition. Hence, it is essentially important for us to design some index to distinguish regular behavior and irregular motion of dynamic systems. In what follows, we discuss some important index.

(a) The Lyapunov exponents for differential equations

We now consider the following nonlinear equation

$$dx/dt = F(x), \tag{A.8.1}$$

where F is a nonlinear vector function of x. Let $x_0(t)$ be a solution of (A.8.1). Introducing $x(t) = x_0(t) + X(t)$, we obtain the linearized equations

$$dX(t)/dt = L(x_0(t))X(t), \tag{A.8.2}$$

where $L(x_0(t)) = (F_i(x_0(t))/ x_j)_{nm}$. The Lyapunov exponents are defined by

$$z = \lim_{t \to \infty} \sup \frac{1}{t} \ln |X(t)| , \tag{A.8.3}$$

It can be shown that depending on different initial values of X(t) at $t = t_0$, different Lyapunov exponents may exist, but not more than n different ones. The following theorem can be found in, for instance, Haken (1983).

Theorem A.8.1.

At least one Lyapunov exponent vanishes if the trajectory x(t) of an autonomous system remains in a bounded region for $t \to \infty$ and does not contain a fixed point.

It should be emphasized that the Lyapunov exponents are a special case of the "generalized characteristic exponents". We know that if all the generalized characteristic exponents are negative, then the differential system is stable.

The Lyapunov exponents can be used to help us distinguish between different kinds of attractors. For instance, in one dimension, there are only stable fixed points, for which the Lyapunov exponents z are negative. In two dimensions, the only two possible classes of attractors are stable fixed points and limit cycles. For a fixed stable point, the two Lyapunov exponents (which may coincide) are negative. For a limit cycle, $(z_1, z_2) = (-, 0)$. In three dimensions, we have some typical cases as follows

$(z_1, z_2, z_3) = (-, -, -)$ for stable fixed point,

$(z_1, z_2, z_3) = (0, -, -)$ for stable limit cycle,

$(z_1, z_2, z_3) = (-, 0, 0)$ for stable torus.

$(z_1, z_2, z_3) = (+, 0, -)$ for strange attractor.

If one Lyapunov exponent is positive, chaos may appear. Since in a chaotic attractor at least one Lyapunov exponent is positive, neighboring trajectories depart very quickly from each other. For instance $(z_1, z_2, z_3) = (+, 0, 0)$ may mean that we are dealing with an unstable torus. If an attractor possesses the exponents $(z_1, z_2, z_3) = (+, 0, -)$, it is considered as a chaotic attractor. It should be emphasized that we have still little knowledge about what Lyapunov exponents mean for attractors and how they can be determined.

(b) The Lyapunov exponents for discrete maps

Consider a discrete map of the form

$$x_{n+1} = f(x_n), \tag{A.8.4}$$

where x_n, $n = 1, 2, \ldots$ are vectors in an M-dimensional space. For a discrete map, the trajectory consists of the sequence of points x_n, $n = 0, 1, \ldots$. We denote the trajectory in the neighborhood of which we wish to study, by x^0_n. Let

$$x_n = x^0_n + X_n, \tag{A.8.5}$$

where x_n and x^0_n satisfy (A.8.4) and X_n are small perturbations. Substituting (A.8.5) into (A.8.4), we get the linearized system

$$X_{n+1} = L(x^0_n)X_n, \tag{A.8.6}$$

where $L(x^0_n) = (f_k(x)/x_j)$ at $x = x^0_n$. This equation may be solved by iteration. We have $X_n = L(x^0_{n-1})L(x^0_{n-2}) \ldots L(x^0_0)X_0$. The Lyapunov exponents are defined by

$$z = \lim_{n \to \infty} \sup \frac{1}{n} \ln|X_n| . \tag{A8.7}$$

Depending on different directions of X_0, we may have different z.

(c) The signal, power spectrum, autocorrelation function and Poincaré map

Now we mention some other possible criteria for chaotic motion. To distinguish between multiply periodic behavior (which can also look rather complicated) and chaos, it is often convenient to Fourier-transform the variable $x(t)$:

$$x(w) = \lim_{T \to \infty} \int_0^T x(t)\exp(iwt)dt . \tag{A.8.8}$$

For multiply periodic motion, the power spectrum $P(w) = |x(w)|^2$ consists only of discrete lines of the corresponding frequencies, whereas chaotic motion (which is completely aperiodic) is indicated by broad noise in $P(w)$ that is mostly located at low frequencies.

To detect chaos, we may also define the change in the autocorrelation function

$$C(v) = \lim_{T \to \infty} 1/T \int_0^T c(t)c(t+v)dt \qquad (A.8.9)$$

where

$$c(t) = x(t) - \lim_{T \to \infty} 1/T \int_0^T x(t)dt.$$

This function remains constant or oscillates for regular motion and decays rapidly if x(t) become uncorrelated in the chaotic regime. It should be mentioned that P(w) and C(v) contain the same information.

A.9 The Logistic Map
- An example of chaos

An important implication of existence of chaos in dynamic systems is that interactions, even simple enough, among various economic variables, can result in very complicated consequences which are beyond our ability to forecast. The following example provides a suitable example of this idea.

Consider the following map discrete logistic map

$$x_{n+1} = \mu x_n(1 - x_n). \qquad (A.9.1)$$

Its behavior is well investigated in the literature. In what follows, we will only discuss the case of $\mu > 1$.

We now examine behavior of equation (A.9.1). Steady states are computed by setting $x^* = \mu x^*(1 - x^*)$. The equation has two steady states, 0 and $1 - 1/\mu$. Let us examine the nontrivial one: $x^* = 1 - 1/\mu$. As μ is greater than unity, the nontrivial fixed point is always positive. The steady state will be stable whenever $|2 - \mu| < 1$, or $1 < \mu < 3$.

As μ increases slightly beyond 3, stable oscillations of period 2 appear. The period 2 oscillations simultaneously satisfy two equations: $x_{n+1} = f(x_n)$, $x_{n+2} = x_n$. As $x_{n+2} = f(f(x_n))$, we may rewrite (A.9.1) as

$$x_{m+1} = g(x_m), \qquad (A.9.2)$$

where $m = n/2$, n is even, $g(x_m) = f(f(x_m))$. The two-point cycles are fixed points of g, where

$$g(x) = \mu^2 x(1 - x)[1 - \mu x(1 - x)]. \tag{A.9.3}$$

The fixed points of g are given by: $x = g(x)$, which has the following solutions:

$$x^* = 1 - 1/\mu,$$

$$x^*_{1,2} = (\mu + 1)/2\mu \pm \{(\mu - 3)(\mu + 1)\}^{1/2}/2\mu.$$

It should be noted that x^* is unstable for our case.

The solution oscillates between two fixed values, denoted by x^*_1 and x^*_2, respectively. The two possible steady states $x^*_{1,2}$ are real if $\mu < -1$ or $\mu > 3$. As we are only concerned with $\mu > 0$, steady states of $g(x_m)$ exist only when $\mu > 3$. The two-period cycle is stable iff $|f_x(x^*_1)f_x(x^*_2)| < 1$. It can be shown that for $3 < \mu < \mu_2$, where μ_2 is approximately equal to 3.3, the cycle is stable.

Beyond μ_2, further bifurcations occur. It can be seen that the fixed points of f^2 also become unstable. Because the derivative is the same at x^*_1 and x^*_2

$$f^{2\prime}(x^*_1) = f'[f(x^*_1)]f'(x^*_1) = f'(x^*_2)f'(x^*_1) = f^{2\prime}(x^*_2),$$

they even become unstable simultaneously. Fig. A.9.1 shows that after this instability the forth iterate $f^4 = f^2 \cdot f^2$ displays two more pitchfork bifurcations which lead to an attractor of period four. In fact, these two examples of bifurcation can be generalized as follows: (i) For $\mu_{n-1} < \mu < \mu_n$, there exists a stable 2^{n-1}-cycle with elements $x^*_0, x^*_1, ..., x^*_{2n-1}$ that is characterized by

$$f(x^{*i}) = x^*_{i+1}, \qquad f^{2n-1}(x^{*i}) = x^*_{i+1},$$

$$|df^{2n-1}(x^{*0})/d^*_0| = |\cap_i f'(x^{*i})| < 1; \tag{A.9.4}$$

and (ii) At μ_n, all points of the 2^{n-1}-cycle become unstable simultaneously via pitchfork bifurcations on $f^{2n} = f^n \cdot f^n$ that, for $\mu_n < \mu < \mu_{n+1}$, lead to a new stable 2^n-cycle.

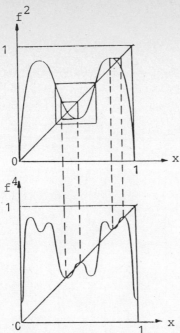

Fig. A.9.1. Generation of an Attractor of Period 4

When the parameter μ is near 3.83 (denoted by μ_∞), a solution of period 3 appears. Li and Yorke (1975) proved that period 3 orbits were harbingers of chaos. This is a solution that appears to undergo large random fluctuations with no inherent periodity or order whatever.

A "bifurcation regime" is defined for $1 < \mu < \mu_\infty$, where the Lyapunov exponent is always negative (it becomes only zero at the bifurcation points r_n). A "chaotic regime" is defined for $\mu_\infty < \mu \leq 4$, where the Lyapunov is mostly positive. The chaotic regime is interrupted by "μ-windows" with the Lyapunov exponent negative where the sequence $\{f^n(x_0)\}$ is again periodic (see May, 1976).

It has been numerically identified that (1) In the periodic regime, a) the values μ_n, where the number of fixed points changes from 2^{n-1} to 2^n, scale like $\mu_n = \mu_\infty - \text{const.}\delta^n$ for $n \gg 1$ where $\delta \approx 4.6692$; and b) the distance d_n of the point in a 2^n-cycle that are closest to $x = 1/2$ have constant ratios: $d_n/d_{n+1} = -\alpha$ for $n \gg 1$ where $\alpha \approx 2.5029$; (2) In the Chaotic regime, a) the chaotic intervals move together by inverse bifurcations until the iterates become distributed over the whole interval [0,1] at $\mu = 4$; b) The μ-windows are characterized by periodic p-cycles (p = 3, 5, 6, ...) with successive bifurcations, p, p.2, p.2^2 etc; and c) Period tripling $p.3^n$ and quadrupling $p.4^n$, etc. occur ar $\mu' = \mu'_\infty$ - const. δ'^{-n} with different Feigenbaum constants δ'. These results can be found, for instance, in Schuster (1988).

The correspondence between the behavior of the map and the Lyapunov exponent z is shown in Fig. A.9.2.

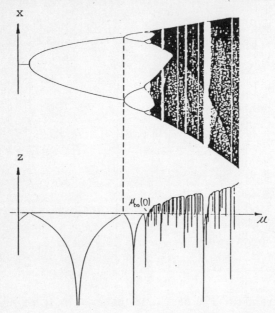

Fig. A.9.2. The Logistic Map x and the Lyapunov Exponent

The above example illustrates how a simple dynamic system may cause very complicated behavior.

REFERENCES

Alchian, A.A. (1963) Reliability of Progress Curve in Airframe Production. Econometrica XXXI, 679-93.

Andersson, Å.E. (1968) From Interest and Prices to Capital and Growth. Swedish Journal of Economics, No. 4, 221-241.

Andersson, Å.E. (1987) Creativity and Economic Dynamics Modelling. In "Economic Evolution and Structural Adjustment" Edited by D. Batten, J. Casti and B. Johansson, Springer-Verlag.

Andersson, Å.E. and Zhang, W.B. (1988) The Two Dimensional Continuous Spatial Input-Output System. Ricerche Economiche XLII, 2.

Andersson, Å.E. and Zhang, W.B. (1988a) Decision Centralization and Decentralization in a Dynamic Economic System. Journal of Computational and Applied Mathematics 22, 317-337.

Andersson, Å.E. and Zhang, W.B. (1989) Endogenous Technology and Economic Growth in a Dynamic Multisector System (mimeo).

Andersson, Å.E. and Zhang, W.B. (1990) Endogenous Technological Changes and Economic Growth. (to appear).

Arrow, K.J. (1962) The Economic Implications of Learning by Doing. Review of Economic Studies 24, 155-73.

Arrow, K.J. and Hahn, F.H. (1971) General Competitive Analysis. Holden-Day, San Francisco.

Batten, D.F. (1982) The Interregional Linkages Between National and Regional Input-Output Analysis. International Regional Science Review 7, 53-68.

Becker, G. (1975) Human Capital, 2nd. New York: National Bureau of Economic Research.

Becker, G. (1981) A Treatise on the Family. Harvard University Press, Cambridge, Mass.

Becker, G. (1988) Family Economics and Macro Behavior. The American Economic Review 78, 1-13.

Benhabib, J. and Miyao, T. (1981) Some New Results of the Dynamics of the Generalized Tobin Model. International Economic Review 22, 589-596.

Bidard, C. and Hosoda, E. (1987) On Consumption Baskets in a Generalized von Neumann Model. International Economic Review 28, 509-519.

Blackhouse, R. (1985) A History of Modern Economic Analysis. Basil Blackwell.

Blinder, A.S. and Weiss, Y. (1976) Human Capital and Labour Supply: A Synthesis. Journal of Political Economy 84, 449-472.

Brody, A. (1970) Proportions, Prices and Planning, A Mathematical Restatement of the Labour Theory of Value. North-Holland Publishing Company, Amsterdam.

Burmeister, E. (1980) Capital Theory and Dynamics. Cambridge University Press.

Burmeister, E. and Dobell, A.R. (1970) Mathematical Theories of Economic Growth. New York: Macmillan.

Cagan, P. (1956) The Monetary Dynamics of Hyperinflation. In M. Friedman (ed.), Studies in the Quantity Theory of Money, Chicago: University Press.

Cigno, A. (1981) Growth with Exhaustible Resources and Endogenous Population. Review of Economic Studies XLVIII, 281-287.

Cigno, A. (1986) Fertility and the Tax-Benefit System. Economic Journal 96, 1035-1051.

Cigno, A. and Zhang, W.B. (1988) Long Waves in Economic Activity. Paper to the European Economic Association Congress, Bologna, 27-29 August 1988.

Corden, W.M. (1966) The Two Sector Growth Model with Fixed Coefficients. Review of Economic Studies XXXIII, 253-263.

Diamond, P.A. (1965) Disembodied Technical Change in a Two-Sector Model. Review of Economic Studies XXXII, 161-68.

Domar, E.D. (1946) Capital Expansion, Rate of Growth, and Employment. Econometrica 14, 137-147.

Domar, E.D. (1951) Essays in the Theory of Economic Growth. New York: Oxford University Press.

Domar, E.D. (1957) Essays in the Theory of Economic Growth. Oxford University Press, Oxford.

Dorfman, R., Samuelson, P.A., and Slow, R.M. (1958) Linear Programming and Economic Analysis. New York: McGraw-Hill.

Drandakis, E. (1963) Factor Substitution in the Two-Sector Growth Model. Review of Economic Studies XXX, 105-118.

Drandakis, E. and Phelps, E.S. (1966) A Model of Induced Invention, Growth and Distribution. Economic Journal LXXVI, 823-40.

Eckaus, R.S. (1963) Investment in Human Capital: A Comment. Journal of Political Economy 71, 501-504.

Fisher, I. (1911) The Purchasing Power of Money. New York.

Friedman, M. (1956) The Quantity Theory of Money: A Restatement. In "Studies in the Quantity Theory of Money, edited by M. Friedman, Chicago: University of Chicago Press.

Ghez, G. and Becker, G. (1975) The Allocation of Time and Goods Over the Life Cycle. New York: National Bureau of Economic Research.

Grandmont, J.M. (1985) On Endogenous Competitive Business Cycles. Econometrica 53, 535-572.

Hadjimichalakis, M. (1971a) Money, Expectations, and Dynamics - An Alternative View. International Economic Review 12, 381-402.

Hadjimichalakis, M. (1971b) Equilibrium and Disequilibriuum Growth with Money - The Tobin Models. Review of Economic Studies 38, 457-479.

Hahn, F. (1969) On Money and Growth. Journal of Money, Credit and Banking I, 172-187.

Hahn, F. (1982) Stability. In "Handbook of Mathematical Economics, Vol. 2., edited by Arrow, K.J. and Intriligator, M.D., North-Holland, Amsterdam.

Haken, H. (1977) Synergetics: An Introduction. Springer, Berlin.

Haken, H. (1983) Advanced Synergetics. Springer, Berlin.

Harrod, R.F. (1948) Toward a Dynamic Economics. Macmillan, London.

Harrod, R.F. (1956) Towards a Dynamic Economics: Some Recent Developments of Economic Theory and Their Application to Policy. London, Macmillan & Co Ltd.

Harrod, R. F. (1973) Economic Dynamics. London: Macmillan.

Hartman, P. (1964) Ordinary Differential Equations. Wiley: New York.

Heckman, J.J. (1976) A Life-Cycle Model of Earnings and Consumption. Journal of Political Economy 84, 11-44.

Hicks, J. (1965) Capital and Growth. Oxford University Press.

Hume, D. (1752) Essays "Of Money", "Of Interest" and "Of the Balance of Trade" in Hume's Writings on Economics, ed. E. Rotwein, 1955. Edinburgh.

Inada, K. (1966) Investment in Fixed Capital and the Stability of Growth Equilibrium. Review of Economic Studies XXXII, 19-30.

Iooss, G. and Joseph, D.D. (1980) Elementary Stability and Bifurcation Theory. New York: Springer-Verlag.

Isard, W. (1953) Some Empirical Results and Problems of Regional Input-Output Analysis. In Leontief, W. (1953).

Johansson, B. and Persson, H. (1983) Dynamics of Capital Formation, Capacity Constraints and Trade Patterns in a Multisectoral Model. IIASA PP-83-3, International Institute for Applied Systems Analysis, A-2361 Laxenburg, Austria.

Johnson, H.G. (1962) Monetary Theory and Policy. American Economic Review 52, 335-384.

Kac, M. (1969) Some Mathematical Models in Science. Science, 166.

Keynes, J.M. (1936) The General Theory of Employment, Interest and Money. London: Macmillan & Co. Ltd.

Kennedy, C. (1964) Induced Bias in Innovation and the Theory of Distribution. Economic Journal LXXIV, Sept.

Kennedy, C. (1966) Keynesian Theory in an Open Economy. Social and Economic Studies 15, 1-21.

Killingsworth, M.R. (1982) "Learning by Doing" and "Investment in Training": A Synthesis of Two "Rival" Models of the Life Cycle. Review of Economic Studies XLIX, 236-271.

Koopmans, T. (1965) On the Concept of Optimal Growth. In "The Econometric Approach to Development Planning." Chicago: Rand McNally, 225-287.

Laidler, D. (1981) Monetarism: An Interpretation and an Assessment. The Economic Journal 91, 1-28.

Leontief, W.W. (1947) Introduction to a Theory of the Internal Structure of Functional Relationships. Econometrica XV, 361-373.

Leontief, W.W. (1949) The Structure of American Economy, 1919-1939. Oxford University Press, London and New York.

Leontief, W.W. ed. (1953) Studies in the Structure of American Economy. New York, Oxford University Press.

Leontief, W.W. and Strout, A. (1963) Multisectoral Input-Output Analysis. In "Structural Interdependence and Economic Development", edited by T. Barna, London: St. Martin's Press.

Leontief, W.W. (1966) Input-Output Economics, Oxford University Press. London and New York.

Levhari, D. (1965) A Nonsubstitution Theorem and Switching of Techniques. Quarterly Journal of Economics LXXIX, 98-105.

Levhari, D. and Patinkin, D. (1968) The Role of Money in a Simple Growth Model. American Economic Review LVIII, 713-753.

Lewis, W.A. (1955) The Theory of Economic Growth. Geoge Allen & Unwin Ltd.

Li, T.Y. and Yorke, Y. (1975) Period Three Implies Chaos. American Mathematical Monthly 82, 985-992.

Marglin, S.A. (1984) Growth, Distribution, and Prices. Harvard University Press, Cambridge, Mass.

Marsden, J.E. and McCracken, M. (1976) The Hopf Bifurcation and Its Applications. New York: Springer-Verlag.

Menger, C. (1892) On the Origin of Money. Economic Journal.

Malthus, T.R. (1933) An Essay on Population. London: J.D. Deut.

Marshall, A. (1890) Principles of Economics 8th edn, 1920; variorum edition, ed. C. W. Guillebaud, 1961. London: Macmillan.

Marx, K. (1867-1894) Capital, 3 vols. Translated by S. Moore and E. Aveling. London: Lawrence and Wishart.

May, R.M. (1976) Simple Mathematical Models with Very Complicated Dynamics. Nature 261, 459-46.

Menger, C. (1871) Principles of Economics. Translated by J. Dingwall and B.F. Hoselitz, 1950. Glencoe, Ill.

Mill, J.S. (1848) Principles of Political Economy.

Morishima, M. (1958) Prices, Interest and Profits in a Dynamic Leontief System. Econometrica 26, 358-380.

Morishima, M. (1960) Economic Expansion and the Interest Rate in Generalized von Neumann Models. Econometrica 28, 352-363.

Morishima, M. (1964) Equilibrium Stability and Growth - A Multi-sectoral Analysis. Oxford University Press.

Morishima, M. (1969) Theory of Economic Growth. Oxford: Clarendon Press.

Morishima, M. (1973) Marx's Economics - A Dual Theory of Value and Growth. Cambridge University Press.

Morishima, M. (1977) Walras' Economics - A pure theory of capital and money. Cambridge University Press.

Morishima, M. (1982) Why Has Japan "Succeeded"? - Western Technology and the Japanese Ethos. Cambridge University Press.

Morishima, M. (1989) Ricardo's Economics - A General Equilibrium Theory of Distribution and Growth. Cambridge University Press.

von Neumann, J. (1937) Ueber ein Dekonomisches Gleichungsystem und eine Verallgemeinerung des Browerischen Fixpunktstzes. In K. Menger (ed.), Ergebnisse eines Mathematischen Kolloquiums (Vienna), Vol. VIII. (English translation: A Model of General Economic Equilibrium, Review of Economic Studies 33, 1945-6, 1-9).

Nikaido, H. (1968) Convex Structures and Economic Theory. Academic Press, New York.

Nikaido, H. (1975) Monopolistic Competition and Effective Demand. Princeton University Press, Princeton, New Jersey.

Pasinetti, L.L. (1979) Structural Change and Economic Growth: A Theoretical Essay on the Dynamics of the Wealth of Nations. Cambridge: Cambridge University Press.

Phelps, E.S. (1966) Models of Technical Progress and the Golden Rule of Research. Review of Economic Studies XXXIII, 133-45.

Prigogine, I. (1980) From Being into Becoming: Time and Complexity in the Physical Sciences. W.H. Freeman and Company, San Francisco.

Prigogine, I. and Stengers, I. (1984) Order out of Chaos: Man's Dialogue with Nature. Boulder, Colo.: New Science Library.

Quesnay, F. (1972) Tableau Economique. Edited with new materials, translation and notes by Kucznyski, M., Meek, R.L., Macmillan, London.

Ricardo, D. (1810) The High Price of Bullion a Proof of the Deprecation of Bank Notes.

Ricardo, D. (1817) Principles of Political Economy and Taxation. Harmondsworth: Penguin 1971.

Robinson, J. (1953) The Production Function and the Theory of Capital. Review of Economic Studies XXI, 81-106.

Robson, A.J. (1980) Costly Innovation and Natural Resources. International Economic Review 21, 17-30.

Rodriguez, C.A. (1975) Brain Drain and Economic Growth - A Dynamic Model. Journal of Development Economics 2, 223-247.

Rosen, S. (1972) Learning and Experience in the Labour Market. Journal of Human Resources 7, 336-342.

Rossi, R.J. and Gilmartin, K.J. (1980) The Handbook of Social Indicators, Sources, Characteristics, and Analysis. Garland STPM Press.

Rothbarth, E. (1946) Causes of the Superior Efficiency of U.S.A: as Compared with British Industry. Economic Journal LVI, 383-90.

Russell, B. (1922) The Problem of China. London: George Allen & Unwin Ltd.

Salvodori, N. (1980) On a Generalized von Neumann Model. Metroeconomica 32, 51-62.

Salvadori, N. (1988) Fixed Capital Within a von Neumann-Morishima Model of Growth and Distribution. International Economic Review 29, 341-351.

Samuelson, P.A. (1957) Wages and Interest: A Modern Dissection of Marxian Economic Models. American Economic Review XLVII, 884-912.

Samuelson, P.A. (1961) A New Theorem on Nonsubstitution. In "Money, Growth, and Methodology and Other Essays in Honour of Johan Åkerman", Edited by H.E. Hegeland. Lund: CWK Gleerup.

Samuelson, P.A. (1965) A Theory of Induced Innovation Along Kennedy-Weizsäcker Lines. Review Of Economics and Statistics XLVII, 343-56.

Samuelson, P.A. (1972) The Collected Scientific Papers of Paul A. Samuelson, Vol. III. Cambridge, MA: MIT Press.

Sato, K. (1966) The Neoclassical Theorem and Distribution of Income and Wealth, Review of Economic Studies XXXIII, 331-336.

Schumpeter, J.A. (1934) The Theory of Economic Development. Harvard University Press, Cambridge, Mass.

Schumpeter, J.A. (1975) Capitalism, Socialism, and Democracy. New York: Harper & Row.

Schuster, H.G. (1988) Deterministic Chaos - An Introduction. Second revised edition, VCH Verlagsgesellschaft mbH, D-6940 Weinheim, F.R.G.

Sheldor, E.B. and Moore, W.E. (1968, edited) Indicators of Social Changes - Concepts and Measurements. Russell Sage Foundation, New York.

Shell, K., Sidrauski, M. and Stiglitz, J. (1969) Capital Gains, Income and Saving. Review of Economic Studies XXXIV, 15-26.

Shinkai, Y. (1960) On Equilibrium Growth of Capital and Labour. International Economic Review I, 107-111.

Smith, A. (1776) An Inquiry into the Nature and Causes of the Wealth of Nations. Chicago: University of Chicago Press, 1976.

Solow, R. (1956) A Contribution to the Theory of Growth. Quarterly Journal of Economics 70, 65-94.

Solow, R. (1957) Competitive Valuation in a Dynamic Input-Output System, Econometrica 27, 30-53.

Solow, R. (1957a) Technical Change and the Aggregate Production Functions. Review of Economics and Statistics XXXIX, 312-20.

Solow, R. (1967) Some Recent Development in the Theory of Production. In "The Theory and Empirical Analysis of Production" edited by M. Brown. New York, Columbia University Press.

Sraffa, P. (1960) Production of Commodities by Means of Commodities: Prelude to a Critique of Economic Theory. Cambridge: Cambridge University Press.

Stein, J.L. (1969) Neoclassical and Keynes-Wicksell Monetary Growth Models. Journal of Money, Credit and Banking 1, 153-171.

Stiglitz, J.E. (1967) A Two Sector Two Class Model of Economic Growth. Review of Economic Studies XXXIV, 227-238.

Stiglitz, J.E. (1974) Growth with Exhaustible Resources. Review of Economic Studies, Symposium, 123-137.

Stiglitz, J.E. and Uzawa, H. (1969) Introduction. In "Readings in the Modern Theory of Economic Growth," edited by the same authors, The M.I.T. Press.

Swan, T.W. (1956) Economic Growth and Capital Accumulation. Economic Record XXXII, 334-61.

Takayama, A. (1965) On a Two-Sector Model of Economic Growth with Technological Progress. Review of Economic Studies XXXII, 251-262.

Takayama, A. (1985) Mathematical Economics, 2nd. Cambridge University Press.

Thornton, H. (1802) An Essay on the Nature of the Paper Credit of Great Britain, edited by F. A. Hayek, 1939. London.

Tobin, J. (1955) A Dynamic Aggregative Model. Journal of Political Economy LXIII, 103-115.

Tobin, J. (1965) Money and Economic Growth. Econometrica 33, 671-84.

Uzawa, H. (1961) On a Two-sector Model of Economic Growth. Review of Economic Studies XXIX, 70-47.

Uzawa, H. (1965) Optimal Technical Change in an Aggregative Model of Economic Growth. International Economic Review 6, 19-31.

Uzawa, R. (1962) On the Stability of Edgeworth's Barter Process. International Economic Review 3, 218-232.

Walras, L. (1874) Elements of Pure Economics: Or the Theory of Social Wealth. Translated by Jaffe, W. from the French original. Allen and Unwin, London.

Weizsäcker, C.C. (1966) Tentative Notes on a Two-Sector Model with Induced Technical Progress. Review of Economic Studies XXXIII, 245-51.

Westin, L. (1987) An Applied Short Run Interregional Equilibrium Model. Working Paper from CERUM, No. 23, University of Umeå, Sweden.

Wicksell, K. (1898) Interest and Prices: A Study of the Causes Regulating the Value of Money. Gustav Fischer (translated by R.F. Kahn, 1962, Augustus M. Kelley, Bookseller).

Zeeman, E.C. (1977) Catastrophe Theory: Selected Papers 1972-1977. Addison-Wesley Publishing Company, Inc.

Zeidler, E. (1986) Nonlinear Functional Analysis and its Applications - Fixed-Point Theorems, Vol. I. (translated from Germany by P.R. Wadsack). Springer-Verlag, New York.

Zhang, W.B. (1988) Brain Drain and Economic Cycles With International Migration: A Case of Minimum Wage in the Unskilled Sector. Journal of Development Economics, No. 2.

Zhang, W.B. (1988a) Limit Cycles in van der Ploeg's Model of Economic Growth and Conflict Over the Distribution of Income. Journal of Economics 48, 159-173.

Zhang, W.B. (1988b) Hopf Bifurcations in Multisector Models of Optimal Economic Growth. Economics Letters 26, 329-334.

Zhang, W.B. (1989) Economic Development - Nonlinearity, Instability and Non-Equilibrium. Doctoral Dissertation presented to Department of Economics, University of Umeå. Umeå Economic Studies No. 198, University of Umeå.

Zhang, W.B. (1989a) Short-Run Inventory Oscillations in the Eckalbar's Disequilibrium Macro Model. Applied Mathematics and Computation (to appear).

Zhang, W.B. (1989b) On Existence of Aperiodic Time-Dependent Solutions in Optimal Growth Economy With Three Sectors. International Journal of Systems Science 20, 1943-1953.

Zhang, W.B. (1990) Synergetic Economics - Dynamics, Nonlinearity, Instability, Non-equilibrium, Fluctuations and Chaos. Springer-Verlag (to appear).

Zhang, W.B. (1990a) An Economic Growth Model. International Journal of Systems Science (to appear).

Vol. 292: I. Tchijov, L. Tomaszewicz (Eds.), Input-Output Modeling. Proceedings, 1985. VI, 195 pages. 1987.

Vol. 293: D. Batten, J. Casti, B. Johansson (Eds.), Economic Evolution and Structural Adjustment. Proceedings, 1985. VI, 382 pages. 1987.

Vol. 294: J. Jahn, W. Krabs (Eds.), Recent Advances and Historical Development of Vector Optimization. VII, 405 pages. 1987.

Vol. 295: H. Meister, The Purification Problem for Constrained Games with Incomplete Information. X, 127 pages. 1987.

Vol. 296: A. Börsch-Supan, Econometric Analysis of Discrete Choice. VIII, 211 pages. 1987.

Vol. 297: V. Fedorov, H. Läuter (Eds.), Model-Oriented Data Analysis. Proceedings, 1987. VI, 239 pages. 1988.

Vol. 298: S.H. Chew, Q. Zheng, Integral Global Optimization. VII, 179 pages. 1988.

Vol. 299: K. Marti, Descent Directions and Efficient Solutions in Discretely Distributed Stochastic Programs. XIV, 178 pages. 1988.

Vol. 300: U. Derigs, Programming in Networks and Graphs. XI, 315 pages. 1988.

Vol. 301: J. Kacprzyk, M. Roubens (Eds.), Non-Conventional Preference Relations in Decision Making. VII, 155 pages. 1988.

Vol. 302: H.A. Eiselt, G. Pederzoli (Eds.), Advances in Optimization and Control. Proceedings, 1986. VIII, 372 pages. 1988.

Vol. 303: F.X. Diebold, Empirical Modeling of Exchange Rate Dynamics. VII, 143 pages. 1988.

Vol. 304: A. Kurzhanski, K. Neumann, D. Pallaschke (Eds.), Optimization, Parallel Processing and Applications. Proceedings, 1987. VI, 292 pages. 1988.

Vol. 305: G.-J.C.Th. van Schijndel, Dynamic Firm and Investor Behaviour under Progressive Personal Taxation. X, 215 pages. 1988.

Vol. 306: Ch. Klein, A Static Microeconomic Model of Pure Competition. VIII, 139 pages. 1988.

Vol. 307: T.K. Dijkstra (Ed.), On Model Uncertainty and its Statistical Implications. VII, 138 pages. 1988.

Vol. 308: J.R. Daduna, A. Wren (Eds.), Computer-Aided Transit Scheduling. VIII, 339 pages. 1988.

Vol. 309: G. Ricci, K. Velupillai (Eds.), Growth Cycles and Multisectoral Economics: the Goodwin Tradition. III, 126 pages. 1988.

Vol. 310: J. Kacprzyk, M. Fedrizzi (Eds.), Combining Fuzzy Imprecision with Probabilistic Uncertainty in Decision Making. IX, 399 pages. 1988.

Vol. 311: R. Färe, Fundamentals of Production Theory. IX, 163 pages. 1988.

Vol. 312: J. Krishnakumar, Estimation of Simultaneous Equation Models with Error Components Structure. X, 357 pages. 1988.

Vol. 313: W. Jammernegg, Sequential Binary Investment Decisions. VI, 156 pages. 1988.

Vol. 314: R. Tietz, W. Albers, R. Selten (Eds.), Bounded Rational Behavior in Experimental Games and Markets. VI, 368 pages. 1988.

Vol. 315: I. Orishimo, G.J.D. Hewings, P. Nijkamp (Eds.), Information Technology: Social and Spatial Perspectives. Proceedings, 1986. VI, 268 pages. 1988.

Vol. 316: R.L. Basmann, D.J. Slottje, K. Hayes, J.D. Johnson, D.J. Molina, The Generalized Fechner-Thurstone Direct Utility Function and Some of its Uses. VIII, 159 pages. 1988.

Vol. 317: L. Bianco, A. La Bella (Eds.), Freight Transport Planning and Logistics. Proceedings, 1987. X, 568 pages. 1988.

Vol. 318: T. Doup, Simplicial Algorithms on the Simplotope. VIII, 262 pages. 1988.

Vol. 319: D.T. Luc, Theory of Vector Optimization. VIII, 173 pages. 1989.

Vol. 320: D. van der Wijst, Financial Structure in Small Business. VII, 181 pages. 1989.

Vol. 321: M. Di Matteo, R.M. Goodwin, A. Vercelli (Eds.), Technological and Social Factors in Long Term Fluctuations. Proceedings. IX, 442 pages. 1989.

Vol. 322: T. Kollintzas (Ed.), The Rational Expectations Equilibrium Inventory Model. XI, 269 pages. 1989.

Vol. 323: M.B.M. de Koster, Capacity Oriented Analysis and Design of Production Systems. XII, 245 pages. 1989.

Vol. 324: I.M. Bomze, B.M. Pötscher, Game Theoretical Foundations of Evolutionary Stability. VI, 145 pages. 1989.

Vol. 325: P. Ferri, E. Greenberg, The Labor Market and Business Cycle Theories. X, 183 pages. 1989.

Vol. 326: Ch. Sauer, Alternative Theories of Output, Unemployment, and Inflation in Germany: 1960–1985. XIII, 206 pages. 1989.

Vol. 327: M. Tawada, Production Structure and International Trade. V, 132 pages. 1989.

Vol. 328: W. Güth, B. Kalkofen, Unique Solutions for Strategic Games. VII, 200 pages. 1989.

Vol. 329: G. Tillmann, Equity, Incentives, and Taxation. VI, 132 pages. 1989.

Vol. 330: P.M. Kort, Optimal Dynamic Investment Policies of a Value Maximizing Firm. VII, 185 pages. 1989.

Vol. 331: A. Lewandowski, A.P. Wierzbicki (Eds.), Aspiration Based Decision Support Systems. X, 400 pages. 1989.

Vol. 332: T.R. Gulledge, Jr., L.A. Litteral (Eds.), Cost Analysis Applications of Economics and Operations Research. Proceedings. VII, 422 pages. 1989.

Vol. 333: N. Dellaert, Production to Order. VII, 158 pages. 1989.

Vol. 334: H.-W. Lorenz, Nonlinear Dynamical Economics and Chaotic Motion. XI, 248 pages. 1989.

Vol. 335: A.G. Lockett, G. Islei (Eds.), Improving Decision Making in Organisations. Proceedings. IX, 606 pages. 1989.

Vol. 336: T. Puu, Nonlinear Economic Dynamics. VII, 119 pages. 1989.

Vol. 337: A. Lewandowski, I. Stanchev (Eds.), Methodology and Software for Interactive Decision Support. VIII, 309 pages. 1989.

Vol. 338: J.K. Ho, R.P. Sundarraj, DECOMP: an Implementation of Dantzig-Wolfe Decomposition for Linear Programming. VI, 206 pages. 1989.

Vol. 339: J. Terceiro Lomba, Estimation of Dynamic Econometric Models with Errors in Variables. VIII, 116 pages. 1990.

Vol. 340: T. Vasko, R. Ayres, L. Fontvieille (Eds.), Life Cycles and Long Waves. XIV, 293 pages. 1990.

Vol. 341: G.R. Uhlich, Descriptive Theories of Bargaining. IX, 165 pages. 1990.

Vol. 342: K. Okuguchi, F. Szidarovszky, The Theory of Oligopoly with Multi-Product Firms. V, 167 pages. 1990.

Vol. 343: C. Chiarella, The Elements of a Nonlinear Theory of Economic Dynamics. IX, 149 pages. 1990.

Vol. 344: K. Neumann, Stochastic Project Networks. XI, 237 pages. 1990.

Vol. 345: A. Cambini, E. Castagnoli, L. Martein, P. Mazzoleni, S. Schaible (Eds.), Generalized Convexity and Fractional Programming with Economic Applications. Proceedings, 1988. VII, 361 pages. 1990.

Vol. 346: R. von Randow (Ed.), Integer Programming and Related Areas. A Classified Bibliography 1984–1987. XIII, 514 pages. 1990.

Vol. 347: D. Ríos Insua, Sensitivity Analysis in Multi-objective Decision Making. XI, 193 pages. 1990.

Vol. 348: H. Störmer, Binary Functions and their Applications. VIII, 151 pages. 1990.

Vol. 349: G.A. Pfann, Dynamic Modelling of Stochastic Demand for Manufacturing Employment. VI, 158 pages. 1990.

Vol. 350: W.-B. Zhang, Economic Dynamics. X, 232 pages. 1990.